AN INTRODUCTION TO THE THEOLOGY OF
RUDOLF BULTMANN

An Introduction to the Theology of Rudolf Bultmann

by

WALTER SCHMITHALS

Augsburg Publishing House

Minneapolis 15, Minnesota

Translated by John Bowden from the German
Die Theologie Rudolf Bultmanns, Eine Einführung
J. C. B. Mohr [Paul Siebeck], Tübingen

Second edition, 1967

First published in the United States of America, 1968
© *SCM Press Ltd 1968*
Printed in Great Britain

To the parish of Raumland
with grateful memories

CONTENTS

CONTENTS

FOREWORD

'MODERN' theology is very much alive both inside and outside the church, and unless the signs are deceptive, it will continue to remain so. Now as ever, for many people the name Bultmann—rightly or wrongly—is the embodiment of all the problems of this modern theology. That itself is justification for publishing the manuscript of a series of lectures which I gave in the winter semester of 1964–65 under the auspices of the *Studium generale* of Marburg University, before an audience from all faculties. The lectures were intended to be an introduction to the theology of Bultmann, for while numerous publications about Bultmann's theology have appeared, to my knowledge there is no introduction to the whole of his theological thought which is written on a more popular level.

I have dedicated this book to the parish of which I have been pastor for more than ten years. When we took leave of one another, the presbytery said with gratitude that the theological work which their pastor had done in these ten years had not been without its effect on the parish. As I thanked them for always having had so friendly an attitude towards this work, I also promised that the first book which I wrote outside the parish would be dedicated to them. I never guessed at the time that it would be an introduction to Bultmann's theology. But as things have turned out this way, I would like to take the coincidence as a sign, which I hope will also be clear to others, that Bultmann's intention in his work is to serve the Church of Jesus Christ, and that the Church already owes considerably more to him than many of its members are inclined to accept.

TRANSLATOR'S PREFACE

'ANYONE who has been brought up to believe in the importance of studying original texts must view with a doubtful eye
the number of digests, interpretations, and evaluations of
other theologians now being offered on the market—
especially if these theologians are still alive and writing. Books concerning the thought of So-and-so who is
still in mid-career are usually a poor substitute (although a
standing temptation to the hard-pressed student) for the actual
works of So-and-so, where his thought can be seen in its living
and developing form. The need for really good translators—
and enterprising publishers—who will help the reader across
the language barrier into another theological *milieu*, remains
greater than the need for popularizers who may so easily dis-
tort the meaning of the creative writers whom they attempt to
interpret.'[1]

These words from a recent number of the *Ecumenical
Review* have seldom needed to be said more than at the present
time, when the sheer weight of published material on theology
threatens to obscure, rather than clarify, what important insights have in fact been gained over the past three generations.
And nowhere has their truth been more clearly demonstrated
than in the case of Rudolf Bultmann. For Bultmann, perhaps
more than any other theologian of the twentieth century, has had
an unenviable fate in the hands of the English and the Americans.

First, the interval between the original publication of some
of his books and their translation into English has often itself
spanned a generation: his fundamental *Die Geschichte der
synoptischen Tradition*, first published in 1921, did not appear

---

[1] P. C. Rodger, Review of *Contemporary Continental Theologians*,
by S. Paul Schilling, *Ecumenical Review*, July 1967, pp. 237f.

in English until 1963; his equally important first volume of collected essays, *Glauben und Verstehen* I, published in 1933, will have had to wait until next year for an English version; the translation of his commentary on the Fourth Gospel, described as 'the best commentary on any book of the Bible in any language', has still to be completed. Furthermore, no publisher has taken a systematic interest in publishing Bultmann in English, with the result that his writings have on the whole been translated in a piecemeal way, all too often included here and there in symposia or anthologies; a glance at the bibliography at the end of this book will give some idea of the situation.

Nevertheless, when all this has been said, there is a good deal of Bultmann's work available in translation—more than might appear at first sight. Here, however, a second difficulty begins, for far too many of these translations are unsatisfactory in various ways. It would be improper at this point to give a detailed review, but the reader should be warned that if he goes on to study other works of Bultmann in English he must be prepared to find an immense variation between fluent English style which obscures the nuances of Bultmann's carefully chosen terminology, and pedantic literalism which transforms Bultmann's excellent German into an almost incomprehensible English equivalent—and mistakes galore into the bargain. Partly because of this situation, and partly to ensure uniformity throughout the present book, I have taken a liberty claimed by the author himself (p. 21) and, while I have tried not to interfere gratuitously with the text, have not hesitated to alter translations from Bultmann where necessary. Some of the alterations and renderings adopted here may not be thought to be an improvement; but in a matter of this kind some difference in personal preferences is inevitable, and I have tried above all to make the author's account as readable as possible for an English-speaking audience.

A third question is raised by the quotation which begins this preface. Why another book about So-and-so, and not more of the real thing, his own work? The present *Introduction* does not in fact incur the criticisms which can so often be raised against treatments of living authors, as Dr Schmithals shows. For as he himself points out, although Bultmann is still very much alive (and has in fact recently completed the manuscript of his long-awaited commentary on the Johannine Epistles), the main outlines of his work have been clear for a long time. Nor is this book a substitute for reading Bultmann; anyone looking for a quick and easy assessment of Bultmann's theology will be disappointed. What he will find is a magnificent *exposition* of Bultmann's work, a chart which will give him some necessary bearings for understanding Bultmann prior to deciding upon his significance. Oddly enough, this is a stage which has been neglected as much in England as it has been in Germany. Despite John Macquarrie's two excellent books, *An Existentialist Theology* and *The Scope of Demythologizing*, there is all too little to introduce Bultmann and, more particularly, to introduce his earliest, fundamental, work; on the other hand, there are a great many assessments at a much more advanced level which, whatever their merits, can prove quite misleading without the fuller knowledge which the best of them presuppose.

Reading this book in itself means reading a good deal of Bultmann, and reading it in a well-ordered way. Of the qualifications of the guide, readers may have no doubt; Dr Schmithals was a pupil of Bultmann, and Bultmann himself has said that this is the best book to have been written on his own theology. If clarity alone can produce understanding, then here is a notable contribution to the current debate.

Unfortunately, however, more is needed for understanding than that. If much of the misunderstanding and misinterpretation of Bultmann can be attributed to limitations in the translation and presentation of his work, a good deal of it can also be attributed to the work of that terrible spirit within the churches which leads men to condemn out of hand what they have not read, to caricature what they do not understand, and to persecute the man responsible for it. Bultmann is not alone in suffering this fate; it is a pattern which is becoming all too familiar, in England and America as well as in Germany. Dr Schmithals, too, points to this phenomenon. How it can be prevented, it is difficult to see; what it is doing to the Christian Church is manifest and frightening.

What, finally, of the man who is at the centre of this study? What emerges from the thorough-going examination of his work? If Bultmann has contributed to some of the most spectacular theological explosions of this century, the overriding impression which is given by these pages is of his conservatism, at least from the perspective of the contemporary theological scene. First, he *is* a Lutheran (see p. 20), and it is quite impossible to understand his theology without some knowledge of Lutheranism and the influence it has had on his thought. Second, Bultmann is an interpreter of something given, the Bible. At the very moment one begins to ask 'Why the Bible?', 'Why the canon?', his answers become thinnest, and the way in which Dr Schmithals, unlike many other commentators on Bultmann, gives proper prominence to Bultmann's interpretations of the New Testament and shows their richness makes this contrast all the clearer. For all Bultmann's later differences with Barth, the basic similarity between the two, though barely referred to here, is quite plain. Here is a 'biblical' theology in the fullest sense. Compared with this emphasis, Bultmann's notorious 'scepticism' takes second place and is seen to be relatively insignificant.

So, paradoxically, if after granting the immense amount that can be learnt from Bultmann, his work is not seen to provide all the answers for which we are looking, it is not because it is too radical, but because it is still too conservative: we cannot be content to stand just where Bultmann does in the firm conviction that that is where God wants us to stand. We must go on asking questions. That does not mean that our answers should be more startling or revolutionary than his—they may in the end prove less so; it does mean that perhaps there are still more dimensions of our freedom and the freedom of God's action still to be explored.

Bloomsbury Street, London
September 1967

1

Introduction: Rudolf Bultmann

ON AUGUST 20, 1964, Rudolf Bultmann—the name on his birth certificate reads Rudolf Karl Bultmann—celebrated his eightieth birthday in Marburg. Considerable note was taken of this event, and it was also the occasion for the present study of Bultmann's theology. But there is more behind this study than that. The real reason for it is neither the warmth with which not only the theological faculty but the whole of the University of Marburg shared in the birthday of their teacher, nor the significance of the person or the personality of Rudolf Bultmann. This study has been made because Bultmann's theology is important, and because we can now look back on it as being already complete in its essentials. I use the word 'complete', not because of the ripe old age of Bultmann himself but because of the consistency of his theological work. And I may surely call it important, because no living theologian's work is noted and discussed more than that of Rudolf Bultmann. Bultmann is for our time what Karl Barth was to the German-speaking world between the two World Wars. The main difference is that Bultmann's theology, even more than that of Barth, has aroused lively interest transcending all boundaries of churches, languages and indeed religions, and has thus led to significant changes. This may be because the specialist area with which Bultmann has been concerned is the exegesis of the New Testament, in which German theological scholarship has long occupied a leading place. Furthermore, exegesis means concern with the problem of hermeneutics, that is, with the proper exposition of texts and other documents of human self-understanding, and this problem is, or should be, familiar to all disciplines. In addition, the contacts with philosophy, classical philology and the history of ancient religion which Bultmann has deliberately cultivated have led to wide areas of contact, and still continue to do so. Above all, however, the decisive influence and significance of the theology of Rudolf Bultmann has been its practical importance as contemporary Christian talk about God's revelation, and it is with this practical relevance that we shall be particularly concerned.

Here is the cause, the cause of Jesus Christ, the cause of the gospel, the cause of the Church, or however we may put it, with which Bultmann has always been concerned. He has been more sorry than glad that his theological work has been so strongly associated with *his* name, and this has always seemed rather inappropriate to him; for the term 'theology' itself already expresses the only name that matters, the name of God. So he would much have preferred this study not to have included his name in the title; his proposal was that it should have been called *Aspects of Modern Theology*. But this proposal was hardly acceptable, even if it is important that we should be concerned with modern theology, that is, theological work which is comprehensible to us and which concerns us, and unimportant that as we do this we should find ourselves dealing with the theology of Rudolf Bultmann. Now, on his eightieth birthday, he has consented to receive the great Cross of Merit with the Star of the Order of Merit of the Federal Republic of Germany from the Hessian Minister for Education and Popular Culture; why should he not also consent to accept the fact that for the sake of greater clarity his name appears in the title of this study? Indeed, he must also allow a few remarks about his personal life, together with observations about his theological development, so that we have a first insight into his

theological work and at the same time are prepared to understand it better.

Rudolf Bultmann was born on August 20, 1884, at Wiefel-
stede in Oldenburg. He was the son of the Protestant pastor
there, Arthur Bultmann, who was later a member of the Oldenburg Church Council. The pietistic heritage of his grandfather
and the moderate Lutheranism of his father, who in Bultmann's student days was turning towards liberal theology,
shaped his home background. He went to the *Gymnasium* in
Oldenburg, and there he was a contemporary of Karl Jaspers.
Jaspers himself has said that from his boyhood on he had a
fellow feeling towards Rudolf Bultmann: 'When I saw you in
the playground of the Oldenburg *Gymnasium* (you were some
years younger than I), I did not dare to strike up a friendship
with you; I saw the gleam in your eye and was glad that you
were there.'[1] This joy was later somewhat disturbed during the
'twenties, when Bultmann was lecturing in Heidelberg, and
preached a sermon in the Peterskirche. He also visited Jaspers,
then ordinarius professor there. Jaspers writes: 'After your
visit, I was disturbed for a long time. I saw you like an im-
movable block of granite. . . . Now on that visit I seemed to feel
the impossibility of making contact, an experience which
became symbolic for me.'[2] The 'seemed to' is evidently a slip
of the tongue. Karl Jaspers *really* found it impossible to make
contact with Bultmann. Does the reason for this lie in Bultmann's personality? Or is it that his concern does not immediately become clear to those who try to make contact? Some
praise the great patience with which Bultmann listens to those
who ask questions of him, the way in which he gives up his
time to them and explains his thoughts; others indignantly
remark how difficult Bultmann is to understand and how much
he compels the person with whom he is speaking to follow his

[1] Rudolf Bultmann and Karl Jaspers, *Die Frage der Entmythologisierung*, p. 113.
[2] ibid.

own thoughts and concepts. It is Bultmann's own view that theology 'does not deal with especially complicated or difficult matters, but with extremely simple ones, so far as theoretical understanding is concerned', 'the understanding of simple things can be difficult, but such difficulty is due not to the nature of the things but to the fact that we have forgotten how to see directly, being too much burdened with presuppositions'.[3] At any rate, we may take it that to follow Bultmann's thought we may be going to have to make some effort. If it should turn out otherwise, all the better.

When Bultmann visited Heidelberg, he was already ordinarius professor in Marburg. He had studied in Tübingen, Berlin and Marburg. At the suggestion of Johannes Weiss, he worked under Wilhelm Heitmüller in Marburg, and received his degree in 1910; he qualified two years later, also in Marburg, under Adolf Jülicher. In 1916 he became extra-ordinarius professor in Breslau, and in 1920–21 he followed in the steps of Wilhelm Bousset as ordinarius professor in Giessen, from where he was called to Marburg in 1921—a quite normal and successful academic career. Throughout this period, that is, right up to the beginning of the 'twenties, Bultmann did not publish very much. True, from 1908 onwards, when he received a scholarship for study in Marburg, he reviewed numerous theological books each year and occasionally some on philosophy and the fine arts. In addition, his only book, his dissertation, appeared in 1910: *The Style of Pauline Preaching and the Cynic-Stoic Diatribe*; if I am right, this is the only book of his which never saw a second edition. His qualification research on *The Exegesis of Theodore of Mopsuestia* has never been published. The years up to 1920 were without doubt years of intensive work, especially as Bultmann could not take an active part in the first World War, and the fruits of this

[3] *Jesus*, pp. 14 f. (*Jesus and the Word*, p. 18).

work became evident later, but at this time Bultmann did not have much to say.

Why was that? He once remarked that until *The History of the Synoptic Tradition*, which appeared in 1921, all his publications had been more or less commissioned. That is a remark worth noting. Bultmann did not choose the area in which he worked through any whim of his own. We should remember this, especially in view of the charge often levelled against him that his understanding of the New Testament is on an based arbitrary selection of the writings which suit his purpose.

Of course, inadequate commissions are not a satisfactory explanation for Bultmann's silence up to the beginning of the third decade of the century. The real explanation may be that in those years he had not yet found any independent theological position and that the theology of his teachers did not satisfy him enough for him to want to or be able to keep to that. When Bultmann was a student and preparing himself for an academic career, 'liberal' theology was dominant in the faculties—'in which camp I also count myself', wrote Bultmann as late as 1920.[4] The term 'liberal theology' can be interpreted very widely. It can be understood to embrace all theological study which since the Enlightenment has not felt itself bound to traditional dogmas as the presuppositions of its work. This was the sense in which Bultmann called himself a 'liberal theologian' in 1920. We shall take the term in a rather narrower sense and limit it to the theological trend which developed after the middle of the nineteenth century in reaction to the speculative systems of Ferdinand Christian Baur and David Friedrich Strauss and was finally superseded by 'dialectical' theology in the early 'twenties of our century. Even when qualified in this way, liberal theology is no simple unity; there are so many characteristic features common to it in all its manifestations and among its leading personalities

[4] 'Ethische und mystische Religion', col. 739.

5

that the description given here is justified only if one also remembers that the reasons for the superseding of liberal theology are to be found in particular manifestations of this theology itself.

The chief characteristic of this liberal theology is its freedom from the compulsion of traditional dogmas. A second characteristic is its freedom towards historical-critical investigation of the biblical documents of the faith. In contrast to the idealist grounding of faith on the eternal Spirit immanent in the world which is to be found in the speculative theology of Baur and Strauss, with its roots in the work of Friedrich Wilhelm Hegel, the liberal theology in which we are interested turns back to history and puts the person of Jesus Christ in the centre of all theological work. But above all, liberal theology is characterized by its concern to incorporate the divine within the horizon of human experience and world history and to regard the realization of the kingdom of God as a development within the world: the Christian world is guided towards its consummation in moral personalities. It is no coincidence that the name of the most influential periodical of this group, edited in Marburg and in which most of Bultmann's earliest publications are to be found, is the *Christian World*. Mankind is expected to rise with increasing strength from its natural state to a perfect culture through the redeeming power of the gospel. Any service to the world is immediate service of God, service which brings in the kingdom of God. The roots of the macabre expression 'Culture Protestantism' lie here. Bultmann describes the interest which governs liberal theology in these words: 'It is a struggle in which the forces of the True, the Good and the Beautiful win the day, and it is a struggle in which man participates, in that he is supported by these forces and thus grows out of his captivity to nature to become a free personality with all its riches. In these forces lies the meaning, the divine quality of history; in personalities, who convey these forces, God reveals himself; and in so far as Jesus, too, is a

6

personality in this sense, he is a bringer of revelation.'[5] Consequently, man himself makes his own access to this revelation 'through a sound judgment, matured by historical study', as Adolf von Harnack writes.

From the beginning of the 'twenties onwards, Bultmann's verdict on this liberal theology is a critical one. Here, he declares, man is in truth divinized; for the supposedly divine forces are only human ones. In 1924 he writes: 'The subject of theology is God, and the trouble with liberal theology is that it has not dealt with God, but with man. God represents the radical negation and sublimation of man; therefore theology, whose subject is God, can only have as its content the word of the cross. This, however, is a scandal for man. So the trouble with liberal theology is that it sought to avoid this scandal or at least to lessen it.'[6]

The recognition expressed here, that God is the 'wholly other' and that man therefore really encounters God only where he and all *his* possibilities are completely brought to nothing, is the basic principle of 'dialectical' theology, which represented a radical departure from liberal theology precisely because of this basic principle. This dialectical theology is associated above all with the names of Karl Barth and Friedrich Gogarten. Its massive intervention in theological thought is marked by the second edition of Karl Barth's *The Epistle to the Romans*, published in 1922, which Bultmann reviewed in the *Christian World* in the same year, thoroughly, and with a considerable degree of agreement. At the time, Karl Barth described this positive review as the most remarkable thing that had happened to his book. Bultmann had published his *History of the Synoptic Tradition* the year before. In it, he dissected the first three Gospels from a form-critical point of view by a strict application of the historical-critical method, and at the same time gave a relatively negative verdict on the historical reliability of the tradition about Jesus. To this

[5] *Glauben und Verstehen*, I, p. 7.   [6] ibid., p. 2.

extent he had showed himself to be a decided liberal, and Barth had not believed that he could agree with an exposition of the Epistle to the Romans which stabbed liberal theology in the heart. Bultmann himself, however, has never disguised the fact that the theological works of Karl Barth and Friedrich Gogarten influenced him decisively. For example, in a discussion with Gogarten which presupposed a common basic approach, he writes: 'That I stand together with Gogarten in this direction is no accident, for I largely owe it to him that this is my situation; and so it is that what I am able to say is also an expression of gratitude for what I have learned from him.'[7]

Of course, Bultmann's few publications before his encounter and liaison with dialectical theology already show the beginnings of a movement beyond the thought-world of liberalism. The year 1917 saw the publication of his article on 'The Significance of Eschatology for the Religion of the New Testament'. The choice of subject was governed by his teacher Johannes Weiss, himself a member of the liberal school, who nevertheless put a decisive question mark against its views when he demonstrated that for the New Testament the kingdom of God represents something breaking in from beyond the world and making an end of the course of the world, that it is an 'eschatological' entity. In his article, Bultmann writes that Christian faith is a relationship of man to God 'which is achieved neither by rational considerations nor by natural necessities but by experiences which are given to man outside reason and nature, which overpower him, to which he surrenders himself freely, which he describes as revelation, as grace; in which he knows that he is not independently creative, as in other areas of culture, but quite simply dependent'.[8] The language used here is that of his teacher Wilhelm Herrmann

---

[7] 'Die Geschichtlichkeit des Daseins', p. 354 (*Existence and Faith*, p. 102).

[8] 'Die Bedeutung der Eschatologie', p. 81.

and of Friedrich Schleiermacher, whom he has always admired and indeed has secretly loved—secretly, because Karl Barth has impressed such a one-sided picture of Schleiermacher on the consciousness of the present that an open love could not have avoided dangerous misunderstandings—but the content is the same as that of two articles by Bultmann, 'Religion and Culture' and 'Ethical and Mystical Religion in Primitive Christianity', published in the *Christian World* in 1920: the kingdom is not worked out by men but received as a gift, because God is the mysterious power of the 'wholly other', 'which dominates man's fate and supports his life'.[9]

The collapse in the theological situation brought about by dialectical theology has been associated with the experiences of the first World War, in which talk of the infinite value of man, the worth of his moral personality and the divine greatness of his soul was condemned to silence. No-one can seriously dispute the significance of these experiences. But they themselves are not a sufficient explanation of the theological explosion of the 'twenties. At any rate, Bultmann has explicitly denied that experience of the war had any influence on his theological thought. In 1926, he wrote to Erich Förster, pastor and professor in Frankfurt: 'Of course, the impact of the war has led many people to revise their concepts of human existence; but I confess that that has not been so in my case. Perhaps I am again going too far towards the other extreme, but I must be frank; the war was not a shattering experience for me. Of course there were a great many individual things, but not the war as such. I am quite clear about this, and I once defended my case in numerous conversations, that war is not so different from peace; a shipwreck, an act of meanness, the sort of thing that happens every day, confronts us with exactly the same questions as the heaping up of events in war. So I do not believe that the war has influenced my theology. . . .

[9] 'Ethische und mystische Religion', col. 743.

My view is that if anyone is looking for the genesis of our theology he will find that internal discussion with the theology of our teachers plays an incomparably greater role than the impact of the war or reading Dostoievsky.' There is a widespread tendency to point to the Dostoievsky renaissance, the discovery of Kierkegaard, the new interpretation of Shakespeare and other events in the intellectual world of the post-war period to explain the theological revolution. But Bultmann's view is that: 'The reason for the influence of Dostoievsky and Kierkegaard lay in the theological situation. A certain degree of parallelism with contemporary phenomena does not mean that we succumbed to such phenomena. It is a real parallelism; in other words, those phenomena in literature art, etc., are also based on an internal discussion with the intellectual situation. That under these circumstances each side learns from the other is, of course, true, but not necessarily a pity.'[10] Bultmann's view, then, is that the new trend in theology derives essentially from the 'university *milieu*', and he concludes: 'For my own part, I am grateful that in my *milieu* I was and am exposed to influences from which I can learn.'[11] Bultmann has constantly maintained this attitude and has always felt that critical discussions between his pupils and himself, their teacher, are appropriate and relevant.

The 'internal discussion with the theology of our teachers' mentioned by Bultmann also finds expression in the fact that, as we have already mentioned, elements in liberal theology contributed to their own eclipse in dialectical theology. We have already indicated the significance of the investigations of Johannes Weiss for the recognition of the 'eschatological', other-worldly character of the primitive Christian preaching of the kingdom of God. Furthermore, the possibility of grounding faith on a picture of the personality of 'Jesus' constructed by the historian, was itself destroyed by scholars of the liberal

[10] In a letter of 1926.

[11] 'Besprechung von Hans Windisch: *Der Sinn der Bergpredigt*', col. 986.

school. In his book *The Quest of the Historical Jesus*, published in 1906, Albert Schweitzer showed that there were as many pictures of the personality of Jesus as there were theologians and psychologists who undertook to write a 'Life of Jesus': each picture of the historical Jesus which apparently breathed life into his personality was an exact reflection of the modern personality which the particular writer himself had as an ideal. In a book on *The Messianic Secret in the Gospels*, published in 1901, William Wrede had given convincing historical reasons for this state of affairs: the Gospels offer us no possibility of reconstructing a course of events in the life and inner development of Jesus because they are not interested in it. Modern liberal questioning was simply alien to them. Bultmann believes that it is clear from the classical document of liberal theology, Adolf von Harnack's *What is Christianity?*, 'that no matter how acutely aware we may be of Harnack's limitations it would be too simple to say that he had no ear for that in the New Testament message which is transcendental and which calls out to men to detach themselves from the "world"'.[12] Above all, there were influences in 'dialectical' theology from the basic thought of the liberal theologian Wilhelm Herrmann, who had been a teacher of both Karl Barth and Rudolf Bultmann in Marburg. Herrmann stressed the independence of religion alongside knowledge and morality, in other words the 'wholly other' of the world of faith, and went on to describe faith as an experience which does not mean something *for me* but *to myself* in the midst of the everyday reality in which I live. Bultmann has constantly acknowledged this legacy of Wilhelm Herrmann's and in so doing has remained a truer and more faithful pupil than Karl Barth.

The examples quoted above show to what extent liberal theology transcended itself in dialectical theology (also called the

[12] Introduction to Adolf von Harnack, *Das Wesen des Christentums*, p. 12 (*What is Christianity?*, p. xii).

'theology of crisis', namely, the crisis of this world with its possibilities) and thus in Bultmann's own theological work. There is no point in arguing whether it is more appropriate to speak of Bultmann's attachment to dialectical theology—as he himself would prefer—or of his share in founding this theological movement. But one thing is certain, that since the middle of the 'twenties Bultmann, together with Karl Barth and Friedrich Gogarten, has been one of the three normative and most influential representatives of 'dialectical' theology and that his work may therefore be said to have played a considerable part in the eclipse of liberal theology.

Bultmann's move towards dialectical theology did not mean a departure from the *legitimate* insights of liberal theology. Bultmann himself wrote about this in 1957, as he looked back at his theological work: 'I try to combine the decisive insight of "dialectical" theology with the heritage of "liberal" theology, though it goes without saying that my attitude to both alike is a critical one.'[13] In fact, theological insights and scientific methods familiar to Bultmann from liberal theology—though they need not necessarily have been 'liberal' in origin—have passed directly and without a break into his theology.

Among these we should make particular mention of the historical-critical investigation of New Testament texts. Here the exegete approaches the texts as he would any texts from the past, whether by Plato, Caesar or Luther, in order to see what is meant by them. Investigation of the New Testament is thus carried on with all the methods of modern scientific textual interpretation, in the conviction that the biblical texts arose in exactly the same way as other profane or religious texts and thus can most appropriately be made to speak if they are investigated and questioned by generally recognized and tried methods. Liberal theology, strongly influenced by the spirit of positivistic historicism, was convinced that in this scientifically irreproachable way it could secure the historical basis of faith,

[13] *Glauben und Verstehen*, 3, p. 178.

namely the 'inner life' of the personality of 'Jesus', against all attacks. Bultmann, too, regards the historical-critical method as the only appropriate way of interpreting texts; he does not, however, expect that Christian faith can be founded on the critical-historical study of academic theology—in other words, in a 'worldly' way. On the contrary, the man who can quote the following clearly approves of Karl Barth: 'Critical historical study represents the laudable and necessary end of *the* "basis" of this knowledge (i.e. the knowledge of *faith*), which amounts to nothing because it has not been laid by God himself. If anyone still does not know that we *cannot* any longer know Christ after the flesh, then he may as well let critical study of the Bible tell him so—and the more frightened he is, the better for him and for the cause.'[14]

We shall learn in due course what Bultmann holds to be the basis of faith. But if the historical-critical method has the function—or at least *also* has the function—of preparing the ground for this basis, there is manifestly no reason for being afraid of critical radicalism and the radical results of criticism. At any rate, Bultmann has never seen any such reason. After a review of his Jesus book by Emanuel Hirsch, he wrote: 'People want to know what expedients I adopt in the situation created by my *critical radicalism*, how many brands I can still snatch from the burning. Wiser people, like Paul Althaus and Friedrich Traub, have even tumbled to the fact that I have taken refuge from my scepticism in Barth and Gogarten. I hope that they will excuse me if their wisdom seems to me to be comic. I have never felt uncomfortable in my critical radicalism; I have always been quite comfortable. But I often have the impression that my conservative colleagues in the New Testament feel very uncomfortable indeed; I keep seeing them involved in rescue work. I am quite happy to leave things to burn, for I see that what is burning is all the fantasy of the Life-of-Jesus theologies, and that this is the "Christ after the

[14] *Glauben und Verstehen*, I, p. 4.

flesh". But the "Christ after the flesh" is no concern of ours.'[15]

Whether and to what extent the *results* of Bultmann's historical investigation of the New Testament may be called radical is a matter for dispute, but it cannot be denied that he is radical, that is, consistent, in the *application* of the historical-critical method. Bultmann regards this radicalness with gratitude as an unbroken legacy from his liberal teacher when he writes: 'Liberal theology received its character essentially from the predominance of historical interest, and this is where its great service lay. It was a service, not only in clarifying the historical scene but above all in training people to criticize, training them for freedom and truthfulness. Those of us who come from a background of liberal theology could never have become or remained theologians had we not met in liberal theology the seriousness of radical truthfulness; we felt the work of orthodox university theology of all shades to be no more than an attempt at a compromise, in which we could have led only inwardly broken existences. . . . Here, we felt, was the atmosphere of truthfulness in which alone we could breathe.'[16] In view of this concern for truthfulness in historical exegesis, it is not surprising that a personal pupil of Johannes Weiss and Adolf Jülicher should have incorporated —too uncritically, in the opinion of many people—many of the results of liberal theological research into primitive Christianity in his own work.

Bultmann's theological development did not end when he turned to dialectical theology. His meeting with the philosopher Martin Heidegger in Marburg was of great significance for him. Heidegger, five years younger than Bultmann, became ordinarius professor of philosophy in Marburg in 1923, where his epoch-making work *Being and Time* appeared in 1927. In 1928 he went to Freiburg. Bultmann and Heidegger soon came

[15] ibid., pp. 100 f.   [16] ibid., pp. 2 f.

in contact with each other, had regular meetings, and also put their common work into practice in joint seminars. When Bultmann published the first volume of his collected articles in 1933, under the title *Faith and Understanding*, he deliberately dedicated the volume to Martin Heidegger; all the articles collected here from the years 1924–30 show the significance of Heidegger's thought for Bultmann's theological work. We may remark in passing that this collaboration also proved fruitful for Heidegger, who was at that time intensively occupied with Paul and Luther, but otherwise this is something with which we need not concern ourselves further. Personal contact between Heidegger and Bultmann broke off after 1933, when Heidegger came suspiciously near to the Brownshirts and their ideology. Nevertheless, in 1954, when the first volume of *Glauben und Verstehen* was reprinted, Bultmann wrote: 'This book is still dedicated to Martin Heidegger in grateful memory of the time we spent together in Marburg.' He regretted that Heidegger did not explicitly withdraw from his position after 1933, but there were still occasional personal contacts between the two scholars in the post-war period. Only Bultmann's encounter with the early Heidegger was, however, important for his theology. The famous 'turn', which happened in Heidegger's work in the 'thirties, did not influence Bultmann's work. It is true that, unlike some others, he does not understand this turn as a 'conversion', a moving away from the insights of *Being and Time*, but sees the 'late' Heidegger in unbroken continuity with the 'early' Heidegger; nevertheless, only the early Heidegger has remained significant for his theology.

The character and extent of this significance will occupy us in detail at appropriate places in this study. At present, the following points might be considered by way of introduction.

Bultmann's encounter with Heidegger did not lead him to depart from the insights of dialectical theology, or even to modify them—at any rate, as far as Bultmann understands it.

But how can an encounter between philosophy and theology take place at all on the presuppositions of dialectical theology? If God is the 'wholly other' and his future is from beyond the world, God and his action are not open to human *thought*—in other words, to philosophy! Karl Barth has therefore regarded Heidegger's influence upon Bultmann with great suspicion. Bultmann, on the other hand, points out that the philosophy of Heidegger is 'atheistic' in the exact sense of this word. This judgment says nothing about Heidegger's belief or unbelief: it merely establishes that God is not the subject of the philosophy of the early Heidegger. God is neither acknowledged nor denied in this philosophical system. For that very reason, Heidegger's philosophizing leaves room for theological work which, in so far as it knows about God, does not owe this knowledge to the thought of the philosopher but to the revelation of God himself.

But what is the subject of the philosophy of the early Heidegger, and what help can this philosophizing offer to theology? Bultmann replies: Heidegger analyses human existence, and here, according to the very insights of dialectical theology, God is not to be found; for God stands beyond men. But, according to Bultmann, theology, too, is concerned with human existence. The Word of God is directed to man, real man, with whom Heidegger is concerned as a philosopher. Therefore the theologian, in so far as he is concerned with the existence of man, can make use of the help which philosophy offers him. It is quite clear to Bultmann that he has to do this on the basis of his own presuppositions and therefore has to do it critically, but Bultmann regards a certain community of interest between theology and philosophy as being beyond question.

Thus, for example, to follow Bultmann: theology is concerned with the character of preaching as address, while philosophy shows what address means for man in general; theology speaks concretely of the 'nature' of human existence, while philosophy demonstrates that human existence must always be a concrete instance on a given occasion; theology speaks of belief and unbelief as definite events, while philosophy can say how the phenomena of belief and unbelief are possible for men at all. But according to Bultmann's conviction philosophy *can* say this, and here he sees a positive relationship between philosophy and theology, of which theology should not be ashamed.

What that means exactly and in detail must be left until later chapters. At present it is clear that Bultmann merely wishes to use philosophy as a means of expression which is at the disposal of the theologian when he thinks and speaks about man. For according to Bultmann, the *concepts* of the theologian have always been those in which 'natural' existence, the world, understands itself: concepts shaped by the world's knowledge, philosophy in the broadest sense—'and how could it be otherwise if what is being talked about has to do with man and if what is said is to be understood'.[17] Thus every theology is dependent upon philosophy for its concepts, whether it realizes the fact or not.

In his disagreements with Karl Barth, Bultmann's charge is characteristically not that Barth falsifies the message of the gospel—that is his charge against liberal theology—but simply that he fails to concern himself over an appropriate language, a precise conceptuality, with which to express correctly what he has understood correctly. For in Bultmann's view, even Karl Barth cannot avoid all philosophical influences. 'In any case, Barth's background is the neo-Kantianism of Cohen and Natorp, who also continued to influence me for a long time; he has—unfortunately!—nothing to do with phenomenology.'[18] In other words, he has nothing to do with a non-theological philosophy, describing phenomena at hand, which is

[17] 'Die Geschichtlichkeit des Daseins', p. 349 (*Existence and Faith*, p. 98).
[18] In a letter of 1926.

17

Bultmann's assessment of Heidegger's work, as we have already seen. Bultmann sees the chief difference between his theology and that of his great theological companion in the fact that the latter works with inappropriate concepts. That is why he discusses Karl Barth's work less than Karl Barth discusses his.

In contrast, Bultmann sees his task as the discovery of the form of expression which best corresponds to the subject-matter of theology; he believes that he has found this in the philosophy of Heidegger: 'I found help for this work in phenomenology, to which I was introduced by my colleague and friend Heidegger. Its purpose is investigation and analysis as opposed to systematic philosophy. I am writing this merely in order to meet the charge that I am selling my soul to a philosophy; it would be fatal for the historian to learn from philosophy only if he became involved in a philosophical system, philosophical impulses or moods which produced definite answers and views instead of questions and methods of questioning.'[19] And: 'No one who understands Heidegger's philosophy can talk about taking over "results" from it. But it can certainly teach him . . . to think about the concepts he is using.'[20] Various statements which claim—sometimes in triumph—to have refuted Bultmann, because here and there or basically or altogether his theology fails to agree with the philosophy of Heidegger, or because Bultmann has misunderstood Heidegger's philosophizing, or because he does not come up to Heidegger or has used Heidegger's analyses in a way which the latter did not intend, do not affect Bultmann's theology even if they are right; for it is not Bultmann's intention to take over *the* philosophy of Heidegger.

Furthermore, it should be remembered and noted that Bultmann was already familiar with the question of the nature of

[19] ibid.
[20] 'Besprechung von Hans Windisch: *Der Sinn der Bergpredigt*', col. 987.

human existence as existence in history—as distinct from mere natural being—which Heidegger poses and works out, even before his encounter with the philosopher. He had encountered it in the 'university *milieu*' which we have already mentioned, in discussion with his teachers. Bultmann writes: 'Like others, I was made to think by the reflections on historical life and its understanding which occupied Nietzsche and Jacob Burckhardt, which lay at the centre of Dilthey's philosophical interest and is the chief theme in his correspondence with Graf Yorck, the concerns to understand the historical in Rickert and Troeltsch and the anthropological analyses of Scheler, not to mention Kierkegaard's insights into the nature of human existence which influence Jaspers and, alongside the themes of Dilthey's work, Heidegger....'[21] But in Heidegger's exact conceptual analysis Bultmann saw the subject of his enquiry worked out in exemplary fashion; he therefore largely followed Heidegger's analyses.

In Bultmann's encounter with Heidegger, his theology took that fixed and characteristic form in which it has confronted us now for about forty years. Bultmann has continued to penetrate more deeply into his theological insights of the 'twenties, but he has never gone beyond them. He has hardly ever felt it necessary to withdraw any of his statements. He has, on the other hand, been constantly concerned to explain and deepen what he has to say. His theology is independent, unmistakeable, and not to be explained as an addition to the works of his teachers; we may have uncovered its most important historical roots, but that does not mean that we have explained it as a combination of liberal and dialectical theology in the garb of Heideggerian conceptuality. It has not been our intention to explain it at all. Indeed, I do not believe that one can explain a theology, and if one can, the explanation is a quite useless undertaking. Bultmann's theology ought to be *understandable*,

[21] ibid., col. 986.

so that in it we understand its subject, God's Word, and in that possibly ourselves. The discovery of its historical roots can help us to such an understanding, and the most important of these have now been mentioned.

On the same grounds we shall also refrain from evaluating or classifying Bultmann's theology. We shall describe him neither as a great teacher of the Church nor as a dangerous heretic. We shall not join the ranks of those who dare to pass judgment on his faith or his lack of it. We shall not follow some in describing him as a model Lutheran—though Bultmann himself would presumably not regard this as being completely wide of the mark—nor others in seeing him as a typical Calvinist, or as a Catholic in disguise—as happens remarkably often today from the Roman Catholic side—or as a crypto-pietist. Wise men may ask whether he stands nearer to Thomas Aquinas or to Immanuel Kant, to Origen or to Karl Jaspers; we shall not be taking them up. It is our concern to understand Bultmann's theology, not to assign it a place in history.

Nor is criticism of Bultmann's theology the task and aim of this study, though it presupposes a critical audience and is intended to provoke the critical judgment of that audience. At this point it is important to realize that Bultmann readily tolerates any judgments on his work, but is cut to the quick if anyone disputes his purpose to serve the Church of Jesus Christ. Any critical judgment must respect this, and I think that anyone who has ever seen Bultmann at the entrance to the parish church in Marburg, which he served as a presbyter, holding out a plate for the contributions of the congregation, will be ready to show him that respect. And so, too, will the pupils of the *Philipp-Gymnasium* in Marburg, who received instruction from him on the Christian faith in the dark days of the last World War.

One last thing: if we want to understand Bultmann's theology, we must listen to Bultmann himself. In 1960, he wrote: 'It is incredible how many people pass judgment on my work without ever having read a word of it . . . I have sometimes asked the grounds for a writer's verdict, and which of my writings he has read. The answer has regularly been, without exception, that he has not read any of my writings; but he has learnt from a Sunday paper or a parish magazine that I am a heretic.'[22] You may certainly doubt whether you are listening to Bultmann himself when you follow the course of this study; for whether I have understood him and can make him understandable are and remain two open questions, which will not be answered adequately even if we let Bultmann himself speak as far as is practicable and make widespread use of his terminology elsewhere. I must therefore ask you to understand this study not only as an introduction to the theological thought of Bultmann but also, and above all, as an invitation to his own writings, which are by no means all hard fare, only to be endured by those with a knowledge of ancient languages.

Each part is complete in itself, but the effect is cumulative, and deliberately so. It should also be noted that the way in which quotations from Bultmann are introduced are not always in accord with the strictest academic conventions: passages in a foreign language are translated without special attention being drawn to the fact, italics often do not correspond with those in the original, omissions are not always marked, etc. Of course this formal freedom, which is meant to help the fluency of the account, does not involve any alteration of the content.

It is our concern, then, to understand Bultmann's theology. But what is theology? Or rather, what does Bultmann understand by theology? The following chapter will be concerned with answering this question.

[22] *Kerygma und Mythos*, I, p. 7.

2

Theology as Talk of God

BULTMANN writes: 'The subject of theology is God';[1] else-where he puts it: 'In his situation, the theologian has now, in our view, the impossible task of talking *of God*. Whatever else would he talk of?'[2] These sentences clearly express the task of theology. They do not say anything surprising or unusual. The concept 'theology', '*theo-logia*' in Greek, simply means 'God-talk', and it would obviously be senseless to call talk which was not of God 'theology'. The concept occurs in various forms in Greek philosophy after the time of Plato in this sense of talk of God, the gods, or the divine. The Church transferred it, at first hesitatingly but after the Constantine era without hesitation, to Christian talk of God, which now emerged victorious over pagan theology as the true theology. God is thus the subject of *all* theology, and to this extent, of Christian theology too. As Bultmann is doing theology, it is quite clear that he, too, wants to talk of God; 'Whatever else would he talk of?'

But Bultmann feels that it is not unimportant to *stress* the fact that theology means 'talk of God'; for in his view Christian theology has not always kept to its subject, and thus has led itself into absurdity. Bultmann's charge against liberal theology, for example, is that 'it has not dealt with God, but with man'.[3] This is a grave charge. But if liberal theology sees

[1] *Glauben und Verstehen*, I, p. 2.
[2] 'Die Frage der "dialektischen" Theologie', p. 52.
[3] *Glauben und Verstehen*, I, p. 2.

God's salvation realized in and through human personalities, and the formation of personality is presented to man as a task that he can fulfil, then the charge is evidently not unjustified. Such criticism makes it clear that Bultmann is concerned that God should be thought of as the only meaningful subject of all theological work.

In that case, of course, the theologian who wants to do theology as '*theologia*,' that is, as 'God-talk', is faced with the inevitable question how one can then speak of God, indeed how one can speak of him at all. Bultmann used this question in 1925 as the title for a significant and much-read article: 'What Sense Does it Make to Talk of God?'[4] In the light of this formulation, we may remember that in the words quoted at the beginning of this chapter Bultmann calls theology's task of talking of God an 'impossible' one, and therefore asks: 'In what way is this task "impossible"? How far is it enjoined on us if it is an impossible task? And finally, how far does it make sense, even though it is impossible?'

First of all, it must be pointed out that Bultmann often uses biblical expressions to talk about an inappropriate *concept* of God.

'*God is not a* datum', that is, not an object, 'which we can recognize in more or less the same way as other objects'.[5] The question of the appropriateness (adequacy) of our knowledge of God, which has at times occupied theology a great deal, is thus to be rejected *completely*; for in any case it imagines God as an object, 'of which direct knowledge is possible'.[6] But whatever the form in which such knowledge may be asserted, 'it could still not take us to God, who can never be something given, something remaining steady, as it were, for the observer'.[7] Anyone who imagines God as an object which is directly accessible to human understanding or to the human heart, is still moving in the context of the Greek view of God, for which

[4] ibid., pp. 26 ff.   [5] ibid., p. 18.   [6] ibid.   [7] ibid.

God, like man, is part of one single world. This world, the cosmos, has for the Greeks a well-ordered form; it is bounded and complete in itself. The unity of the cosmos 'embraces gods and men. There is no place for any transcendent sphere.'[8] Bultmann is fond of quoting Plato, *Gorgias* 507e–508a, according to which the wise men say: 'Heaven and earth and gods and men are held together by communion and friendship, by orderliness, temperance and justice; and that is the reason why they call the whole of this world by the name of order (cosmos), not of disorder or dissoluteness. . . . Now you have failed to observe the great power of geometrical equality amongst both gods and men.' If gods and men belong to the same order, are subject to the same cosmic laws and both share in the one nature, the gods are naturally the object of rational human knowledge, and this reason recognizes that the transcendence of the divine is to be understood 'as transcendence over everything concrete and individual, over all coming to be and passing away',[9] everything that is characteristic of the human element in the cosmos.

In Judaism, however, 'a wholly different conception of God' prevails.[10] 'The transcendence of God is not thought of in the Bible in terms of the spirit which is beyond the sphere of the material and the sensible, as timelessness in contrast to coming to be and passing away, but simply as authority, the indisposability and constant futurity of God.'[11] 'In his relation to the *world*, God is . . . the creating will. He commands, and it happens; he decrees, and it exists (Ps. 33.9). For his glory he created the world, and all his works must praise him.'[12] 'In his relation to *man*, God is the sovereign Lord who deals with man according to his will as the potter with the clay, who rejects whom he will and has mercy on whom he will. His will

[8] *Das Urchristentum*, pp. 121 f. (*Primitive Christianity*, p. 152).

[9] *Glauben und Verstehen*, 3, p. 156.

[10] *Jesus*, p. 94 (*Jesus and the Word*, p. 99).

[11] *Glauben und Verstehen*, 3, p. 157.

[12] *Jesus*, p. 94 (*Jesus and the Word*, p. 99).

has prescribed for man what is good and evil.'[13] Man does not make God the object of his reason: 'Man has only to ask what the Lord requires.'[14]

It is exactly the same in the New Testament. 'That God's existence is not an objectively perceptible, mere existing like that of a thing, is indicated by I Cor. 8.4–6.' At the beginning of this passage, Paul first asserts that 'there is no God but one'. 'If God were being spoken of as only a cosmic Thing,' runs Bultmann's interpretation, 'the statement, "there is no God but one", would not be right at all; for in this sense of "is", other gods and lords are',[15] as Paul explicitly declares in the verses mentioned. But 'for us' the apostle asserts, 'there is only one God, the Father . . .', Paul is thus obviously speaking of the one true God not as of a 'higher being', as an object that is to hand. The real God is rather *our* God, the God with whom man has unconditionally to reckon.

But we must move on. Bultmann writes: *'Nor is God "self-actualizing" or "unactualized"* in the sense of an idealist philosophy.'[16] God appears as self-actualizing, for instance, in Hegel's philosophy and among the theological Hegelians, according to whom he realizes himself in the continuing process in which the 'Spirit' finds the way to itself. As the unactualized, God is real 'in the Logos, which lies at the roots of rational human life';[17] God occurs in this way, for example, in the pantheism of Stoic philosophy 'as the law ruling in the universe which gives form to all phenomena – law which differs from the modern natural law because it is not wholly and essentially defined by the concept of cause and effect, but rather by the concept of a creative, active, form-giving power',[18] which is identical with human reason. In the light

[13] ibid. (ibid., p. 100).   [14] ibid., p. 95 (ibid.).
[15] *Theologie*, p. 229 (*Theology*, I, p. 229).
[16] *Glauben und Verstehen*, i, p. 18.   [17] ibid.
[18] *Jesus*, pp. 93 f. (*Jesus and the Word*, p. 99).

of the biblical concept of God, such talk of God seems to be the 'divinization of man'. 'But God represents the total sublimation of man, his negation, his questioning, indeed judgment for man.'[19] The biblical God stands over against the world and is not immanent in it. So we do not have God in any form as the given, the self-actualizing or the 'unactualized' whom we could have at our disposal in thought or action.

It is clear that all these remarks do not present statements which are characteristic only of Bultmann's theology. What has been said so far simply expresses a fundamental recognition of all proper biblical theology, that God is the 'wholly other'. Man can speak of him, only if he makes him an object of knowledge, only by the *via negationis*, by denying him the properties of the cosmos. This certainly leads the way to an appropriate *concept* of God. But it need hardly be said that in this process one still does not come up against God himself. For as God is not in any way a *datum*, he is not a *datum* for our conceptual thought. God is there only when he *gives himself*. So Bultmann fully agrees with Karl Barth in claiming that God is only known 'when he reveals himself';[20] and this revelation, as *God's* revelation, is necessarily contingent, that is, an event introduced by God alone, a free act of God. Theology as talk of *God* is possible only in 'talking of the *revelation of God* as an event—an eternal event, but still an event'.[21] Without revelation, it would in fact and without question be an 'impossible task' to talk about God.

This is not the place to discuss the understanding of revelation in Bultmann's theology; that will be done at the appropriate time. Even without further discussion of the concept of revelation, it seems clear that *if* God reveals himself, *if* he makes himself known, it becomes possible to speak of God, by speaking of his revelation. 'God is never there at all apart from

[19] *Glauben und Verstehen*, 1, p. 18.
[20] ibid.
[21] 'Die Frage der "dialektischen" Theologie', p. 45.

revelation',[22] but 'in the event of revelation . . . God is accessible to man'.[23]

At this point, however, where our introductory questions seem to have found an answer, the real problem for Bultmann begins. When he calls talk of God an 'impossible task', he does so as a Christian theologian, that is, as a theologian who wants to talk of God on the basis of revelation and only on this basis. He thus calls the very talk of God enjoined by revelation an impossibility! But in that case, how is even talk of the God who reveals himself an 'impossible task'?

I shall begin by quoting the first paragraph from the 1925 article 'What Sense Does it Make to Talk of God?', which I have already mentioned. Bultmann writes: 'If we understand "talking of God" to mean "talking *about* God", then such talk has no meaning at all, for the moment it takes place it has lost its object, God. Wherever the thought of "God" comes to mind, it suggests that God is the omnipotent, that is, the reality that determines everything. But this is not the thought that is expressed when I talk *about* God, i.e. when I regard God as an object of thought about which I can take my bearings, if I occupy a standpoint from which I can approach the question of God in a neutral way and make hypotheses about God's reality and his nature, which I can either reject or, if they are illuminating, accept. Anyone who has been influenced by particular considerations to accept the *reality* of God can be quite certain that he has grasped nothing of the reality of *God*; and anyone who thinks that he can say something about the reality of God by means of proofs for the existence of God is arguing over a phantom. For any kind of "talking *about*" presupposes a standpoint outside the object of the discourse. There is, however, no standpoint outside God, and so God cannot be spoken of in general statements, general truths,

[22] *Glauben und Verstehen*, 1, p. 142.
[23] ibid., p. 265.

which are true without reference to the concrete existential situation of the person who is speaking.'[24]

These statements can be understood in themselves without any great difficulty. First of all they repeat what we have already outlined: as the 'wholly other', God cannot become an object at the disposal of our thought and our knowledge. But they go far beyond an assertion of this kind. Wherever 'God' is mentioned in this paragraph we could substitute 'God's revelation', and perhaps we should; for Bultmann speaks of no other God than the God of the Christian revelation. But the problems of the statements remain the same. It is as meaningless to speak about *God's revelation* as it is to speak about *God*. To want to prove the reality of *God's revelation* is as foolish as to want to prove the *existence of God*. And if there is no standpoint outside *God*, then of course there is no standpoint outside *God's revelation*, in so far as this really is *God's* revelation.

But how is it that I have nothing to do with God or God's revelation when I talk *about* God, that is, about God's revelation? Bultmann's assertion that I am not speaking about *God* at all when I speak *about* him, is not as easy to understand as his assertion that God, as the 'wholly other', cannot immediately, that is, without his revelation, be the object of my thought and speech. Of course, if there can be no standpoint outside God, then we cannot in fact talk *about* God, or, we can only talk about God in such a way that we are at the same time talking about ourselves. But why cannot we have a standpoint outside God? Bultmann does not want to say that God is immanent in the world of men or the human spirit. On the contrary! He stresses—as we have seen—very strongly that God stands *over against* man. So according to Bultmann, man cannot occupy any standpoint outside *the* God who encounters him as the 'wholly other' from beyond all that is human.

Here we come up against one of the basic phenomena of Bultmann's theology, which is not only significant for the

[24] ibid., p. 26.

question of meaningful talk about God but also permeates all
his theological thought. We must therefore acquire an adequate grasp of it. The phenomenon is that of the subject-
object pattern of thought and the overcoming of it. According
to Friedrich Gogarten, the subject-object pattern 'is inextric-
ably linked with the Cartesian view of the world and of
reality';[25] Bultmann is of the same opinion, that, 'since the
Renaissance and the Enlightenment it has dominated our
thought, under the influence of the view of the world held by
Greek science.'[26] The subject-object pattern is thus a modern
form of thought. In this pattern Descartes, by means of the
cogito, posits an isolated subject and thus, inevitably, an
equally isolated object; and between subject and object there
is a gap. This isolation of subject and object does not, however,
correspond to the original authentic understanding of man,
world and God. Whereas for modern thought 'encounter'
means the grasping of objects *by me*, 'encounter' originally
meant that what encounters me discloses itself *for me*. For
example, it is impossible for the Bible to regard man as an
isolated being over against God and the world, or God and the
world as objects for human consideration and at human disposal, in other words, to 'objectivize' them. Anyone who, as a
Christian theologian, thinks and speaks within the subject-
object pattern is no longer in harmony with what is meant in
the Bible. Christian theology thus has the urgent task of overcoming the subject-object pattern. 'Since our thinking,
especially in the sciences, has been conducted in accordance
with this pattern for the past three hundred years or so, the
subject-object pattern cannot be overcome except by a very
considerable effort, an effort which requires time'[27]—a statement the truth of which will certainly (and unfortunately!) be

[25] Friedrich Gogarten, *Entmythologisierung und Kirche*, pp. 43 ff.
(*Demythologizing and History*, pp. 50 ff.).

[26] *Glauben und Verstehen*, I, p. 31.

[27] Gogarten, *Entmythologisierung und Kirche*, p. 44 (*Demythologizing
and History*, p. 51).

confirmed during the course of this study. Gogarten, who made the statement in an attempt to defend Bultmann against attacks on his theology, sees some hope in the fact that modern science, which stamped the subject-object pattern on our consciousness in the nineteenth century, is at present in process of overcoming this pattern. Bultmnan derives his recognition of the danger of the subject-object pattern and his view of ways of overcoming it from his time as a pupil of Wilhelm Herrmann, and has constantly made full use of this recognition. In his encounter with Karl Barth and Martin Heidegger, his concern was intensified and his concepts further clarified.

Bultmann is fond of elucidating the problems involved here by referring to the phenomena of love, friendship or trust. Can I, as subject, present love to myself as an object, 'objectivize' it, so that it becomes the object of my thought, speech and judgment? Or, can I make the person I love the object of an investigation into the phenomenon of love? *If* I do this, I am in any case putting myself outside love. But that is to deny love itself; for love is there only where someone is loved, where I am 'in love', and not where I talk *about* love. As an object of my consideration, love has already come to an end, whatever I may say about it; the loved one is no longer *my* loved one however much I might like to have it otherwise. One can also look at it this way: I cannot love another person *after* I have established that they deserve my love; only *in* love itself do I perceive that they are worthy of my love. Bultmann writes: 'Love is no *datum*, in respect of which it would be possible to act or not to act, to speak or not to speak. It exists only as a determination of life itself; it is there only if I love or am loved, not alongside this or behind it.'[28] Love, therefore, is not an object. A father who talks *about* love to his child can in so doing deny *love* to his child, even if he says the right thing. I do not have control over love as I do, for example, over an

[28] *Glauben und Verstehen*, 1, p. 27.

apple, which I can leave hanging on a tree, or pluck off and eat. Whatever I do or do not do with the apple, it is a *datum* for me, before all my action. Not so love; that is real only in its accomplishment. 'A young man who wants to find out about his (future) bride by means of a detective agency will not get to know her at all as she is, because that does not disclose itself to objective inspection, but only to existential encounter.'[29]

It is just the same with trust, friendship, the relation of father and child. I can talk about friendship and in so doing say a good deal that is to the point; I can write a psychology of friendship. Nevertheless, in all this I encounter no real friendship. Friendship does not happen this way. Here I am nobody's friend and do not have or make a friend unless this writing or talking about friendship happens by chance to be itself an act of friendship, perhaps because I am acceding to the request of a friend in communicating my thoughts. But that itself makes it clear that friendship is something other than an object of my reflection. Were I, for example, to investigate the tokens of my friend's friendship with a view to discovering whether or not they were genuine, the relationship of friendship would already have been destroyed. So I cannot objectivize friendship in a meaningful way; I can only live it and experience it. Now the experience of friendship does away with the subject-object pattern; for in that case I am no longer setting my friend or friendship over against myself as an object; I am *in* friendship, I am 'myself' only *with* the friend, whether I am receiving or showing friendship.

Now it is just the same with God and our relationship to him. Bultmann points out[30] that Luther, in his lectures on Genesis, saw that the real sin of Adam was not that he ate the forbidden fruit, but that he allowed himself to ask: 'Did not God say?' In so doing he made God, or his word, his revelation, a matter for dispute. He set himself up against God's demand, in order to pass judgment on it. This *disputare de Deo*, in which man makes God his object, brings about the division into subject and object, which is inappropriate to the reality of God. The objectified God is no longer

---

[29] *Glauben und Verstehen*, 3, p. 116.   [30] ibid., 1, p. 27.

the true God, but an idol; the revelation which is reduced to the status of an object is no longer God's revelation, but a religious word of man. As a result, it is clear why Bultmann[31] should declare that the atheism of a discipline does not only consist in its denying the existence of God with scientific means. A discipline which asserts or proves the reality of God is no less atheistic; for in both cases God is made the object of human thought; man imagines him as an object and encounters him in just the same way as a heavenly body or an atom—in other words, he no longer encounters *God*.

Martin Heidegger calls the age in which man objectifies everything that encounters him 'the age of subjectity'. Bultmann calls this understanding of reality 'the disposition of an entire epoch to the world and history, a disposition which is now taken for granted'.[32] In this age God is seen and talked about in analogy to the world. But anyone who talks in this way has already lost the object of his discourse, God, for God cannot properly be spoken of within the subject-object pattern if he is *the* reality that governs man in his concrete situation. If God is portrayed as one entity among others, even as the supreme entity in the world or as an entity beyond the world, 'God' may of course be the object of thought and discourse. But according to Bultmann's interpretation of biblical statements, God is in no way the supreme entity, but the all-determining power, so that we are still a long way from the notion of 'God' if we conceive of God as supreme being. The Bible does not portray God and his revelation as part of the world of entities, indeed it cannot do so, for the subject-object pattern is still alien to it. 'The distinction of subject and object must therefore be kept quite separate from the question of our existence (before God).'[33]

[31] ibid.
[32] 'Der Gottesgedanke und der moderne Mensch', pp. 336 f. ('The Idea of God and Modern Man', p. 85).
[33] *Glauben und Verstehen*, 1, p. 32.

We can now understand why for Bultmann there can be no standpoint outside God. Not because God would be immanent in the world or in man, but because God is only real where he determines the existence of man, where his claim on us is perceived in such a way that 'for anyone to put himself outside God would be a repudiation of God's claim on us. It would be godlessness, sin. The situation would only be different if there could be a neutrality towards God. That, however, would be the end of the idea of God.'[34]

Encounter with God as the 'wholly other' is therefore not the isolated encounter of the subject which portrays the world for itself, or of the object, which man portrays for himself; it represents man's being determined from beyond himself, and that really does mean his *being determined* by this encounter from beyond. Here is something which he is not in himself: he encounters it, and indeed only encounters it, where he is related to the encounter in all his reality. As the 'wholly other', God is not reached by religious exaltation to a sphere beyond man, but is revealed to the man who lives in the midst of his world in encounter with him. Thus if one separates the statement that God is the 'wholly other' from the other statement that he is 'the reality that determines our existence','the statement can only mean that God is *something* quite different from man, a metaphysical being, some sort of ethereal world, some sort of complex of mysterious forces, a creative source or, finally, the Irrational'.[35] To talk of God in this way is, however, in terms of talk of the real God, godlessness; for when I talk in this way I return to *my* interest, *my* understanding, *my* feeling and *my* imagination, but I do not venture my life, my concrete existence. I cannot know of God outside myself, without exposing myself to the claim of God. The God who is *something* wholly other is an idol; only the God who encounters me as *the one who* is the wholly other, is God.

[34] ibid., p. 28.
[35] ibid., pp. 29 f.

In common with this idea of God, *God's transcendence* is not to be understood locally, but is determined by the meaning of 'this world' —what is at man's disposal. Thus anyone who talks about God's transcendence is not speaking of his remoteness in space but of the fact that he is not at man's disposal. The true idea of God thus excludes his being localized beyond the earth, just as it includes his not being at man's disposal. To this extent, talk of God's transcendence is tautological, which it would not necessarily be were God's transcendence understood in spatial terms; for if he is conceived of as an entity, must God not necessarily be understood to be remote in space, if the definition 'transcendent God' is to be meaningful?

A further implication of a true idea of God is that talk about *God as a person* is misunderstood if God is imagined as a metaphysical being. Such talk has significance in the fact that God *encounters* me; for encounter is always a personal event. God is reality for me only as a reality which encounters me. According to Bultmann, that is the meaning of John 1.1: 'In the beginning was the Word and the Word was with God and the Word was God.' That God is 'Word' means that his reality discloses itself only in encounter, in his claim and promise which goes out as Word.

A final implication of the true idea of God is the insight that the confession of *God as creator* is not taken seriously if God is seen merely as the *prima causa*, the first cause of all entities. If God, the first and the last, is the *origin* of all that is, then this must be understood in the right sense, that he makes me a new creature, in other words, that he encounters me here and now in the midst of my sin and thus makes possible for me new life, life in truth, in forgiveness, life from himself.

What we have said results in a principle for all legitimate talk about God. We can only talk about God in talking about ourselves: 'Any talk about reality which ignores the element in which alone we can have what is real, i.e. our own existence, is self-deception. God is never something to be seen from outside, something at our disposal, an "objective".'[36] God's revelation would not be *God's* revelation if 'we spoke of it in general statements, general truths, which are true without reference to the concrete existential situation of the speaker'.[37] Or: 'The Christian faith speaks of a revelation which it under-

[36] ibid., p. 33.   [37] ibid., p. 26.

stands to mean God's act as an event which is not visible to the objectivizing thought of reason, an event which as revelation does not communicate doctrines, but concerns the existence of man and teaches him, or better, authorizes him, to understand himself as sustained by the transcendent power of God.'[38] That is why theological discourse is *in itself* anthropological discourse, talk about God is talk about man, knowledge of man is a necessary condition of the possibility of legitimate talk about God or about revelation as the action of God.

The doctrine of creation may once again serve to illustrate this. Bultmann writes: 'The affirmation that God is creator cannot be a theoretical statement about God as *creator mundi* in a general sense. The affirmation can only be a personal confession that I understand myself to be a creature which owes its existence to God. It cannot be made as a neutral statement, but only as thanksgiving and surrender.'[39]

The following paragraph from Bultmann's *Theology of the New Testament*, for example, makes it clear that in Bultmann's conviction, the New Testament never speaks in one way about God and in a completely different way about man: 'Pauline theology is not a speculative system. It deals with God not as he is in himself but only as he is significant for man, for man's responsibility and for man's salvation. Correspondingly, it does not deal with the world and man as they are in themselves, but constantly sees the world and man in their relation to God. Every assertion about God is simultaneously an assertion about man, and vice versa. For this reason and in this sense, Paul's theology is, at the same time, anthropology.' More exactly, 'every assertion about God speaks of what he does with man and what he demands of him. And, conversely, every assertion about man speaks of God's deed and demand—or about man as he is qualified by the divine deed and demand and by his attitude towards them.'[40] In a similar way, Bultmann interprets Pauline christology directly as soteriology; that is, talk about Christ is only meaningful

[38] 'Der Gottesgedanke und der moderne Mensch', p. 342 ('The Idea of God and Modern Man', p. 89).

[39] *Jesus Christ and Mythology*, p. 69.

[40] *Theologie*, pp. 191 f. (*Theology*, I, pp. 190 f.).

35

as talk about man's salvation. Even Jesus talks of God only 'to affirm that man's will is claimed by God and is determined in his present existence through God's demand, his judgment, his grace. The distant God is at the same time the God near at hand, whose reality is not to be grasped when a man seeks to escape from his own concrete existence, but precisely when he holds it fast.'[41]

For discourse about God which transcends the subject-object division, Bultmann is fond of referring to the Reformers' understanding of scripture. He quotes Luther: 'And here we also see that to believe in Christ does not mean to believe that Christ is a person who is God and man; for that would never help anyone; but that the same person is Christ, that is, that for our sakes he went out from God and came into the world. . . .' He often takes up Melanchthon's well-known saying '*Christum cognoscere id est beneficia eius cognoscere*' ('To know Christ is to know his benefits').[42] He further refers to his teacher, Wilhelm Herrmann, who attacked the separation of the act of thinking and the act of living and untiringly stressed that God is experienced only in the totality of living. At one point he quotes him: 'We cannot make a picture of him (the Almighty) for ourselves. For what an almighty being is in himself remains hidden from us. But he has appeared to us in what he has done for us. We can only say of God what he does for us.'[43] In his first publication, a review of a few lines in the *Christian World*, in 1910, Bultmann praises the book he is reviewing along the lines his teacher would take, because it teaches the reader 'to consider what is more important to him about Jesus, *thoughts about* him or the *life* that he kindles'. Bultmann, of course, feels that the decision must be made for the latter. Today he quotes younger theologians like Dietrich Bonhoeffer: 'God is the beyond in the midst of our life'; or 'The transcendent is not the infinitely remote but the nearest

[41] *Jesus*, p. 104 (*Jesus and the Word*, p. 110).
[42] 'Die Frage der "dialektischen" Theologie', p. 54.
[43] *Kerygma und Mythos*, II, p. 185.

at hand';[44] Gabriel Vahanian: 'Faith is an attempt to reconcile subject and object, subjective truth and objective reality, without overwhelming either one of the terms,'[45] and others. He understands all these quotations as a more or less precise and explicit expression of the one intention: *'If we are to speak of God, we must evidently speak of ourselves.'*[46]

To sum up: theology as talk of God is possible for Bultmann only if it takes place on the basis of revelation. Theology as talk of God on the basis of his revelation is possible only if in talking of God it does not talk *about God* but *of man.*

But in that case *is* it possible to talk of God? Does this cease to be an 'impossible task'? 'Not at all!' says Bultmann. Even as talk of man, talk of God still remains impossible talk, and the task of theology remains an impossible task! How is that?

Bultmann's assertion will become clear as soon as we grasp what it means to talk about man, about one's self. That, Bultmann thinks, is not always understood properly, and is very often completely misunderstood.

It would be a misunderstanding, for instance, if I were to conclude from the statement that 'to talk of God' means 'to talk of myself', that God is not outside myself. That could be a correct conclusion if 'to talk of myself' meant 'to talk of my experiences'. But it does not mean that at all. Anyone who talks about his religious experiences, his inner life, his convictions, his faith, and thinks that he is talking about God would at least have to ask how the 'wholly otherness' of God is revealed or can be made visible in such talk. Could these experiences not be an illusion? Is not doubt perhaps a more appropriate attitude? In that case, is it not self-deception if in temptation a man consoles himself with his experiences? How can I be certain that I am not giving someone else a stone

[44] 'Der Gottesgedanke und der moderne Mensch', p. 342 ('The Idea of God and Modern Man', p. 90).

[45] ibid., p. 343 (ibid., p. 90).

[46] *Glauben und Verstehen*, 1, p. 28.

instead of bread when I want to help him with my experiences? My experiences are never safeguarded against the charge that God is only my cipher for processes that go on within my soul, which has no reality apart from these processes. Talking of oneself in talking of God can only make sense if what we mean is talking of God's action towards us. In that case, it is of course *possible* that we are talking of God 'when we confess, when our inner life speaks, when our experience is expressed,'[47] namely, when this confession is an act of encounter with God, when it is itself God's act in us.

But what happens 'when we consider our confession, our inner life, our experience, as something *on the basis of which* we trusted in God, as what we commended to others something *on the basis of which* they should be sure of God'?[48] Bultmann replies: 'At that moment we speak *about* our existence, and have detached ourselves from it.'[49] We no longer live in God, but make our life in God the object of reflection. Once again we fall victim to the subject-object pattern. For our life, *about* which we speak, is obviously a phantom or a past reality but not lived, genuine, authentic life. In the life *about* which we speak, we ourselves are dead. God is not to be found in this 'objectivized I', which no longer represents ourselves; for God is present only in the accomplishment of existence. God is event. When I speak *about* the occurrence of God in my existence, the same thing happens as when I speak about God; I objectivize the occurrence, become removed from it and thus from God himself. The God outside my concrete existence is an idol. If I find a place for God in my existence once it has become the object of my reflection, I show myself to be in fact godless. It is therefore the case that since God, as faith knows, is no higher being, but the power which determines our reality, and since we therefore do not really exist without God, we cannot talk *about* our existence any more than we can talk *about* God. The existence *about* which I talk is godless, and as

[47] ibid, p. 29.　　　[48] ibid.　　　[49] ibid.

such it is no longer authentic human existence. 'If our existence is grounded in God, i.e. if it is not to hand outside God,
then to grasp our existence means to grasp God,' writes Bultmann,[50] and he would agree if we added: thus the objectification of our existence amounts to the objectification of God and
thus to the loss of our existence, i.e., the loss of God. Nor can
we really speak about our sin; for 'otherwise I should be able
to distinguish myself from my sin, whereas in reality I am
myself the sinner'.[51]

Now, however, we are up against an apparently insoluble
difficulty which helps us to understand Bultmann's remark
that the task of theology, to speak about God, is an impossible
one. We cannot speak about God because he is not at our disposal; we must speak about ourselves if we want to speak about
God. But we cannot really speak about ourselves, for as soon as
we do that we separate ourselves from ourselves, we make the
experiences in which God encounters us the object of our consideration and thus become removed from God, namely, from
encounter with God, and so no longer deal with our authentic
selfhood. 'A man has no control in his ideas over this existential
self, for he cannot stand to one side and observe it, he *is* it.'[52]

So: 'We cannot talk about our existence because we cannot
talk about God; and we cannot talk about God because we
cannot talk about our existence.'[53] We could only do both at
the same time, and in fact we can do neither. Of course we can
say—as we did at the beginning of this chapter—what the
general significance of the idea of God is and what faith in
God would have to mean; in other words, that the concept of
'God', used meaningfully, embraces the concepts of 'eternity',
'omnipotence', 'indisposability', that God is the reality which
determines me, that he is not part of the world of entities, that
he cannot be objectified, etc. But in such talk God is only a

[50] ibid., p. 36.   [51] *Jesus*, p. 135 (*Jesus and the Word*, p. 140).
[52] ibid., p. 141 (ibid., p. 147).
[53] *Glauben und Verstehen*, 1, p. 33.

39

possibility, presupposed in thought. If I want to encounter his reality, talk *about* him is meaningless; for I do not have his reality in any word about him, but only in my existence—and not in any talk about my existence but in the concrete act of existing. Thus according to Bultmann the paradox of theology as an 'impossible task' does not consist in the fact 'that—like all sciences—it must speak objectively of faith, in the knowledge that all talk finds its meaning only in the transcending of objectification'.[54]

In that case, is talk about God in fact impossible? Are we left with nothing but silence? Bultmann puts this question and adds: 'Of course, at the same time that would mean that we should not act at all!'[55] by which he does not mean that we cannot do anything more at all. The fact that we cannot talk about God does not mean that we cannot talk any more at all. Rather, Bultmann apparently means: if there is no longer any possibility of talk of God, then the possibility of *authentic* human action, that is, conscious action from God, is exhausted. In that case, quietism in speech and action would be the appropriate attitude. But 'anyone who thought in this way would be making the old mistake; he would be regarding the idea of God as something *on the basis of which* a particular attitude was possible or appropriate; the mistake that the idea of God can in fact be taken into account for our conduct as something given which we have at our disposal.'[56] Who, then, can tell me that God *commands* me not to talk about him because it is an 'impossible task' from a human point of view, because *he* wants to make this task a meaningful one? My reflection about God no longer centres on God if it excludes this possibility. It is thus the same thing whether I hold that God is accessible to my knowledge and act and speak accordingly, or feel that he is inaccessible and therefore refrain from acting and speaking. In both cases I make God my object and

[54] Bultmann and Jaspers, *Die Frage der Entmythologisierung*, p. 72.
[55] *Glauben und Verstehen*, I, p. 33.   [56] ibid., p. 34.

am thus no longer with *God*. Silence as a result of reflecting on the impossibility of speaking about God would thus in fact simply be silence before an idol which was regarded as God. Silence about God is no nearer to him than talk about him.

Bultmann's positive view is that: 'To renounce theology would be to renounce faith.'[57] He does not mean by this statement that if theology ended faith would eventually come to an end—though this might well be true; his argument is that to renounce theology would itself be an act of unbelief and is therefore impermissible, because such a renunciation 'would not recognize the significance of justification for the particular man and his undertakings—in this case the undertaking of theology—and would make the promise for him and his work null and void'.[58] That is a statement which might hardly have been expected at this point in our study, and it cannot be understood without further explanation. Our attempts to understand it will at the same time help us to see what Bultmann means when he regards talk of God as at the same time both impossible *and yet* required of theology.

To recapitulate: according to Bultmann we cannot speak either about God or about our existence; for God determines our existence. If we make our existence the object of reflection, we make God the object of reflection, too, and we lose God. If we reflect about God, we reflect about our own existence, and so we have already surrendered that. We have neither God nor ourselves as *object*.

We could only speak meaningfully of God—and that means about ourselves before God—if we could speak about him *from* God; in other words, if speaking of God or our authentic existence as determined by God were a concrete act of existing in encounter with God. That might happen if God encountered us in such a way that our acknowledgment of him took

[57] 'Das Problem einer theologischen Exegese', p. 353.   [58] ibid.

41

place *in* this encounter, or if he so encountered the hearer of our words that they led him to a concrete encounter with God by God himself encountering him in our words. Put in dogmatic terms: talk about God *from* God is talk which is brought about through the Holy Spirit, and is itself a 'demonstration of the spirit and of power'. In such talk, *God* changes talk about him into talk from him, by making man's word about him into *his* word *to* man. Talk *from* God is therefore God's own talk in the inadequate form of human talk about him. In this talk *from* God, the subject-object pattern is overcome through the Spirit of God; God is no more the object of my reflection than is my existence; rather, by such talk I know myself encountered by God; I do not experience something new, whether about God or myself, but something new *happens* to me through the address of God.

Talk about God *from* God is therefore meaningful, and to this extent it is also legitimate talk about God. But does this recognition make talk about God become possible for *men*? Obviously not! Talk *from* God is talk of the Holy Spirit, is God's own talk. So how could it be possible for *us* to talk *from* God! God and his Spirit are not at our disposal. So what are we to do? To be silent about God instead of to talk about God is, as we have seen, no solution to the problem. On the contrary! Silence avoids impossible talk about God, but at the same time it prevents talk from God; talk of God makes talk from God possible, but as we do not have control over talk from God it can only be undertaken by us as impossible talk *about* God.

The only way out of this dilemma is the recognition 'that neither a tentative question nor a carefully thought out decision whether we speak or keep silent is within our power; this decision is God's decision, and for us there is only a *having-to*-speak or a *having-to*-keep-silent, a *having-to*-do or a *having-not-to*-do. And in fact that is the only answer to the question if and when we can speak of God: when we have to.'[59]

[59] *Glauben und Verstehen*, 1, p. 34.

In that case we are relieved of the responsibility whether our talk of God is talk from God or talk about him.

In this context we may remember Paul, who writes in I Cor. 9.16: 'For if I preach the Gospel, that gives me no ground for boasting, for I have to. Woe to me if I do not preach the Gospel!' Bultmann, of course, does not understand this 'have to' any more than Paul as a compulsion, as the necessary effect of a cause, as a consequence of enthusiasm or passion, in other words, as a natural process. This 'have to' rather means obedience to God's demand and as such is a free act, in which we accede to God's claim.

But *when* have I to—and that means at the same time: may I—speak of God? How and where do I experience God's command to me to speak? Bultmann feels that one can never put this as a general question and know beforehand. The 'have to' only emerges in and from the concrete situation; it is grounded only 'by the moment', and any acceptance of such a 'have to' happens 'as a concrete act of faith in obedience to the demand of a concrete situation'.[60] The 'have to' is not there before and outside our obedient talk of God, but is only given in it and with it. From a Christian point of view, therefore, the reality of this 'have to' can only be believed; that means that there is nothing on the basis of which this 'having-to-speak' presents itself convincingly to me, so that *there and then* I could accept it or withdraw from it. Rather, this 'have to' is experienced as such only where I accept it, where I *venture* to talk of God in obedience. Talk of God as a human work is impossible; as an act of obedience it is constantly a venture. The 'have to' that Bultmann means is not the 'have to' when the pastor *has to* preach on Sunday mornings at ten, the professor of theology *has to* lecture from five to six o'clock, and the teacher *has to* give religious instruction according to the timetable; but each 'has to' of this kind can lead to a genuine 'have to', when talk of God is ventured as a free act of

[60] ibid., p. 312.

43

obedience towards God, obedience which trusts God to make human talk of God *his* talk, his word *from* God.

Now what do all these remarks about talk of God add up to? Not, at any rate—to repeat what has already been said—that it is ever possible as human talk. Talk of God which takes place in faith or in the power of the Holy Spirit, that is, talk *from* God, is, from the human point of view, also impossible talk *about* God, or *about* man. If God lets man speak from God, that does not mean 'that something special, something verifiable happens in our lives, that we are imbued with special qualities and can do special things or speak special words which are not human by nature. What could we ever do and say that was *not* human?' [61] That such human words *about* God are words *from* God cannot be demonstrated by the person who utters them; the claim, explicitly raised, that particular words are words *from* God, at most means that the person who speaks in this way has not understood how talk of God and understanding of such talk is possible at all, namely, only when God himself plays a part. The person who hears these words will perceive that they are spoken from God only 'when it pleases God' [62] to encounter him; that is, not when he learns something new from them by which he arranges his speaking and acting, but when he understands himself anew, when he becomes new through God's grace (II Cor. 5.17).

Even the talk of God that happens because man has to do it is, because it is human talk, sinful talk. It is talk *about* God, and will possibly be understood by all only as this: as talk about an object, even though it is about the supreme being. 'It always remains sinful, in so far as it is always something undertaken by us.' [63] But in trust in the Holy Spirit, who alone can make my talk about God into talk from God, it is at the

---

[61] ibid., pp. 36 f.
[62] 'Die Frage der "dialektischen" Theologie', p. 53.
[63] *Glauben und Verstehen*, I, p. 37.

same time justified, 'as it is God's will to justify the sinner'.[64]
Theology thus produces under all circumstances a movement
of unbelief. 'And it is only justified if it knows what it is doing
and does not delude itself that it can ever in any way be anything but a movement of unbelief, which can only be justified
if it recognizes itself for what it is.'[65] If talk of God takes place
under the sign, 'Woe is me if I preach not the gospel', under
the 'has to' of faith, then Luther's *pecca fortiter* applies here
too,[66] and to renounce theology because I do not have firm
assurances that it happens *from* God and leads the hearer into
an encounter with God himself 'would be to renounce faith,
because it would not recognize the significance of justification
for the particular man and his undertakings—in this case the
undertaking of theology—and would make the promise for
him and his work null and void'.[67] From a human point of
view, then, the undertaking of theology constantly remains a
'sin', and meaningful talk of God is for men an 'impossible
task'. It is only possible in view of the justification of the sinner, who ventures the impossible in trust that God will justify
the venture as it pleases him.

This is the perspective from which Bultmann occasionally
defines the concept 'dialectical theology'. Christian theology
is *essentially* dialectic in the character which has been described in this chapter. It speaks of God in its insight that
man cannot speak of God; in this talk it takes control of God,
of whom it speaks as the one who cannot be controlled; it
resolves to work in the obedience of faith and at the same time
with its talk departs from the existence of faith; it means to
awake faith and is a demonstration of unbelief. That is its
dialectic, in which it must persevere if it is not to fall into
either objectification of its subject or silence.

---

[64] 'Das Problem einer theologischen Exegese', p. 353.
[65] *Glauben und Verstehen*, I, p. 312.
[66] cf. 'Das Problem einer theologischen Exegese', p. 353.
[67] ibid.

Even what we have set out to do by thinking about and discussing Bultmann's theology, that is, his talk of God, is thus, to put it in Bultmann's words, 'talk about God and therefore, if there is a God, sin, and if there is no God, nonsense. Whether it is meaningful and whether it is justified is not a matter for any of us.'[68]

At the beginning of this chapter, we asked why Bultmann called theology an impossible task; the answer is: because it is impossible for man to speak *about* God. We further asked to what degree this impossible task remained incumbent on us; the answer is: in so far as we *have to* speak about God. Finally we asked how the impossible task of theology is to be realized meaningfully: Bultmann replies: if it pleases God to make talk about him into talk *from* him.

All that has been said is, of course, true not only about theology in the narrow sense but also about the proclamation of the Word in general, in which the problems of talking about God become particularly clear and at the same time significant. Bultmann distinguishes between theology and preaching without separating the two. The two have in common above all the fact that theology and proclamation have no other or no higher knowledge than that which is given to every believer—the preacher and the theologian do not stand above the so-called 'layman', rather, theology and preaching are 'nothing but a movement of faith'[69] in the dialectical way that we have described. The only difference is that in theology 'the knowledge inherent in faith' is lifted 'into the clarity of conscious knowing',[70] which is again a presupposition for proper proclamation.

Bultmann defines 'theology' more exactly as 'the conceptual account of the existence of man as being determined by God'.[71] 'Thus theology is in any case a scientific undertaking,

---

[68] *Glauben und Verstehen*, I, p. 37.   [69] ibid., p. 90.
[70] *Theologie*, p. 191 (*Theology*, I, p. 190).
[71] 'Das Problem einer theologischen Exegese', p. 353.

as it is the task of conceptual thought.'[72] 'On the other hand, theology can never raise the claim to be direct proclamation of the word';[73] the character of theology, as opposed to that of preaching, is that it does not speak to particular hearers. 'For as scientific work it can never produce more than statements of relative validity, whereas the proclamation of the word only makes sense if its statements lay claim to being definitive for the concrete situation (and proclamation is only possible for the concrete situation). . . . The conceptual work of theology, even the exegetical work, can never be regarded as finished at a particular moment; its characteristic is that it must always become better. It would be senseless to demand the same thing of preaching the word if this really is what it should be. The Church must demand an ever-improving theology; it cannot demand an ever-improving proclamation of the word—all it can demand is that the word be proclaimed.'[74]

The last sentence in the quotation does not, of course, mean that we could not improve our sermons; it means that preaching has always to be the best possible on any particular occasion and that a new situation demands a new sermon, not a 'warmed-up' one. (The reason why many sermons are so bad is probably that they are 'warmed-up' sermons.)

Bultmann can also express what he means by saying that theology is indirect address and preaching direct address.[75] He has therefore quite understandably published a volume of his Marburg sermons only with great reluctance.

To conclude, we note Bultmann's definition that theology is 'the conceptual account of man's existence as being determined by God'. That is itself a theological statement. It shows itself to be a proper theological statement in that it only speaks of God in relation to man and of man strictly as he is related to God. That was indeed one of the basic insights of this chapter, that we can speak of God only when we speak of man. This

[72] ibid., p. 354.   [73] ibid.   [74] ibid., pp. 354 f.
[75] *Glauben und Verstehen*, 1, p. 176.

does not, of course, mean that the relationship between God and man must be explained in every single theological statement. The demand for appropriate theological discourse is not a formal one, but a material one. Therefore it is not illegitimate, but in accordance with Bultmann's own procedure, for our next chapter to be called 'Man' and for a later one to deal with 'God's Revelation'. This procedure would be illegitimate only if the chapters with these titles led up to a later one which was meant to combine them under the heading 'Man and God'. When we speak of man we are *at the same time* speaking of God, and vice versa.

To speak first of man and not of revelation as God's saving act corresponds to the method which Bultmann constantly applies, the appropriateness of which must be demonstrated in its application, in Bultmann's case and in ours.

3

Man

WE BEGIN once again with the basic statement of Bultmann's theology, around which the previous chapter revolved: 'If theology is not to speculate about God, to talk of the *concept* of God, but of the real God, then in talking of God it must at the same time talk of man.'[1] Bultmann is fond of using the concept of *existence* in talking about man. That, too, was clear from the last chapter, which showed that for Bultmann, speaking of man or of human existence amounts to the same thing. This fact in itself already shows that for Bultmann man does not have 'existence' as something in itself or as a possible way of behaving, but that he *is* an existence. Man cannot 'construct an existence' for himself, nor can he 'lack something in his existence'. No-one can 'destroy man's existence' or 'deprive him of the basis of his existence': man, rather, always exists as man. According to Bultmann, existence is the form of being characteristic of man, without which man would not be man.

Occasionally we have already noticed in Bultmann the concept 'authentic existence', which presupposes its counterpart 'inauthentic existence'. 'Authentic existence' was Bultmann's expression for existence determined by the reality of God, for existence in faith. 'Inauthentic existence' is accordingly existence in unbelief, existence not determined by God. It is still too early here to develop and interpret Bultmann's understanding of faith and unbelief in terms of authenticity and

[1] *Glauben und Verstehen*, I, p. 117.

49

inauthenticity of human experience. At this point we are only interested in the fact that according to Bultmann man in any case *exists*, whether in faith or in unbelief, that existence is his nature, whether he lives in the authenticity or the inauthenticity of his existence.

But what does it mean to speak of man as an existence? What understanding of the nature of man is expressed in this designation? The present chapter will be concerned with this question.

Bultmann writes: ' "Existence" means something more than being-at-hand, that is, the fact that something "exists" = is at hand. Existence is the specifically human mode of being.'[2] This is the sense, as Bultmann sees, in which Kierkegaard coined the concept of existence. He believes that the specifically human mode of being, 'existence', is rightly understood when man's being is understood as an *ability to be*; that is, he believes 'that man's being is removed from his control. Sometimes it is at risk in the concrete situations of life, and goes through decisions in which man never chooses *something for himself*, but *chooses himself as his possibility*.'[3] Man is thus *possibility*, his own possibility.

The significance of these remarks will become clearest if we compare the understanding of human existence described in them with another understanding of human existence. Bultmann is fond of using the Greek understanding of the nature of man as a comparison; for it is contemporaneous with the biblical picture of man and has, moreover, retained its influence right up to the present day.

The Greek calls the world 'cosmos', which means 'order', 'adornment'. The characteristic feature of the cosmos, which is the world of gods and men, is therefore that it represents a well-ordered unity. Each individual happening at any given time happens according to the eternal laws which give the

[2] *Glauben und Verstehen*, 3, p. 107.   [3] ibid., 1, p. 118.

cosmos its elaborate form. Everything in the world has a place which is provided for it—the concept of 'providence' in particular plays a considerable role in the Stoa—and fulfils its purpose when it occupies this place. The reality of the cosmos, understood in this way, is presupposed for each concrete reality in the world.

Man, too, is part of the cosmos. He is a prominent part of the cosmos; for 'there are many marvellous things, but none more marvellous than man' (Sophocles). But man, like even the gods, is subject to the laws of the cosmos. These laws, i.e. the forms appointed for the world, are what is eternal, 'and man is eternal when he participates in them'.[4] Man 'understands the world as a unity pervaded by divine power, and himself as incorporated in this cosmos and safeguarded in it, if he grasps the place that is properly his and affirms the ordering of the world which is identical with the law of his own being'.[5] The world is understood by analogy with a work of art, 'in which the raw material is shaped and has taken shape. It is important to know the laws of its forms and of all the development of forms. In this way man understands himself, that is, as a part of the great *cosmos*.'[6] The reality of all human being is already given through the ordering of the cosmos independently of and before each concrete historical reality of the individual man.

Thus the Greek understands himself as 'a particular instance of the general, and understands the enigmas of his existence, in understanding the conformity of the *whole* to law'.[7] That means that he is 'an object of observation like the other objects of nature'.[8] He measures himself by the ideal standard of the cosmos which he can observe and calculate, and conforms himself to this ideal. To do this he must make himself free 'from life in its concrete attachment to whatever is

---

[4] *Glauben und Verstehen*, 2, p. 64 (*Essays*, p. 73).
[5] ibid., p. 65 (ibid., p. 73).   [6] ibid., p. 63 (ibid., p. 72).
[7] ibid.   [8] ibid.

given, whatever encounters him, the particular and the transitory' and strive 'to exist beyond the sphere of the temporal or the incidental, in the sphere of timelessness and eternity';[9] for concrete historical reality with its manifold potentialities is calculated to distract man's attention from his authentic reality, given through the eternal regularity of the cosmos. Each individual thing at any given time is thus only rightly understood when it is comprehended 'in relation to the laws which give it form, and make the universe a work of art'.[10]

It is possible for man to realize the ideal which is set before him, for the law, i.e. the ideal that is set before him, is nothing strange to him, coming from outside him, but his own law. Man is 'spirit', and in this way is related to the Godhead, which like him is itself a part of the cosmos. By virtue of his spirit he can understand the cosmos and realize himself in it; for the law of the spirit is the law of the cosmos itself.

Bultmann describes the Greek picture of man as a *Weltanschauung*: 'A *Weltanschauung* seeks to make even my destiny comprehensible on the basis of a general understanding of man and the world, as an instance of what happens generally.'[11] In a *Weltanschauung* there are controls over man prior to his concrete reality. What happens at any given time cannot introduce anything new in principle; above all, it cannot teach man to understand himself anew, but must be interpreted in such a way as to fit in with the existing *Weltanschauung*.

Does this picture of man correspond to the understanding of man presupposed in the New Testament? Bultmann answers with a decisive 'No!' 'In the view of the New Testament, that is the very way in which I evade my authentic existence. I do not achieve my existence in the sphere of the abstract, but in a concrete situation, in the here and now, in my individual responsibility and decision, where in hazarding myself I can gain or lose myself.'[12]

[9] ibid., pp. 64 f. (ibid., p. 73).   [10] ibid., p. 64 (ibid., p. 73).
[11] ibid., p. 69 (ibid., p. 78).   [12] ibid.

Man

According to the Greek understanding of existence, man is at his own disposal in so far as he knows of his own ideal determination in the context of a general world-view and can shape himself to it, with whatever success he may have. According to the biblical understanding of existence, I am not at my own disposal, for my determination as a man is to choose myself as existence in all concrete situations, i.e. whatever I may choose in particular, (also) to choose myself as my own possibility. I am not always already myself; I become myself at particular times in particular concrete situations. I never know what I will become; I only know that I am possibility, and my authentic reality is to keep myself as possibility, in other words to keep surrendering, or putting at risk what I already am, so as to gain myself as my possibility. But in that case I am taken out of my own control, for I have no control over my encounter at any given time in the concrete moment, which demands a decision which is constantly new.

In accordance with this, while the Greek speaks of providence, this concept is completely alien to the Bible. For the Greeks, everything in the world is ordered with a purpose and is clear to man, so that in his insight into the universe, in looking at the cosmos, he has the world and its eternal laws at his disposal. For the Bible, however, God's action cannot be seen; *his* ways are unfathomable; man therefore has no control over God but is man precisely by virtue of the fact that he stands open at all times to incalculable encounter with God, who does with man what pleases *him*.

Over against the Greek understanding of existence, 'the New Testament asserts that the authentic life of man is not that of the cosmos, but runs its course in the incidental, the individual, in the sphere of history: that what the Greek regards as the appearance of reality is in fact the authentic reality of life; and that it is here and nowhere else that man's fate is decided for good or ill, once he has become open to the future which presents itself to him on each several occasion in the "now". It is in this world of concrete historical happening that God and what he asks, what he demands, what he gives

53

are to be found. God is not manifest in the eternal orders of the world to the thought that soars into a timeless sphere—and that is where for the Greek *Weltanschauung* the scandal lies. These orders are ambivalent, and they can just as easily conceal God as reveal him. God is to be met with in the historical happening which is his free, arbitrary action. The quest for truth is to the Greek a search for the disclosure of the world of entities in its totality; to the New Testament it is the question of the demand, or the gift, of the moment.'[13]

Among other things, it follows from all this that man has his authentic being only as life in the moment. 'For existence in the moment is his authentic being.'[14] How else could it be, if 'to exist' means 'to proceed by decisions'! For true decisions can only be made in the face of the demand or the gift which always comes to me in the moment and comes to me anew in each moment.

This once again helps us to understand why Bultmann has to 'exclude completely the distinction between subject and object' from the question of our existence.[15] 'True, one can of course reflect objectively upon existence, that is, upon what existence means in theory, upon the nature of existence. But reflection of this kind recognizes that on each occasion existence is mine and can only be taken over or achieved by me; that means: existence is on each several occasion *event* in the decisions of the moment. It is not to hand, but is something which happens on each several occasion';[16] in other words, I do not understand myself sufficiently as man if I understand myself only as a natural being existing as a thing, instead of as someone who happens on each occasion.

Finally, it follows from all this that the nature of authentic human existence according to the New Testament, as Bultmann understands it, is man's radical openness for the future, i.e. for what comes to him anew on each several occasion. As long as he is prepared to exist in decisions, man remains man,

[13] ibid., p. 73 (ibid., pp. 83 f.).
[14] *Glauben und Verstehen*, 3, p. 30 (*Existence and Faith*, p. 86).
[15] *Glauben und Verstehen*, 1, p. 32.   [16] ibid., 3, p. 117.

no matter whether he grasps God or the world, grace or sin, life or death in his particular decisions.

In each such attempt he is essentially man, he grasps his existence; for at the same time he grasps himself as a being which constantly exists as its potentiality. If, on the other hand, he is no longer willing to have this status, if he shuts himself off in principle from encounters in which he is at risk at each several moment, he loses himself, surrenders his existence, or better, surrenders himself as existence, no matter how he may now see his life, no matter what view of the world now governs him.

It should be noted that man is not authentic man by *having* possibilities, but by deciding about *himself* in view of the possibilities which he has. That is what Bultmann means when he says that man is his own possibility. An animal, too, *has* possibilities, but it does not have the possibility to choose itself; it *is* not possibility, it is nature. Man, on the other hand, is not authentically understood if he is understood as nature. He is possibility, i.e. his authentic being stands newly before him at each moment, and if he exists *authentically*, he does not know today who he will in fact be tomorrow, what he will in fact do tomorrow. He can only decide about that tomorrow, and his decision—the one which he ultimately makes in all concrete decisions, amounts to being open to the future and having in the end to decide nothing except *to exist*, that is, to will to be man in unconditional openness to whatever encounters him at any given moment.

For Bultmann, the Greek understanding of existence is not just a thing of the past. On the contrary, it has been given new shape by the 'idealism' of the nineteenth century, and many people even today unwittingly identify the idealist picture of man with that of the Bible and Christianity. In 1926, Bultmann wrote—with the idealistic picture of man characteristic of liberal theology in mind: 'We are accustomed to regard a man as an individual of the species "man", a being endowed with definite capacities, the development of which brings the human ideal in him to realization—of course with variations in each individual. As "character" or "personality", man achieves his end. Harmonious development of all human facilities, according to the individual endowment of each man, is the way to this ideal. Perhaps no man can travel this road to the end, but progress along the road, bringing the ideal nearer to realization, justifies human existence.'[17] All this, says Bultmann, is completely alien to the Bible, for which the worth of man 'is not determined by his human quality or the character of his spiritual life', which is a feature of all concrete humanity, but only 'by the decision the man makes in the here-and-now of his present life. . . . Only what a man now does gives him his value.'[18] The Bible is therefore concerned 'that just this necessity of decision constitutes the essential part of his human nature'.[19]

Bultmann sees the Greek understanding of existence still maintained in principle in the scientific picture of man which characterized the nineteenth century. This is no coincidence; for according to Bultmann man is fond of evading the recognition that he is really man only as existence. He looks much more intensively for a '*Weltanschauung*', i.e. for a picture of the world in which he knows himself to have a place as a particular instance of the general. 'It is quite understandable that such "*Weltanschauungen*" are very popular, even if they are not very flattering about man and explain him, say, as a chance product of a combination of atoms, as the highest vertebrate and cousin of the apes, or as an interesting phenomenon of psychological complexes. For once again they do man the great service of detaching him from himself, of excusing him from the problems of his concrete existence, concern for it and responsibility for it. Man's desire for a "*Weltanschauung*" is grounded in this fact, that he can withdraw to it in the face of the riddles of destiny and death, that at the moment when his existence is shattered and becomes questionable he can avoid taking it seriously and understand it more as an instance of the general rule, put it in a context, objectify it, and thus find a way out of it.'[20] Bultmann is far from disputing that these somewhat unflattering remarks about man have a scientific basis and may or may not be justified. It is just that he believes that they do not describe man authentically and that it is the 'first lie' of man that he is convinced that he has understood himself sufficiently with such remarks about his humanity.

[17] *Jesus*, p. 39 (*Jesus and the Word*, p. 45).
[18] ibid., p. 40 (ibid., p. 46).
[19] ibid., p. 39 (ibid., p. 44).
[20] *Glauben und Verstehen*, I, p. 31.

We have said, and now have seen, that this understanding of existence developed by Bultmann under the concept of 'existence' represents in his view the picture of man contained in the New Testament. That does not, of course, mean that somewhere in the New Testament we can find the presentation of an anthropology in a developed conceptuality, as happens in Bultmann's own writings. But Bultmann sees this understanding of man taken for granted in all the theological language and concrete proclamation of the New Testament.

This is the case in the *proclamation of Jesus*, which announces the kingdom of God and in so doing does not simply communicate some interesting information to man but summons him to decide for God and his kingdom. For the Jews, of course, the idea of the 'kingdom of God' was connected with cosmic catastrophes and a drama set in heaven in which the wicked were destroyed and the people of God redeemed. For Jesus, however, Bultmann writes, the real significance of the kingdom of God does not depend 'on the dramatic events attending its coming, nor on any circumstances which the imagination can conceive. It does not interest him at all as a describable state of existence, but rather as the miraculous event which signifies for man the great Either-Or, which constrains him to decision.'[21] The real basis of Jesus' preaching of the coming kingdom of God was not the nearness of God's rule but Jesus' understanding of the nature of human existence, namely, 'that man realizes standing in decision to be his authentic nature. Because Jesus sees man thus in a crisis of decision before God, it is understandable that in his thought the Jewish Messianic hope becomes the absolute certainty that in this hour the kingdom of God is coming. If men are standing in the crisis of decision, and if precisely this crisis is the essential characteristic of their humanity, then every hour is the last hour.'[22] Jesus thus put the apocalyptic expectation

[21] *Jesus*, p. 32 (*Jesus and the Word*, p. 37).
[22] ibid., p. 39 (ibid., p. 44).

of the coming kingdom of God 'at the service of this concept of human existence'; [23] his interest was directed towards
man as 'existence', not towards apocalyptic. Bultmann thus
expressly stresses that one can understand Jesus' proclamation
'only when one considers the conception of man which in the
last analysis underlies it, and when one remembers that it can
have meaning only for the one who is ready to question the
habitual human, i.e. self- interpretation and to measure it by
the interpretation of human existence which encounters him
here', namely, 'the conception of man as forced to decision
through a future act of God'.[24]

Bultmann develops the biblical picture of man at length by
means of *Pauline theology*. His extensive treatment of the
Pauline literature in his *Theology of the New Testament* begins
with a section on 'The anthropological concepts'.[25] By way of
introduction, Bultmann remarks that Paul always sees man in
his relationship to God. To understand this relationship it is
necessary first to 'clarify for ourselves the peculiarity of human
existence, i.e. the formal structures of this existence',[26] for
Paul sees *everything* that is and takes place in relationship to
God. 'What, then, is the specifically human—that which gives
man's relation to God its peculiar character?'[27] Obviously Paul
no more developed a scientific anthropology than did Jesus;
the understanding of the nature of human existence presupposed by him must be inferred from concrete statements
about the relationship between God and man which he makes
from time to time.

The most characteristic term which Paul uses to describe
human existence in general is, according to Bultmann, the
concept *soma*, which is usually translated 'body'. This translation is inadequate; for we are accustomed to regard the body
as a *part* of man and the 'soul' or 'spirit' as other parts of man

---

[23] ibid. (ibid., p. 45).   [24] ibid., p. 41 (ibid., p. 47).
[25] *Theologie*, pp. 192–226 (*Theology*, I, pp. 191–227).
[26] ibid., p. 193 (ibid., p. 192).   [27] ibid. (ibid., p. 191).

which are to be distinguished from his body. For us, man *has* body *and* soul *and* spirit. But this does not match Paul's specific use of the concept *soma*; for Paul, *soma* is a description of the *whole* man. Man does not *have* a *soma*, he *is* a *soma*. Bultmann points out that in Paul one can often replace the term *soma* with the corresponding personal pronoun. In Phil. 1.20, for example, Paul expresses the hope that 'Christ will be honoured in my body', i.e. in his *soma*. That does not mean, as the context clearly shows, 'in my body', but 'in myself'. Bultmann also calls attention to Rom. 6.12 f., where *soma* is interchanged with 'self' without the meaning being altered: 'Let not sin therefore reign in your mortal *bodies* . . . but surrender *yourselves* to God.' It would therefore be more appropriate to translate *soma* as 'self' instead of 'body'; for *soma* describes the person as a whole.

Now Paul does not always speak of man as a *soma*. *Soma* evidently describes man in a particular respect. 'But what is the specific respect in which man is regarded when he is called *soma*?'[28] Bultmann replies: 'Man is called *soma* in respect to his being able to make himself the object of his own action or to experience himself as the subject to whom something happens. He can be called *soma*, that is, as having a relationship to himself—as being able in a certain sense to distinguish himself from himself. Or, more exactly, he is so called as that self from whom he, as subject, distinguishes himself, the self with whom he can deal as the object of his own conduct, and also the self whom he can perceive as subjected to an occurrence that springs from a will other than his own. It is as such a self that man is called *soma*.'[29] As the concept *soma* describes man in general, to have such 'a relationship to himself' is in itself the nature of man.

In this terminology, which is still strange to us, Bultmann is simply saying what we have hitherto kept hearing from him

[28] ibid., p. 196 (ibid., p. 195).
[29] ibid. (ibid., pp. 195 f.).

about his understanding of human existence: that man essentially lives in decisions in such a way that in all these decisions he decides about himself; that 'to exist' means constantly to be open for encounters; that human existence is rightly understood only as 'being in the moment'. 'To have a relationship to oneself' in fact means to begin something with oneself, to put oneself at risk, to be able to gain and lose oneself, never to be devoted to oneself but always to have surrendered oneself, in short: to be able to exist, to stand before oneself as potentiality in all concrete possibilities.

Of course, misunderstandings are easily possible if one does not note sufficiently carefully that Bultmann here distinguishes man as object from man as subject. Did he not tell us that 'the distinction of subject and object must be kept quite separate from the question of our existence'?[30] Now if he is understood rightly, he is not going back on that remark, but showing what it means in practice. The man who makes himself the object of his reflection or his talk, i.e. the man who *talks about himself*, is removed from his existence; for he is existence only in what he does, in decision, in action. The man who makes himself the object of his *action*, i.e. who *decides about himself*, on the other hand, proves his existence; for as the object of his action he is not alienated from himself but actually brings his existence to fulfilment. So when Bultmann speaks of the man who stands over against himself as object in his decision, he is speaking of the man in existence who, whether as the subject who decides or as the object of his decision, is the one, same, total man in the fulfilment of his existence. He is called 'subject', because while existing in everyday possibilities *he* always decides about himself; he is called object, because he decides *about himself*. However, in order to avoid misunderstanding, we shall as far as possible avoid the terms 'subject' and 'object' in the sense last introduced; what Bultmann means can also be clarified sufficiently without these concepts.

[30] *Glauben und Verstehen*, 1, p. 32.

Once again: Paul calls man *soma* in so far as he is regarded as a being who can decide about himself, or more accurately, in so far as man feels responsible to himself as to his own decision. This being *soma* 'is in itself neither good nor bad'.[31] But only because man is *soma* does he have the potentiality of being either good or evil, and therefore the potentiality of having, positively or negatively, an authentic relationship to God. As *soma* he can open himself to the future and live from what encounters him. 'If man were no longer *soma*—if he no longer had a relationship to himself—he would no longer be man.'[32]

Bultmann interprets the zeal with which Paul defends the resurrection of the body (=*soma*) against his Corinthian opponents in the light of this recognition; for the man who is no longer *soma* is no longer man. The Greek is interested in immortality, through which he hopes to avoid what is temporal, fortuitous and historical, in order to achieve his timeless being in pure contemplation of the idea which gives form to the cosmos. In defending the resurrection of the *soma*, Paul, on the other hand, asserts specific human existence in the sense we have just described of 'being in the moment', even beyond death. So Bultmann is fond of referring to I Cor. 13.13: 'So faith, hope, love abide'—in contrast to knowledge, which is partial—even in the consummation. By virtue of their structure, faith, hope and love are never an assured possession, but must be grasped by decision, realized in action, in each several moment. Consequently, in I Cor. 13.13 Paul presupposes that the openness of Christian existence has no end; rather, the characteristic quality of man as 'existence' remains constant in time and in eternity.

If *soma* in Paul characterizes man in so far as he is the *object* of his own action and decision, other concepts characterize the same man in so far as he is *subject* of this action and decision. Among these, Bultmann includes *psyche* (soul); *pneuma* (spirit); *zoe* (life); *nous* (understanding); *syneidesis* (conscience) and

[31] *Theologie*, p. 199 (*Theology*, I, p. 198).   [32] ibid.

kardia (heart). As *syneidesis* man knows about himself as *soma*; as *nous* he decides about himself as *soma*; as *kardia* he desires himself as *soma*, and so on. The connection between the concept *soma* and the groups of concepts just mentioned thus makes it quite clear, in Bultmann's view, that man has a relationship to himself, that he can contemplate himself, can gain himself and lose himself, surrender himself, to life or death, in other words, that he is his own possibility.

The analysis of human existence in general, carried out by Bultmann and reported by us so far, is not a specific element of his theology as far as its content is concerned. Bultmann is, however, fond of introducing his theological work from time to time with such a detailed anthropological analysis. The reason for this is, of course, that according to Bultmann, theology as talk of God is significant only if it talks of the *man* whom God encounters. Wherever the biblical faith has been maintained, Bultmann notes that the picture of man which underlies it has also been maintained, mostly unconsciously or not explicitly, but occasionally brought to consciousness and established in a terminology, as with Kierkegaard.

Now of course the description of human existence which Bultmann feels to be appropriate on the basis of the New Testament occurs not only in the realm of theology, but also in the realm of philosophy, particularly in 'existentialist' philosophy, and most markedly in the philosophy of Martin Heidegger. This fact has led to a lively discussion within the controversy over Bultmann's theology, especially as Bultmann himself often draws attention to it and has even made it the subject of explicit reflection. But even if Bultmann had not drawn direct attention to the fact, his analysis of existence would itself have indicated the problems of its relationship to philosophy; for the conceptuality with which Bultmann develops the New Testament understanding of existence is essentially that used by Heidegger and, in parts, also coined by him.

Martin Heidegger raises the question of *Being* in a new way. In his view it has never been investigated since the time of the early Greek philosophers, but has been presupposed as something which is quite obvious. Unlike the Greeks, Heidegger looks for an answer to the question of Being not in a view of the cosmos, but in an analysis of human existence, whose relationship to Being is obvious, seeing that man as an individual entity *asks* about Being. The question of Being thus begins, appropriately enough, as a question of human existence, the being of *Dasein* (Heidegger's word for distinctive human existence). In this question the philosophical work of Martin Heidegger, who asks about Being, coincides with that of Rudolf Bultmann, who asks about God: both begin, despite the fundamentally different positions from which they start, with the question of man.

Following Kierkegaard, Heidegger calls the being of *Dasein*, so to speak 'the substance of man', *existence*. Existence means literally: 'to stand out (in) . . .' Heidegger understands the term 'existence' in this literal sense. The being of *Dasein* as existence is being-able-to-be, the standing-out of *Dasein* in its own possibility; the fact that man *is* (not *has*) existence means that he always has himself before himself as his own possibility; to exist in an authentic way therefore means to keep oneself open at all times for encounters, for the future, etc.

From these few sentences it is already clear that Heidegger's understanding of human existence corresponds exactly to what Bultmann outlines as the biblical understanding of human existence. Bultmann finds nothing surprising in this; for existentialist analysis is in his view simply 'the systematic development of the self-understanding given with existence'.[33] No matter who undertakes it, this development can only take place 'in profane reflection'; it is the 'business of the philosophical analysis of existence',[34] even when it is undertaken

[33] *Kerygma und Mythos*, II, p. 193 (*Kerygma and Myth*, p. 194).
[34] ibid., p. 192 (ibid., p. 192).

by the theologian. So philosophy and theology meet here; for 'the object of an existentialist analysis of man is . . . man; and man . . . is likewise the object of theology'.[35] Bultmann can call philosophy which is concerned to 'develop the understanding of existence given with human existence in appropriate terminology',[36] a 'right' philosophy. He regards Heidegger's philosophy as a 'right' philosophy in this sense. It shows man 'that human Being, as distinct from all other Being, means *existing*, a form of Being which assumes complete responsibility for itself. It tells us that our authentic existence is realizable only in existence, which means existing always in the concrete here and now.'[37] Bultmann feels that it is unjustified prejudice to think that it is impossible to outline a 'purely formal' analysis of existence in philosophical reflection which can lay claim to general validity. 'How far such an attempt can succeed is of course another question, but in the last resort it is no more relevant than the insight that conclusive knowledge is impossible in any science or philosophy. Any resultant analysis is still open to correction, and here as elsewhere discussion is the *sine qua non* of progress.'[38] True, one can ask whether the nature of man, that is the peculiar human mode of being as existence, could have been discovered without the New Testament. But Bultmann rejects this question: 'As a matter of fact it has not been discovered without the aid of the New Testament; there would be no modern philosophy at all without the New Testament and Luther and Kierkegaard. But this merely indicates the place of existentialism in the intellectual history of man; as far as content is concerned, the understanding of existence in modern philosophy is justified by something other than its historical

[35] 'Die Geschichtlichkeit des Daseins', pp. 339 f. (*Existence and Faith*, p. 93).
[36] *Kerygma und Mythos*, II, p. 192 (*Kerygma and Myth*, p. 193).
[37] ibid., p. 193 (ibid., p. 193).
[38] ibid., p. 194 (ibid., p. 195).

origin.'[39] It would be right, even if it did not correspond to the biblical picture of man.

Perhaps it is remarkable to some that Bultmann so repeatedly and extensively discusses the relationship of the philosophical analysis of existence to talk about man in his theology; or, more exactly, how Bultmann is so vigorously attacked for taking his anthropological terminology from the philosophical elucidation of existence, and how he feels himself obliged to make prolific apologies. For the analysis of human existence which we have put forward by means of Bultmann's remarks is in fact very formal, and in no way removes what the New Testament calls faith.

The polemic against Bultmann and his intensive defence against that polemic can, however, be understood better if we see that the correspondence between Heidegger's philosophical analysis of existence and Bultmann's theological talk of man is more comprehensive than we have so far noticed. To be 'existence' means, as we saw, to stand in possibilities, to be open to encounters in which a decision is made about oneself. In each true decision I always decide for myself as existence; that means that in decision I prove my permanent openness for what comes to me on each several occasion. But, Bultmann explains, according to the New Testament man has surrendered this very openness by handing himself over to the world that he can see, that is at his disposal, letting himself be led astray to live on this basis and thus has fallen victim to the world. In this way he has cut himself off from encounter with God, the one who is not at his disposal. In that man no longer simply keeps himself open for the future, he no longer exists *authentically*. He has surrendered himself as possibility. In surrendering to the world he has lost his 'authentic existence'; he lives in 'inauthenticity'. The question is, whether he will or can renounce this inauthenticity and regain his authentic

[39] *Kerygma und Mythos*, I, p. 35 (*Kerygma and Myth*, p. 26).

existence, and this question is, from a Christian point of view, the question of man's salvation.

At this point we need not go further into what is hinted at in these last sentences about 'sin' and the 'salvation' of man; we shall be developing the hints in the following chapters. The point that interests us here is simply that on the basis of a philosophical analysis of existence Martin Heidegger seems to be saying the same thing as the Bible, as Bultmann understands it. At any rate, according to Bultmann, 'Martin Heidegger's existentialist analysis of the ontological structure of being would seem to be no more than a secular, philosophical version of the New Testament view of human existence; man, existing historically in care about himself, on the basis of anxiety; on each occasion in the moment of decision between the past and the future, as to whether he will lose himself in the world of what is to hand, of the "they", or whether he will abandon all security and commit himself unreservedly to the future, and thus achieve his authentic Being! Is not that also the New Testament understanding of human life?'[40]

In view of such a question we can see how necessary it is to make a thorough investigation of the relationship between the content of the philosophical analysis of existence and that of Bultmann's theology. For very soon the problem comes to a head in the question whether the Christian understanding of existence is not also possible without Christ, as a philosophical, natural one. As we have already seen Bultmann remark, the fact that Heidegger's existentialist analysis in fact presupposes the New Testament may not be relevant at all. One may certainly ask to what extent in their years together not only Bultmann learnt from Heidegger, but also Heidegger, who at that time was intensively occupied, among other things, with Luther, learnt from Bultmann. But even if this were so—and without question that was the case—the New Testament understanding of existence also appears today, at any rate to

[40] ibid., p. 33 (ibid., pp. 24 f.).

the extent we have outlined, as a natural, profane, secularized understanding of human Being. Therefore it could 'well appear possible to have a Christian understanding of Being without Christ, as though what we had in the New Testament was the first discovery and the more or less clear expression, in the guise of mythology, of an understanding of Being which is at bottom man's natural understanding of his Being, as it has been given clear expression in modern existentialist philosophy. . . . In that case—and a respectable historical argument could be produced in support—theology would simply be the precursor of philosophy, now outmoded by philosophy and nothing more than an unnecessary and inconvenient competitor.'[41] Thus the question of the relationship of Bultmann's theology to philosophy still remains open. It will occupy us further when in the next chapters we go on to develop the New Testament understanding of man, first as 'inauthentic', then as 'authentic'; it will occupy us further, in order to shed more light on this development and at the same time to help us to find an answer.

Before that, however, in view of what has been said in this chapter, it would be a good thing to clarify two terms which are particularly important for Bultmann, 'existentialist' (*existential*) and 'existential' (*existentiel*). The first of these two terms has occupied us continually during this chapter. It may become even more precise if we contrast it with what 'existential' means for Bultmann.

Karl Barth makes fun of the distinction we have just mentioned. 'Anyone who engages in a discussion with Bultmann or his pupils should beware of confusing "existentialist" and "existential", if he does not want the conversation to come to an abrupt end. Other misunderstandings may be forgiven, this one never!'[42] Nevertheless, Bultmann uses these concepts

[41] ibid., p. 32 (ibid., p. 23).
[42] Karl Barth, *Rudolf Bultmann, ein Versuch, ihn zu Verstehen*, p. 35 (*Kerygma and Myth*, II, p. 111).

regularly; he makes a strict distinction between them; with this distinction they are an expression of a fundamental problem in Bultmann's theology. Anyone who does not keep the two expressions distinct in a discussion of Bultmann shows that he does not have the most elementary background for such a discussion, namely, an understanding of what Bultmann is saying.

Both 'existentialist' and 'existential' are terms which refer to existence, but each does so in a different way.

Existentialist analysis, according to Bultmann, elucidates the nature of human existence in the abstract. It analyses the structure of existence. It explains conceptually what it means for man, unlike a mere natural being, to be his own possibility. It sketches out the different possibilities of existence. It is not itself an act of achieving existence, for in such an analysis no real decision has yet been made, except the decision to see the Being of man in his existence.

Where man decides for a concrete possibility of existing, or for existing itself as the being of his existence, he is no longer occupied in an existentialist analysis, he is engaged *existentially*. Thus on the basis of his existentialist structure—of which he need not of course be conscious—man chooses in existential decision on each several occasion one of the possibilities of his concrete existence. He exists, and existence never *happens* existentialistically, but always existentially.

The establishment of the existentialist structures of existence necessarily takes place within the subject-object pattern. True, man is not objectified so that he becomes a natural being, but the understanding of existence given with his existence is itself made an object of reflection. *This* objectification takes place in existentialist analysis. But the division between subject and object is always overcome in the achievement of existential existence.

Existing, of course, has priority over existentialist analysis. Bultmann writes: 'Clearly, existentialist analysis is founded upon the existential questions of existence, for otherwise it is hard to see how it could know anything about existence. Indeed, its work consists in systematizing the understanding of existence involved in existence itself.'[43] Without the achievement of existential existence, then, there would be no existentialist analysis. To exist existentially (if one may keep putting it so tautologously) and to make an existentialist analysis of existence are related to one another without the surrender of their fundamental difference. Their relationship is therefore not interchangeable. There is only existentialist analysis because there is existence, but there are existential decisions even without existentialist analysis.

Moreover, the distinction between 'existentialist' and 'existential', in Bultmann as in Heidegger, corresponds to that between 'ontological' and 'ontic', which is more common in philosophy. Existentialist analysis is concerned with ontology in so far as it describes the mode of being of existence. 'Ontic', on the other hand, describes the actual achievement of existence or the concrete mode of acting of existence itself. Even if the ontological structure of human nature is clarified existentialistically, we have only the presupposition for making ontic statements about men, though of course it is the necessary presupposition for the right conceptual understanding of the existential achievement of existence. Anyone who discloses existentialist structures is doing ontology; the concrete possibilities which man puts into existential realization are ontic. Thus, for example, philosophy can disclose the ontological possibility of something like 'faith' in human existence without saying anything about the ontic reality of faith.

As far as the problem of the relationship between Bultmann's theology and philosophy is concerned, the distinction between 'existentialist' and 'existential' can also be put in the following way: philosophy 'does not pose the problem of existence as an existential question, but asks in existentialist

[43] *Kerygma und Mythos*, II, p. 193 (*Kerygma and Myth*, p. 194).

analysis about the meaning of existence in the abstract: for it is aware that the existential problem can be answered only in existence itself'.[44] 'It does not tell man: "You ought to exist *thus!*" It simply tells him: "You ought to *exist!*" Or perhaps that is going too far. It might be better to say that it shows him what existence means.'[45]

In these statements Bultmann's view is evidently not that philosophy *may* not say: You ought to exist *thus*—who would want to prohibit that?—but that it *cannot* say this, in other words, that it cannot help man to his authentic existence. In this explanation of Bultmann's we can already see his final assessment of the relationship between philosophy and theology and his solution of the question whether there can be Christian existence on a philosophical, natural basis. This is the question which we shall be carrying forward into the coming chapters in which we shall investigate the ontic reality of human existence on the basis of the ontological analysis of human existence.

[44] ibid., p. 192 (ibid., p. 193).
[45] ibid., p. 193 (ibid.).

4

Inauthenticity and Sin

BULTMANN says—and thus far we have understood him—
that one can only talk meaningfully of God if one talks of man.
But to talk of man cannot be a specifically theological task. At
all events, philosophy also talks of man, and such talk is its
legitimate business; furthermore, such talks is *its* legitimate
business, and not that of theology, which has to talk of God.
Now because theology can only talk of God by talking about
man, its work is closely associated with that of philosophy. It
need not necessarily be conscious of this fact: Bultmann makes
it conscious of it. The theologian does not necessarily need a
philosopher: he can be his own philosopher. But wherever the
theologian analyses human existence and seeks to grasp it
conceptually, he is doing the work of a philosopher.

We saw how Bultmann makes use of Heidegger's analysis of
existence in his theological work, as in it he sees the nature of
man as existence, as it is presupposed in the New Testament.
developed appropriately and in suitable terms. Now the
analysis of existence carried out by Heidegger in *Being and
Time* in some ways goes beyond the description of the ontological structure of human existence to which we devoted our
attention in the previous chapter. We have already indicated
that this is the case. Heidegger discloses not only the fact *that*
man exists, i.e. that human Being is 'being-able-to-be'; he also
analyses how in fact man realizes his existence. In that he
infers the ontological basic structure of *Dasein*, namely

71

existentiality, from the *ontic reality* of man—where else would he find this structure?—he also analyses existence in respect of its factical movement.

At this point we find the concepts 'authentic existence' and 'inauthentic existence', which also recur repeatedly in Bultmann's theology. The present chapter is concerned with human existence as 'inauthentic'. This concept of 'inauthenticity' alternates in Bultmann's writing with the concept of 'sin', which is of course lacking in the philosophy of Heidegger; the concept of 'sin' gives theological qualification to what appears in the philosophical elucidation of existence as 'inauthenticity'. We have yet to show how far this qualification is at the same time a correction, or goes beyond the philosophical understanding, giving the latter the character of a 'preunderstanding'; first of all, however, we must look briefly at the understanding of inauthenticity in Heidegger's analysis of existence. He himself is of the conviction that faith and 'world view', 'in so far as they make any such assertions', 'must come back to the existentialist structures . . . set forth, provided that its assertions are to make a claim to *conceptual* understanding.'[1]

According to Heidegger, as we saw, the 'nature' of human *Dasein* is 'existence': man stands in possibilities in such a way that it is ultimately he himself who is at risk in these possibilities. In his decisions, man does not choose this or that; whatever his concrete choice, he chooses himself as his ownmost possibility. If man is his own possibility he can gain himself, but he can also lose himself. In other words, he can exist in the mode of authenticity or in that of inauthenticity.

In authentic existence, in which man gains himself, he keeps himself open in the midst of the everydayness of the world for the future, for the encounters which present themselves to him and in which he receives himself again and again as his own. In authentic existence he holds fast to himself as possibility, he *is himself* and thus, literally, '*authentic*'.

[1] Martin Heidegger, *Sein und Zeit*, p. 180 (*Being and Time*, p. 224).

Now in Heidegger's view *Dasein* has, however, always fallen away from itself and into the 'world'. It abandons itself to the world. It goes over to the world. It allows itself to be determined by the way in which 'they' are involved together in the world, by 'talk', curiosity and ambivalence. It 'falls victim' to everydayness, to the dictates of the public, which is really no-one, to the levelling of averageness, in which each man is the other and no-one is himself. As a consequence: 'The supposition of the "they" that one is leading and sustaining a full and genuine "life", brings *Dasein* a *tranquillity*, for which everything is "in the best of order" and all doors are open.'[2] 'Idle talk and ambiguity, having seen everything, having understood everything, develop the supposition that *Dasein's* disclosedness, which is so available and so prevalent, can guarantee to *Dasein* that *all* the possibilities of its being will be secure, genuine and full.'[3] This tempting tranquillity heightens the fall. Men surrender to the impulse which seems to give them everything and which in fact merely keeps tearing man away from his authenticity. All this happens on the basis of an anxiety in which the insignificance of my *Dasein* and the nothingness of the world dawn upon me, an anxiety which therefore, of course, can also lead to authentic being by disclosing nothingness.

That man *can* exist though fallen in this way shows that he is an existing being. To this extent, fallenness reveals an ontological structure of *Dasein* itself which also continues through to the authenticity of existence. The 'truth' of human Being embraces both authentic and inauthentic existence. For a man to take his fallenness for authentic existence is, on the other hand, a conviction which endangers *Dasein* itself and alienates man from himself; for in this fallenness he surrenders freedom of choice together with openness for encounter and thus surrenders himself as possibility, as *Dasein* in its *authenticity*.

[2] ibid., p. 177 (ibid., p. 222).
[3] ibid.

73

So much, in excessive brevity, for Heidegger's analysis of *Dasein*.

'Is not that exactly the New Testament understanding of human life?',[4] asks Bultmann. He thinks that this question must be answered in the affirmative, and therefore interprets the statements of the New Testament about sin in the concepts of the philosophical analysis of human existence, without attaching great importance to the fact that Heidegger's philosophy is hardly conceivable without the New Testament and Luther. A brief extract from an article by Bultmann written in 1928, to the details of which we shall be returning later, may make this clear: 'For man to commit himself to his fallenness means for him to surrender his own possible being. The view of the "world" is that man *has* possibilities on each occasion. It forgets that man always *is* himself possibility, that his being is a being-able-to-be, that man is on each occasion called to decision and stands at risk. The "world" rejects such decision; it has thus already decided for itself, and therefore cut off its being as being-able-to-be. In this way it has cut off its own future; for being-able-to-be is to have future. Therefore the world is always already past; everything that it has is false, is a lie, is past because it always keeps to the old and never leads to the future. The "world" is in death.'[5] To those who take exception to the nearness of this interpretation of the Bible to the philosophical analysis of *Dasein*, Bultmann retorts that they are blind to the problem which in fact exists of the relationship between philosophy and theology. He writes: 'I think that they should really be afraid that the philosophers are saying the same thing as the New Testament and saying it quite independently,'[6] especially as philosophy does not have its 'biblical' insights by chance. As philosophy makes human existence its theme, what faith calls 'sin' must come under its

---

[4] *Kerygma und Mythos*, I, p. 33 (*Kerygma and Myth*, p. 25).
[5] *Glauben und Verstehen*, I, pp. 139 f.
[6] *Kerygma und Mythos*, I, p. 33 (*Kerygma and Myth*, p. 25).

province *somehow*, 'and I think I may say that philosophy knows about sin in so far as it knows about man's fallenness and the authenticity which he must achieve'.[7]

Now it is, of course, clear that the New Testament goes further than Heidegger in what it has to say, as he does not in fact talk about 'sin'. Heidegger's statement that *Dasein* 'has fallen away from itself as an authentic possibility for Being its Self, and has fallen into "the world" ' is no 'negative evaluation'.[8] He is interested in the movement of falling only as an expression of the basic structure of human existence. From the fact that man *is* fallen, Heidegger concludes that he *can* fall, that he is thus his own potentiality; more than this Heidegger will not venture. Nor will he regard the fallenness of *Dasein* 'as a "fall" from a purer and higher "primal status"',[9] nor does he decide 'whether man is "drunk with sin" and in the *status corruptionis*, whether he walks in the *status integritatis*, or whether he finds himself in an intermediate stage, the *status gratiae*'.[10] He therefore does not qualify the ontic fallenness of man in the same way as faith does; still less does he qualify this fallenness as godlessness.

The New Testament does otherwise, calling man's inauthenticity 'sin' and thus showing that it is interested not in ontological structure but in ontic reality, not in existentialist comprehension, but in the existential conduct of men. Anyone who gives a theological interpretation of what the New Testament says about man *before* faith, man in sin, must be quite clear about that. Bultmann therefore writes at the beginning of the relevant paragraphs of his *Theology of the New Testament*: 'If, up to this point, the ontological structure of human existence, as Paul sees it, has been clarified, this nevertheless only affords the presuppositions for his ontic statement about

[7] *Kerygma und Mythos*, I, p. 224.
[8] Heidegger, *Sein und Zeit*, p. 175 (*Being and Time*, p. 220).
[9] ibid., p. 176 (ibid., p. 220).
[10] ibid., p. 180 (ibid., p. 224).

man in which his real interest lies',[11] i.e. for the statements about sin and faith as statements about the theologically qualified inauthenticity or authenticity of man.

How does Bultmann find man's inauthenticity described in the *New Testament*? Or rather: how does he develop the biblical understanding of *sin* as the inauthenticity of human existence?

If we are to understand the nature of sin, Bultmann believes that we must first clarify the idea of God which underlies the concept of 'sin'. For the Bible, God is not 'the mythological designation for an ontological state of affairs but the personal God, man's Creator who demands obedience of him'.[12] Both these points, that God is man's Creator and that he demands man's obedience, necessarily belong together; for the fact that God is the Creator does not represent 'a cosmological theory which professes to explain the origin of the world and its existence as it is. Rather, it is a proposition that concerns man's existence.'[13] Above all, 'knowledge of God as Creator contains primarily knowledge of man—man, that is, in his creatureliness, and in his situation of being one to whom God has laid claim. . . . To know God means in itself to acknowledge God, obey his demand, bow before him in grateful adoration.'[14] When Paul writes in I Cor. 8.6: 'We have *one* God, from whom are all things and for whom we exist', Bultmann understands him to mean that God's uniqueness is his being-for-us, i.e. 'his being is understood aright only when it is understood as significant-for-man being; hence, it is not understood aright unless at the same time man's being is also understood as springing from God and thereby oriented towards him'.[15]

If man has his authentic life in the moment, then according to the New Testament it is God who is Lord of this moment; if

[11] *Theologie*, p. 227 (*Theology*, I, p. 227).
[12] ibid., p. 228 (ibid., p. 228).   [13] ibid. (ibid., pp. 228 f.)
[14] ibid. (ibid., pp. 228 f.).   [15] ibid., p. 229 (ibid., p. 229).

he has his authentic life in radical openness to the future, then according to the New Testament it is God who gives this future; if he lives 'authentically' only in his decisions, then according to the New Testament it is God for whom he has to decide; if he has his authentic life when he holds on to himself as possibility, then according to the New Testament he thus holds on to God, who wills to encounter him.

It is the peculiarity of man's creatureliness, his existentiality, that he *can* orient himself on God, and that shows that he, whom Paul describes as 'God's image and glory' (I Cor. 11.7), 'is endowed by God with special dignity and responsibility'.[16] True, in his creaturely transitoriness he is creation like the rest of the world, but in his exceptional being 'he stands between God and the creation and must decide between the two',[17] for if he can have a relationship to God, so too he can have one towards the world.

Thus the created world, with which man can form a relationship, just as he can with God, has the same ontological quality as God. This fact is expressed by the New Testament in the way it often speaks of *world-powers*, of cosmic angel powers of demonic character, which rule the world and—rightly or wrongly—claim man in the same way as God does. So even the world is not primarily regarded in the way in which it is found, but in its power.

Now man, existing as his own possibility between God and the world, looks in his existence for life, that is, for himself; for all human searching, Bultmann argues, even in its perversion, is a search for life, and 'human existence knows, openly or covertly, of its dependence upon that from which it can live'.[18] This knowing and searching is good, and what is good is at the same time what is demanded; for as Creator, God is the origin of life and his command is a command to live (Rom. 7.10). Because God and only God is the giver of the life in which man has his authentic being, and because God

[16] ibid.　　[17] ibid.　　[18] ibid., p. 379 (*Theology*, II, p. 26).

demands man as a living being, Bultmann can write: 'The alternative, to lay hold of one's true existence or to miss it, is synonymous with the alternative to acknowledge God as the Creator or to deny him.'[19]

The ontic constitution of human nature is, according to the unanimous witness of the New Testament, its sinfulness. Man has continually fallen short of his authentic being; he denies God. How does this sinfulness happen? What in fact is sin? Man, searching for life, seeks it from the world and not from God. In this way he perverts the creation so that it becomes 'world', and in so doing loses his life.

How does such sin happen? What is there tempting in the world that attracts man away from God and towards what is created? Bultmann replies: the uniqueness of the world as compared with God is that it stands at man's disposal; 'hence, to seek life in it means to have the presumption to seek life in the disposable, i.e. to presume to have life at one's own disposal. Hence the ultimate sin reveals itself to be the false assumption of not receiving life as the gift of the Creator but procuring it by one's own power, of living from one's self rather than from God.'[20]

Why does man succumb to this temptation? Bultmann replies: because he is afraid of the insecurity of his existence in which he lives if he seeks his life from God. For God is never at his disposal; God always stands before him. A life which is lived in trust towards God never has itself in hand, but has surrendered itself completely. It is simply possibility in every moment, namely, God's possibility, and man's possibility in so far as man keeps himself open for the encounter with God which is not at his disposal. From this uncertainty, which seems to him to be uncanny and threatening, man flies, by turning to the world which is at his disposal.

This must now be developed further.

[19] ibid., p. 233 (*Theology*, I, p. 232).   [20] ibid.

Inauthenticity and Sin

Paul often describes life in sin as life 'after the flesh' or 'in the flesh'. In his writings, as elsewhere in the Bible, the expression 'flesh' usually means simply the creatureliness of man. Man is flesh and not spirit, he is creature and not creator. But being a creature does not necessarily mean being a sinner. How does it come about that 'flesh' can imperceptibly become a description of the human state of being a sinner? Certainly not because sin is primarily understood as physical-sexual conduct; this is to misunderstand both the biblical concept of flesh *and* the biblical concept of sin. We must start from the fact that 'flesh' describes the neutral sphere of what is natural and earthly, of what is to hand and at man's disposal. In that case sin has its origin 'in the flesh' *in so far as 'conduct that directs itself according to "flesh"*, taking "flesh" for its norm, is sinful'.[21] Bultmann points to Rom. 8.5, where Paul gives an almost explicit definition of the phrase 'after the flesh': 'For those who live according to the flesh *set their minds on* the things of the flesh', where 'flesh' again means what is to hand.

The corresponding terminology in John is less open to misunderstanding. Where Paul speaks of the 'flesh', John speaks of the world, ' "World" here does not mean the world of nature, nor the world as the field of possibilities, gifts and tasks for human thinking and creative effort. "World" here is not the world as the creation of God, but "world" in a quite specific sense,'[22] namely, as the power by which we allow ourselves to be seized because we expect our life from it and to this extent long for it. 'Such is the mysterious power of the world that it presumes to claim us wholly, so that we are cheated into thinking it the ultimate reality; this is its uncanny tendency, to delude us into thinking that it can satisfy us completely with its gifts, can absorb us utterly with its duties. The consequence is that the world itself becomes a god, rounded in itself, closed and all-sufficient.'[23]

[21] ibid., p. 238 (ibid., p. 238).
[22] *Marburger Predigten*, p. 51 (*This World and the Beyond*, p. 61).
[23] ibid., pp. 51 f. (ibid., p. 62).

The man who longs for life therefore reaches out *as a sinner* for the things of the world because they are at his disposal, in order to receive and guarantee his life from them. But that is a delusion; 'a man is determined by his origin and in each present moment does not have himself in hand; he has only the alternatives: to exist either from God (reality) or from the world (unreality)'.[24] But unreality gives no life. 'This self-delusion is not merely an error, but sin, because it is a turning away from the Creator, the giver of life, and a turning towards the creation—and to do that is to trust in one's self as being able to procure life by the use of the earthly and through one's own strength and accomplishment. It is in this sense, then, that "fixing the mind on the things of the flesh" is to be at war against God (Rom. 8.7).'[25]

This sinful illusion can take different forms, for 'flesh' and 'world' is much more than the sphere of the 'life of instinct or sensual passions, but is just as much that of the moral and religious efforts of man.'[26] 'We must not deceive ourselves. It is not here a question of the "world" which tempts man astray into "paths of evil", into bad immoral actions. No, the world exercises its tyrannous sway just as much over moral men as over immoral men, and it must never be forgotten that the struggle of Jesus against the world was precisely a struggle against very moral men.'[27] Of course sensibility can also become 'world' and thus vice; desire which is good in itself can assume the form of self-seeking lust and thus be qualified as 'flesh'. In the same way the zealous fulfilment of the law can be an expression of the fallenness of man into the world of what is at his disposal, when 'a man supposes that he can thereby achieve righteousness before God by his own strength. The Galatian Christians who want to adopt the Torah and be circumcised are indignantly asked: "Having begun with the

[24] *Theologie*, p. 372 (*Theology*, II, p. 20).
[25] ibid., p. 239 (*Theology*, I, p. 239).   [26] ibid.
[27] *Marburger Predigten*, p. 51 (*This World and the Beyond*, p. 61).

Spirit, are you now ending with the flesh?"—ending, that is, not in sensual passions, but in observance of the Torah (Gal. 3.3).'[28] 'Pride in all the pious Israelite's merits and titles of honour' is also 'fleshly'.[29]

The Hellenistic world qualifies itself as 'world' by its striving for wisdom and its confidence in knowledge and spiritual endowments. According to Bultmann, our modern age tries to possess the world with the help of the natural sciences, so as to live by them in a world 'possessed' in such a way: man understands himself as master of the world and his life.

Typical concepts which are used in the New Testament to describe this sinful attitude are 'covet', 'care', 'boast', 'put one's trust in the flesh'. 'The evil "*desires* of the heart" are the desires of such as have turned to the worship of creation (Rom. 1.24)', and life with such a desire is a 'life of self-reliant pursuit'.[30] Human care, which in the form of planning dictatorially reaches into the future with the intention of securing man's future is for Paul a care which has fallen victim to the world (I Cor. 7.32 ff.), 'which rests upon the illusion that a man can insure his life by that which is worldly, controllable'.[31] Man's attitude of sinful self-reliance takes its extreme expression in '*boasting*': 'In "boasting" is revealed a misconstruing of the human situation, a forgetting of the fact implied by the question, "What do you have that you have not been given? And if it has been given you, why do you boast as if it had not been given you?" (I Cor. 4.7).'[32] In the same way, all '*putting one's confidence in the flesh*' bears witness to 'the supposed security which a man achieves out of that which is worldly and apparent, that which he can control and deal with'.[33]

Note that it is not the flesh, not the world, not the creation that are sinful or perverted, for 'man can understand it as the

[28] *Theologie*, p. 240 (*Theology*, I, p. 240).   [29] ibid.
[30] ibid., p. 241 (ibid., p. 241).   [31] ibid., p. 242 (ibid., p. 242).
[32] ibid.   [33] ibid., p. 243 (ibid., p. 243).

gift of the Creator, from which God's question is continually addressed to him, and God's future is constantly brought before him'.[34] But if man bases his life on the transitory creation instead of on God, this creation becomes 'a hostile, destructive power. It owes to man himself such independence as it has towards God.'[35] So Bultmann can write: 'The world indeed is simply the sphere which men have made into a power over themselves by whatever they have done in the past.'[36] To live from the world thus means 'to live from one's own past'; that is sin, and freedom from sin would thus be freedom from one's own past.

Even if man makes the creation his God, the world remains God's creation; for the expectations with which sinful man enters the world into which he falls can never be fulfilled. The misuse of the world does not give it the power to supply life, 'man can produce only a specious reality which actually is a lie, a nothing. For, being a creature, he does not, like God, live out of his own resources, but ever lives out of an uncontrollable origin which has power over him. He always comes from a Whence and for him there is only the possibility to be from God or from the world, which means: from God or from falsehood, from God or from Nothing. If he repudiates his origin from God, then his origin is Nothing, to which he has given power over himself.'[37] So the misuse of creation makes no difference to this.

In his fallenness into the world man himself becomes another. His sin does not remain without 'consequences'. In being concerned to live from what is at his disposal, he 'in reality makes himself dependent upon that which he supposes he can control'.[38] He is delivered into the *slavery of sin*. 'Thus the

[34] *Glauben und Verstehen*, 2, p. 71 (*Essays*, p. 81).
[35] *Theologie*, p. 231 (*Theology*, I, p. 230).
[36] *Glauben und Verstehen*, 2, p. 71 (*Essays*, p. 81).
[37] *Theologie*, p. 372 (*Theology*, II, p. 20).
[38] ibid., p. 244 (*Theology*, I, pp. 243 f.).

eerie fact is that the "cosmos", the world of men, constituted by that which the individual does and upon which he bestows his care, itself gains the upper hand over the individual.'[39] 'We can see in our times to what degree men', who want to take possession of the world, 'are dependent on technology', over which they would like to become masters, 'and to what degree technology brings with it terrible consequences. By means of science men try to take possession of the world, but in fact the world gets possession of men.'[40] Man is delivered over to this slavery of sin because he convulsively clings to what he can himself achieve, and is driven further and further into fallenness by anxiety that he has not yet secured his life sufficiently. 'Everybody tries to hold fast to his own life and property, because he has a secret feeling that everything, even his life, is slipping away from him';[41] 'secret anxiety . . . moves in the depths of the soul at the very moment when man thinks that he must obtain security for himself'.[42] How could it be otherwise? The man who has chosen life from what is at his disposal as *his* impossible *possibility* must keep grasping more and more vigorously at the 'world', the more he feels that this is denying him authentic life: sin, once awakened, always breeds new sin.

According to Bultmann, this situation finds its strongest expression in Rom. 7.14: 'I am carnal, sold under sin.' At the very point at which man vaunts himself in his last possible freedom by freeing himself from all ties and, abandoning himself to whatever happens to be at his disposal, lives for the day, he lives in the depths of slavery, trapped by the chance and arbitrariness of the moment. Paul thus sees man as *totally fallen*. He can accordingly speak of the powers of the flesh, the world and sin as personal powers against which man is helpless: sin ' "came into the world" (Rom. 5.12) and "achieved

---

[39] ibid., p. 257 (ibid., p. 256).
[40] *Jesus Christ and Mythology*, p. 40.
[41] *Kerygma und Mythos*, I, pp. 28 f. (*Kerygma and Myth*, p. 20).
[42] *Jesus Christ and Mythology*, p. 40.

dominion" (Rom. 5.21). Man is enslaved to it (Rom. 6.6, 17 ff.) sold under it (Rom. 7.14); or man places himself at its disposal (Rom. 6.13), and it pays him wages (Rom. 6.23).'[43] 'The personification of these powers expresses the fact that man has lost to them the capacity to be the subject of his own actions';[44] he has handed himself over to them as his possibility. Man is not only a sinner; he is, as the Gospel of John says, *of sin*. He cannot regard his sin as a weakness 'which forms no part of his true nature, or as a mistake which is an exception to be outweighed by appealing to his normal self';[45] as fallenness in the world, sin determines man's whole existence.

True, man wants life, but *in fact* he grasps death. Paul describes this paradoxical condition of man with the words: 'I do not do what I want, but I do the very thing I hate' (Rom. 7.15); 'I do not understand my own actions' (Rom. 7.15), for 'It is no longer I that do it, but sin which dwells within me' (Rom. 7.17). These words do not simply reproduce what goes on in the consciousness of a Christian who is not completely successful in transforming his good will into action. These words of Paul's describe 'the gruesome contradiction which characterizes human striving . . . : it wants to gain life and only achieves death'.[46] 'This is the domination of sin: all man's doing is directed against his true intention.'[47] Man, called to his authenticity, seeks to realize it from his own potentialities and is thus led against his will into inauthenticity.

Because sin is not a momentary failure of man, but an expression of the direction of his whole life, it brings *death* with it. 'If sin is man's false pursuit of life, and if this consists in leading one's life "after the flesh", i.e. out of the created, the earthly-natural and transitory—then sin leads with inner necessity into death: "If you live according to the flesh you

[43] *Theologie*, p. 245 (*Theology*, I, p. 245).   [44] ibid.
[45] *Jesus*, p. 135 (*Jesus and the Word*, pp. 140 f.)
[46] *Theologie*, p. 249 (*Theology*, I, p. 248).
[47] ibid., p. 246 (ibid., p. 246).

will die" (Rom. 8.13). He who derives life out of the transitory must himself perish with the perishing of the transitory.'[48] Paul expresses this situation juristically in the well-known phrase, 'The wages of sin is death' (Rom. 6. 23). 'Fundamentally, then,' says Bultmann, 'death is already a present reality, for man "sold" under sin has lost himself, is no longer at one with himself.'[49]

Whereas the man who is with himself in authentic existence has his life in the moment, i.e. in every present encounter and decision, man in the slavery of sin is *chained to his past*, and, because he never lives authentically, *cut off from the future*. For 'as our action always results in our finishing something, it carries concealed within it the temptation to understand ourselves from what we have done and to tighten our grip on what we have done. In fact we keep succumbing to this temptation and so succumb to the past; for what is done is always past. In so far as we understand ourselves from the past, even our future action—although it is a future action—is always already past, stamped with the past and with death. Indeed it stands before us as a work, as a contrived condition which we have attained.'[50] Man's way into sin is characterized 'as that of the man who is already conditioned by his precious decisions. To this extent he is not really free, but tied to his past. Hence he never finds his authentic self. In order to be free, and to find himself, he would actually have to be freed from himself—that is from the self which he has previously made of himself—from the past which ties him down—or, in Christian terms, from his sin.'[51] He would have to surrender 'everything that the past contained of which a man might boast, that might tempt him to dwell on it and reassure himself, everything on which he might base his confidence and in which he might find his security, whether the gifts of fate, the achievements wrought by his own abilities, or the attainments of his knowledge'.[52] He would in fact have to surrender himself as he already is in order to regain himself as possibility. He would have to give up all securities in order to live in each moment from what encounters him from beyond whatever is

[48] ibid., p. 247 (ibid., pp. 246 f.).
[49] ibid., p. 249 (ibid., p. 249).
[50] *Glauben und Verstehen*, 1, p. 223.
[51] *Glauben und Verstehen*, 2, p. 278 (*Essays*, p. 309).
[52] *Marburger Predigten*, p. 42 (*This World and the Beyond*, pp. 51 f.).

to hand or at his disposal. But his sin consists in the fact that he wants to gain his life from that over which he has control, and therefore he is constantly concerned with the past and the future, instead of being himself for the moment. On this theme, Bultmann quotes Pascal (*Pensées*, 172) in a sermon: 'Never do we live whole-heartedly in the present. We anticipate the future, as though it were too slow in coming, as though we wished to hasten its advent; or else we recall the past, as though to arrest it in its swift flight. We are so foolish that we allow our thoughts to stray in periods of time which are really not ours, and we do not think of the sole point of time which veritably belongs to us. We are so stupid that we dwell on a past which no longer subsists, and thoughtlessly miss the time which is present with us. The truth is that the present is normally offensive to us. We refuse to face it because it vexes us; and if it is pleasant we idly deplore its passing. We try to keep it by merging it with the future, and we fondly think we can arrange matters which do not lie within our control, with a view to a point of time which we have no certainty of reaching. Let each one examine his thoughts. He will discover that they are all concerned either with the past or the future. We hardly ever think of the present; and when we do think of it, it is only to shed its light on the future. The present is never an end for us. Thus we never live, but only hope to live; and since we are always preparing ourselves to be happy, it is inevitable that we never in fact are happy.'[53]

But there is still more. Bultmann writes: 'The power of sin operates not only in the fact that it completely dominates the man who has become its victim, but also in the fact that it forces all men without exception into slavery: "for all have sinned" (Rom. 3.23; cf. 3.9, 19), "Scripture has encompassed all men under the power of sin" (Gal. 3.22).'[54] I John 5.19 runs: 'The whole world lies in evil.'

Bultmann remarks that this verdict could, 'unless the guilt-character of sin were to be denied, only have its origin in experience',[55] in other words, it must be clear that sin comes through sinning and does not adhere to men as a natural

[53] ibid., pp. 219 f. (ibid., pp. 241 f.).
[54] *Theologie*, p. 249 (*Theology*, I, p. 249).
[55] ibid., p. 250 (ibid., p. 250).

quality or seize them relentlessly as a curse from a primeval happening. Bultmann is convinced that it is the intention of the New Testament to maintain the universality of sin *and* to maintain its character of guilt. John does this expressly in the prologue of his gospel. In these introductory sentences man's determination towards sin 'is not attributed to a mythical cause but simply shows itself to be a fact':[56] 'The light shines in the darkness and the darkness did not grasp it. . . . It was in the world and through it the world had come into being, yet the world did not recognize it' (John 1.5, 10).

Paul also asserts the universality of sin in Rom. 1.18–3.20 with his remarks that God has been recognizable in his Godhead from the creation of the world but that mankind as a whole has never recognized him as God, but has turned its attention to what is not. Of course we also find mention in Paul, as happened frequently in late Judaism, of the fall of Adam (Rom. 5.12 ff.), through whose sin all men became sinners, in other words, the idea of 'original sin'. Without question this idea is appropriate for expressing the universality of sin; it is, however, unsuitable for showing the character of sin as guilt. Paul himself feels what is the inappropriateness of such expressions in this respect when he expands the statement that sin came into the world by *one* man and death through sin, by another statement, that death came to all men because they had *all* sinned (Rom. 5.12).

What is the explanation of the experience of the universality of sin? Bultmann writes: 'At the root of the idea of inherited sin lies the experience that every man is born into a humanity that is and always has been guided by a false striving. The understanding of existence so derived applies as a matter of course to every man; and every man brings himself explicitly under it by his concrete transgression, thereby becoming jointly responsible for it.'[57] 'So everyone exists in a world in

[56] ibid., p. 377 (*Theology*, II, p. 25).
[57] ibid., p. 253 (*Theology*, I, p. 253).

which each looks out for himself, each insists upon his rights, each fights for his existence, and life becomes a struggle of all against all even when the battle is involuntarily fought. So sin is always already here, and the divine command always encounters man as a "thou shalt" or "thou shalt not" which he must transform into an "I will" or "I will not" by first conquering himself. The fact that the good always demands a sacrifice testifies that in his living man has a tacit understanding of himself that is basically sinful.'[58] Man has 'put himself in the place of God. And every man comes out of a history that is governed by this misunderstanding. He comes out of a lie; he is determined by the "flesh" whose power he cannot break.'[59] He may therefore 'make ever so many criticisms of the traditional mythological version of the doctrine of original sin and talk idly about man's original goodness, but in actual fact each one of us acknowledges that the doctrine is true, namely, in his judgments concerning the concrete man with whom he has to deal and in his relations with them. We mistrust one another from the beginning, and in our mistrust there is at the same time resistance against others, refusal to have anything to do with them, hate.'[60]

At this point we take up once again the question of the relationship of Bultmann's theology to the philosophical elucidation of existence. First, in order to bring it to a provisional conclusion; secondly, to make a transition to the following chapters; and finally, because this will clarify further the nature of inauthenticity as man's sin, as Bultmann understands it.

The close parallel between the existentialist analysis of inauthenticity by Heidegger and the biblical understanding of

[58] ibid., p. 254 (ibid.).
[59] *Glauben und Verstehen*, 3, pp. 26 f. (*Existence and Faith*, p. 83).
[60] 'Der Sinn der christlichen Schöpfüngsglaubens', p. 12 (*Existence and Faith*, p. 217).

sin, as Bultmann develops it, is evident. Inauthenticity and sin have a similar ontological structure, indeed they have *the same* ontological structure; for sin *is* the inauthenticity which Heidegger describes. By falling into the world of what is to hand, attaching himself to what is at his disposal, man surrenders himself; for he cuts himself off from the incalculable and uncontrollable encounters of the future in which he is himself, because in them he can decide afresh each time about himself. In unqualified openness to the future he would exist authentically; but in his attachment to the world he has held fast to his inauthenticity.

Of course the differences between Heidegger's philosophical description of inauthenticity and Bultmann's theological one are clear. Heidegger's analysis of existence is pure ontology. It therefore does not describe the ontic determination of the inauthenticity of existence as *sin*; it neither asserts nor disputes the sinfulness of man. In speaking of the fallenness of existence it makes it clear that there can be such a thing as 'sin' but it does not decide whether there really is sin. It does not characterize fallenness as apostasy from God, but it does not exclude the possibility of understanding fallenness in this way.

This, however, is precisely what Bultmann does assert. In explaining the biblical understanding of sin, he describes inauthenticity from the standpoint of faith, and we have followed him here. 'From the standpoint of faith' does not mean in the light of his personal belief that his account is some sort of confession of faith (that indeed may be the case, but unbelief, too, can understand and describe the biblical understanding of sin). 'From the standpoint of faith' means rather from the conviction, from the evidence of faith, and at the same time, on the presupposition that the *truth* of the ontic determination of inauthenticity as sin can never be experienced objectively, but only in faith, i.e. existentially. So whether what the New Testament—or Bultmann—says about the inauthenticity of existence is true is not to be discovered from a description of inauthenticity as sin, but only from my own experience of *myself as a sinner*. In other words, what sin *really* is can only be understood if man encounters himself as a sinner. But man encounters himself as a sinner only if he stands before God, who frees him from his sin, and because God can be experienced only in faith, the understanding of inauthenticity as sin is possible only in faith. Bultmann is never tired of pointing to the fact that sin is not experienced by reflection *about* sin, of which the present chapter is just one example; it is *authentically* experienced only in faith: 'Only the man who knows *himself* to be a sinner can know what grace is. He only knows himself as a sinner in so far as he stands before *God*; thus he can only know of sin if he knows of grace. The nature of faith is made up of the sight of God's judgment and the sight of God's grace *together*.'[61] Thus faith asserts that man's being is only revealed *fully* as sin, in the light of faith. This position finds its most extreme expression in Jesus' words in the Gospel of John: 'If I had not come and spoken to them, they would not have sin' (John 15.22).

These last remarks have already suggested the basic difference between the philosophical elucidation of existence and Christian faith. Philosophy can recognize the fallenness of man in the world; it can thus reveal man's inauthenticity to him and make it ontologically comprehensible. But in addition to this it is convinced that man can find the way to his authenticity on the basis of the philosophical elucidation of existence, and thus overcome his fallenness, or, from a Christian point of view, free himself from his sin.

'Is this self-confidence of the philosophers justified? Whatever the answer may be, it is at least clear that this is the point where they part company with the New Testament. For the latter affirms the total incapacity of man to release himself from his fallen state. That deliverance can come only by an act

[61] *Glauben und Verstehen*, 1, p. 23.

of God. The New Testament does not give us a doctrine of "nature", a doctrine of the authentic nature of man; it proclaims this divine act of deliverance, the saving event which was wrought in Christ.'[62] The philosopher thinks 'that all man needs is to be shown his plight, and that then he will be able to escape from it. In other words, the corruption resulting from the fall does not extend to the core of the human personality. The New Testament, on the other hand, regards the fall as total.'[63] In the New Testament, then, inauthenticity is understood in radical term as *slavery* to sin. According to Bultmann, the assertion of the philosopher that man's knowledge of his own authenticity makes him master of it expresses the same human attitude as that which makes the pious Jew with whom Paul argues look for justification in his own works. It is 'self-glorying and self-assertion, a desperate attempt to control one's own destiny. If the true life of man is one of surrender, then that life is missed not only by those who live by controlling what is at their disposal instead of surrendering, but also by those who understand surrender as a goal which is at their disposal. They fail to see that authentic life can be received only as a gift.'[64] In so far as the philosopher feels 'that man can achieve authenticity by his own efforts, he repeats the primal sin and holds fast to it.'[65] So according to the New Testament, man is one who has totally fallen victim to the world: true, he can know that he exists in inauthenticity, but he cannot gain his authenticity by his own efforts precisely because in so doing he remains inauthentic, that is, master of himself. Faith knows of this situation on the basis of the saving event, i.e. on the basis of the fact that God has acted for man because man cannot act. The believer thus learns to understand fallenness more radically than he could through the philosophical elucidation of existence.

[62] *Kerygma und Mythos*, I, p. 35 (*Kerygma and Myth*, p. 27).
[63] ibid., p. 36 (ibid., p. 28).   [64] ibid., p. 37 (ibid., p. 29).
[65] ibid., p. 224.

Of course the New Testament cannot prove that this is the case with fallenness 'any more than the philosophers can prove the intelligibility of Reality. It is a matter for decision',[66] which can never be affirmed theoretically and objectively, but only in existential experience of the action of God. According to Bultmann, this question of decision brings to light the basic difference between Christian faith and philosphy: 'The New Testament speaks and Christian faith knows of an act of God through which man becomes capable of surrender, capable of faith and love, of his authentic life.'[67]

Thinking of such statements, Karl Jaspers calls Bultmann's position 'absolutely and utterly orthodox and illiberal in this respect'.[68] Whether the reproach contained in this verdict is justified or not can evidently only be decided by each individual on the basis of his understanding of Christian existence. Whether the concept 'orthodox' is appropriately used here by Jaspers may also be left unanswered. At any rate, it is clear that Jaspers uses the term 'orthodox' to characterize Bultmann as a *theologian* in the sense of the Christian understanding of theology. In this respect, the philosopher's verdict is without doubt an apt description of Bultmann's self-understanding. Bultmann is consciously a Christian theologian and wants to be nothing but this, as his interpretation of the biblical concept of sin has adequately made clear. He merely wants to do his theological work more adequately than some others.

We have one last and not unimportant problem to deal with in connection with Bultmann's interpretation of the New Testament understanding of sin. It has perhaps struck the reader that we—like Bultmann in his quotations—have always used the term 'sin' in the singular. This is not necessarily obvious, for in everyday language we speak of *sins*, as transgressions of

[66] ibid., p. 38 (*Kerygma and Myth*, p. 30.)
[67] ibid., p. 40 (ibid., p. 33).
[68] Bultmann and Jaspers, *Die Frage der Entmythologisierung*, p. 49.

divine commandments, and this terminology is without question also that of the New Testament. The New Testament speaks of sins as often as it speaks of sin, thereby suggesting that while the two must be distinguished, they may not be separated. Bultmann's interpretation of the inauthenticity of man as his sin related primarily to the biblical concept of sin (singular!) which he also calls 'original sin', in which man is always finding himself involved: in wanting to secure his life with what is at his disposal, he denies God. So we could say, anticipating the terminology of the next chapter, that sin is the attitude of 'unbelief'.

This sin is not 'a sort of appendage to man', but 'his essential character'.[69] Sin (singular!) is man's disclaimer of himself as the one who is always his *possibility*: it is the disclaimer of the man who 'cannot bear to live in uncertainty before God, but longs to secure his existence and endeavours to create such security—whether by naïvely living out of the disposable world in care or sensual pleasure or by self-consciously seeking grounds for boasting before God in a formal legal correctness. Sin is to want to live out of oneself, out of one's own power, rather than out of radical surrender to God, to what he demands, gives and sends.'[70] Bultmann calls this *real* sin when he asserts 'that real sin does not consist in individual transgressions of the law at all, but in the *basic attitude* of man—his striving to establish his own righteousness'.[71] Sin is thus by no means regarded as immorality, and this is clear from the fact that *being* a sinner and the *universality* of sin can certainly not be asserted in respect of immorality.

It is easy to understand why 'the world' is fond of understanding sin in the sense of moral failings and sinful actions, and is also very ready to condemn the understanding of sin in these terms. For this attitude denies the seriousness of sin. 'It

[69] *Jesus*, p. 135 (*Jesus and the Word*, p. 140).
[70] *Glauben und Verstehen*, 3, p. 42 (*Existence and Faith*, p. 225).
[71] *Glauben und Verstehen*, 2, p. 41 (*Essays*, p. 47).

thinks of sin as something occasional, fortuitous, a deviation which can occur. It does not realize that if anyone sins he is the slave of sin (John 8.34). And if anyone suggests that it, the world, is sinful, it derides him or is angry. For it is of the very essence of the self-consciousness and need of the world, that it should consider itself to be good. It holds the question of sin to be a question which it has to decide and settle within its own sphere, before its own forum and according to its own laws.' It does not realize that the verdict of sin is not 'a question of any particular piece of conduct but of the characteristic basic attitude of the world, an attitude which may go with good as well as with bad deeds: . . . to close one's eyes to the intrinsic finitude of earthly things, to consider the world the final authority both in what it claims and in what it offers, to shut oneself off from the grace which is open to this world from God's holy world as soon as it confesses that it needs divine grace. This is sin.'[72]

But what is the relationship between *sins* and this *sin* of man? It is already clear that the former do not first constitute sin in their totality; for sin is always there and is in one respect independent of sins. Looking back to the time of his life in unbelief, i.e. in sin (singular!), Paul can therefore say that in fulfilling the law, i.e. in freedom from individual sins, he was in advance of many of his contemporaries (Gal. 1.14; Phil. 3.6). His view of the relationship between sins and sin is that God has given men over to their *sins* because they did not recognize him as God in their *sin*, but turned to what is not, 'to a base mind and to improper conduct. They were filled with all manner of wickedness, evil covetousness, malice. Full of envy, murder, strife, deceit, malignity, they are gossips, slanderers, haters of God, insolent, haughty, boastful, incentors of evil, disobedient to parents, foolish, faithless, heartless, ruthless. Though they know God's decree that those who do

[72] *Marburger Predigten*, pp. 55 f. (*This World and the Beyond*, pp. 66 f.).

such things deserve to die, they not only do them but approve those who practise them' (Rom. 1.28–32).

Bultmann interprets these sentences at the beginning of Romans to mean that Paul understands by *sin*, 'the proto-sin of apostasy which repeats itself in every Now in the face of that possibility of knowing God which is open to every Now', and that God gives the sinner over to sins means 'that the proto-sin of apostasy necessarily draws the vices after it'.[73] Sins are thus the consequence of sin. Immorality is only a secondary aspect of sin, indeed only *one* secondary aspect; morality can equally well be a secondary aspect of sin, for example, if it is practised so that a person can be noticed by people or if a man means to gain merit before God with it. Thus, from the proto-sin 'comes every individual guilty act: selfishness, which is not open to the other man, and does not let a man surrender himself freely in love for his neighbour. . . . From it come envy and strife, the struggle of each against all, discord and want, which men cause each other.'[74]

It is therefore also true that it is wrong to suppose that 'faith in the grace of God requires a sense of sin or a confession of sin, in the sense that man must admit to himself how much, how often and how grievously he has sinned and keeps sinning. He does not need to brood frantically and artificially on his immoralities, and does not need to contort his good works into bad. He is to consider the ground of his being, and to ask himself whence his life comes: whether it is from the grace of God or from his own power, and whether his life is sustained from the effort to gain glory, whether he is driven this way and that by the need for recognition, or whether in the knowledge of his vanity he has seen through the comedy of this effort and so has become conscious of his sin in the sight of God.'[75]

[73] *Theologie*, p. 251 (*Theology*, I, pp. 250 f.).
[74] *Glauben und Verstehen*, 2, p. 72 (*Essays*, p. 82).
[75] ibid., p. 43 (ibid., pp. 48 f.).

5

Authenticity and Faith

THE PRESENT chapter makes up a pair with the one which preceded it. Whereas that dealt with the inauthenticity of man, which is understood in the Christian message as sin, we must now examine the authenticity of man, which is described and explained in the New Testament above all with the help of the concept of 'faith', a concept which can readily be misunderstood. When approaching this concept, it is advisable as far as possible to leave on one side any of the usual ideas, if we are to understand how Bultmann defines the understanding of 'faith' in the New Testament. He himself challenges us to do this by often using the word 'self-understanding' as an alternative to 'faith', to combat the usual confusing or even false ideas of the nature of Christian faith. It might be better to say 'new self-understanding', for Bultmann regards even sin as a self-understanding, namely, as the self-understanding of the existence which exists inauthentically. The extent to which the Christian understanding of 'faith' is clarified by the concept of 'self-understanding' will be seen in the course of this chapter.

Our present task is easier than that in the previous chapter; the understanding of inauthenticity which we have achieved already determines our basic ideas of what 'authenticity' is; moreover, sin, as we have already seen provisionally, is the same as unbelief, so that in some respects the understanding of sin includes the understanding of the concept of faith. It would be different if 'sin' and 'faith' were two possibilities of existence among many. But in fact, according to Bultmann, 'sin' can only be correctly understood as non-faith, so that there is no neutral possibility for man other than sin or faith.

It will already be clear from these observations that the 'by faith alone' of Paul and the Reformers is so obvious for Bultmann that it hardly can and need be emphasized further, because it is itself given with the concept of faith. Paul's statement, 'What does not come from faith is sin' (Rom. 14.23), is absolutely vital for Bultmann's theology, and the way in which it occurs in Bultmann's interpretation of Johannine theology points in the same direction: 'For John, as for Paul, faith is the way to salvation, the only way. However, "by faith alone" is so taken for granted by John that he does not explicitly emphasize it.'[1]

Of course, even for the philosophical analysis of existence which Bultmann uses, man has no status apart from the exclusive modes of being of authenticity and inauthenticity. The fact is indeed expressed clearly enough in the concepts themselves. To return to them once again: Heidegger's philosophical analysis of existence describes the being of human *Dasein* as existence, i.e. as ability to be. In his Being, man is concerned with himself. He loses himself, his authenticity, his *own*ness, when he falls victim to the 'they', the world, and thus surrenders himself as *possibility*. It is the nature of this condition of fallenness that man does not let death come anywhere near him—to fallen man, the thought of death seems to be an inopportune and dubious thing—and where he does so he is driven to it by care about his life, not about his death. However, death belongs to the totality of our being, not only as the terminus of life, but because it is constantly present in life; for death gives human existence the character of *finite* existence. Furthermore, death is man's ownmost potentiality. Here no

[1] *Theologie*, p. 427 (*Theology*, II, p. 75).

one else can take his place. Every man has to accept death for himself. 'They' do not relieve him of death. With death, says Heidegger, *Dasein* stands before itself in its ownmost ability to be. But because of this, even the preliminaries to death can liberate the authenticity of man's existence for himself. This liberation consists in the fact that man accepts his whole existence as a *finite* one, for which he is responsible at every minute. It is existence of such a kind that he allows himself to be thrown back on the 'now' by death, in each particular situation, by being radically open to everything that is coming to him (the 'future'). It is an existence in which he is momentarily for his time. For being in the moment is man's authentic being. In this sense Heidegger understands human being as future and at the same time as an everlasting dying, as long as man exists. For if man exists *authentically*, he is never finished. He always stands before himself; he constantly leaves what he already is behind himself, in order to 'project' himself into the future, i.e. to become himself anew over and over again.

It is clear that this analysis of human authenticity is hardly conceivable without the New Testament, but also that it is *possible* without reference to the New Testament. It is not developed as the understanding of a revelation, but as the understanding which is given with existence itself, which shows itself to the man who, with death, brings the totality of human existence to mind.

Bultmann is also fond of using Heidegger's analysis of authenticity which we have just outlined and the concepts which Heidegger uses in his own development of the Christian understanding of faith. In so doing he can describe the *structure* of existence in faith without resorting to theology, i.e. without reference to revelation. There is an illuminating description of this character in an article which deals with the relationship between faith and science. In Bultmann's view, the crisis in faith produced by natural science 'fundamentally consists in the question posed by natural science to man, whether he will understand his existence in the light of the reality lying open to scientific observation and research—the reality of what is to hand, perceptible to the senses, the systematic integration of which is perceptible to the thinking mind, the unity of which can be constructed—or in the light of the reality of the "moment". I might even say, whether he seeks to derive the "moment" from the natural happening that lies behind it, in order to understand it as a necessary derivative; or whether he is willing to acknowledge that the "moment" cannot be derived from anything, to acknowledge its openness to the future, its demand, its character as decision. Is he willing to acknowledge that the "moment" has a richer content than can be established by observation, measurement and calculation, rich in possibilities for joy and thankfulness, pain and repentance, duty and love—rich in possibilities demanding decision in the present, a decision which no science can remove, a decision in which man gains or loses his authentic existence? The question is, therefore, whether he acknowledges the responsibility of the present or not. . . . Faith never has to struggle against the findings of natural science, but solely against its possible claim as a *Weltanschauung*, to understand the purpose of Being.'[2] In these statements the *structure* of authentic human existence is developed very impressively without reference to the revelation of God, and Bultmann thinks that the situation which he describes must be understandable and clear even to the unbeliever. The well-known words of Paul from II Cor. 6.9 f., which Bultmann is particularly fond of quoting, can also be understood as an existentialist description of the existential Christian self-understanding which receives the richness of life at a remove from what is controllable in the world. They therefore also occur frequently in Heidegger: '. . . as unknown, and yet well known; as dying, and behold, we live; as chastened, and not killed; as sorrowful, but always rejoicing; as poor, yet making

[2] *Glauben und Verstehen*, 2, pp. 15 f. (*Essays*, p. 17).

many rich; as having nothing, and yet possessing all things.' One could also compare a sentence like: 'But *this* is life: to regain oneself as possibility, once again to be-able-to-be, once again to have future,'[3] a sentence which is meant to describe the life of the *man of faith*.

Bultmann is, of course, conscious that authenticity is understood more radically in the biblical concept of faith than in philosophy. Thinking of Heidegger's philosophy—here we are once again developing what was said at the end of the last chapter—he explains, 'taking up his thrownness in resoluteness for death is man's radical self-assertion'.[4] Here man regards his authentic existence—in biblical language his 'life' —'as a task grasped by him and to be overcome'.[5] But for faith that is sin; and so man still finds himself in inauthenticity. The Bible says that life is always a gift: 'What have you that you did not receive? If then you received it, why do you boast as if it were not a gift?' (I Cor. 4.7). The authenticity of existence is thus possible only in accepting the gift of life, i.e. in surrender to God as the giver of life. In view of the total fallenness of existence, the gift of authentic life becomes event only in the liberation of man from *himself* in his fallenness. The realization of this event the Bible calls 'faith'. Consequently Christian faith is by its very nature 'faith in', for the believer knows 'that at the very point where man can do nothing, God acts— indeed has acted already—on his behalf',[6] he knows 'of an act of God which first makes surrender, faith, love, the authentic life of man possible'.[7] 'Certainly existentialist analysis may assert that free openness for the future is a mark of human Being in its authentic existence. But is this knowledge sufficient to enable man as he actually is to attain this openness? It cannot do this any more than it can impart existence. All it can do is to tell man that if he wants to attain authentic existence he

---

[3] *Glauben und Verstehen*, 1, p. 140.
[4] *Kerygma und Mythos*, I, p. 37 (*Kerygma and Myth*, p. 30).
[5] ibid., p. 38 (ibid., p. 31).　　　　[6] ibid., p. 39 (ibid.).
[7] ibid., p. 40 (ibid., p. 32).

must be free for the future.'[8] God alone gives freedom from fallenness into the past and the present might of the world, in his saving action. Faith is indeed simply openness for the future, which can be described equally well in philosophical terms, as 'readiness for dread' in the face of the future and what is not at one's disposal. But faith knows that it is not human work, but a gift of grace. 'Readiness for dread is thus the gift of faith, and is identical with freedom from the vanity which lies at the root of sin, that we can ground our own existence on our own resolve and thus attain free openness for the future. As Paul put it: "Death is swallowed up in victory" (I Cor. 15.54)', namely, in the victory of God's saving act over death.

True, existentialist analysis can bring home to man the frightening character of the fact that his authenticity lies in openness for the future, namely, when it establishes that 'each man's particular future can in the last resort be defined as "nothingness", and when it can understand free openness for the future solely as "the readiness for dread", which man has to accept by an act of resolve'.[9] But if faith is simply this readiness for dread, it is still so in face of the divine saving act. Therefore faith knows 'that *God* encounters us at the very point where the human prospect is nothingness, and only at that point'.[10] Faith cannot describe authentic existence differently from unfaith: 'To live from the future means to be open for whatever the future brings. . . . Hence life is not determined by a self-chosen aim, to which all a man's energies and hopes are bent; but his life is rather characterized, in a certain sense, by lack of specific aim, i.e. by an inner freedom from self-chosen aims; the faith . . . that the future will bring him his true self, which he can never capture by his own self-appointed courses.'[11] Faith knows itself to be *freed by God* for

[8] *Kerygma und Mythos*, II, p. 203 (*Kerygma and Myth*, p. 205).
[9] ibid.   [10] ibid.
[11] *Marburger Predigten*, p. 66 (*This World and the Beyond*, pp. 77 f.).

such a future and therefore lives 'in the assurance and conviction that all must work together for good, and that every future is the blessing and gift *of God*'.[12]

In this way 'faith' means 'to be prepared for the moment which is always the decisive moment! The Christian faith of course is no static possession. It is not simply the conviction of the truth of certain doctrines which can be appropriated once for all. The Christian faith is a certain direction of the will. It is only alive in us if its reality is proved ever anew. It is not sufficient for us once to have decided to have faith in God, but our decision for God has to be consummated ever afresh when we are confronted by him in the actualities of living and his call strikes us. Again and again it is the decisive *now* on which everything turns. By his encounters God puts us to the test. To hold ourselves in readiness for his call requires us to be inwardly detached from all that claims our attention, from work and care, from sorrow and joy, and to see that nothing claims and absorbs us *wholly*, with the consequence that we become blind to his encounter and deaf to his call.'[13] 'It then remains to keep oneself open at any time for the encounter with God in the world, in time. It is not the acknowledgment of an image of God, be it ever so correct, that is real faith in God; rather, it is the readiness for the eternal to encounter us at any time in the present—at any time in the varying situations of our life. Readiness consists in openness in allowing something really to encounter us that does not leave the I alone, the I that is encapsulated in its purposes and plans, but the encounter with which is designed to transform us, to make us ever new selves. The situation can be heartening just as well as disheartening, can be challenging as well as requiring endurance. What is demanded is selflessness, not as a pattern of moral behaviour, but as the readiness not to cling to ourselves, but to receive our authentic self ever anew. This readiness can be interrogative, but it can also be completely unconscious. For surprisingly God can encounter us where we do not expect it.'[14] 'I cannot myself say in detail—nor may I do so—where and at what point God's summons encounters the individual, you and me, in the course of our daily life, in the routine of our work and our social contacts. For it is the mystery of Jesus' encounter with us that he meets us disguised in ever new forms; it is the mystery of God's call that it comes to us

[12] ibid.   [13] ibid., p. 134 (ibid., pp. 151 f.).
[14] 'Der Gottesgedanke und der moderne Mensch', p. 347 ('The Idea of God and Modern Man', p. 94).

clad always in a different shape, that it sounds ever new, and in circumstances where we least expected it. Hence I can only give a general warning that each of us should be prepared and vigilant and alert both to hear the summons and to obey it.'[15]

Bultmann reminds those to whom faith seems to be somewhat reduced if it is described as 'free openness for the future', and gives nothing but the transitory moment now and again in such openness, of a verse by Andreas Gryphius:

> Not mine the years that time has led astray,
> Not mine the years that still may come my way;
> Mine is the moment, and I make my sign—
> So HE, the Lord of time and heaven, is mine.

And also a passage from T. S. Eliot's *Four Quartets*:

> Time past and time future
> What might have been and what has been
> Point to one end, which is always present.[16]

In this chapter we are still not considering God's saving act itself, the saving event as the ground and object of faith. That needs a more thorough treatment. We are outlining only the *structure* of faith, a decisive feature of which is that faith has an object, the Christ-event, which we shall be describing later. It is therefore 'faith in . . .'

What does it mean for the structure of faith that an action from beyond is part of its make-up, is the condition for its possibility? It means, for example, that 'faith' is not ' "piety" or trust-in-God *in the abstract*'.[17] It has historical basis, and as trust in God is therefore trust in . . . , trust in God's saving act.

It further means that the new existence in faith is not brought about by human effort, is *not a work*. Faith is conscious that 'nothing is owed to itself, but everything to the

---

[15] *Marburger Predigten*, p. 134 (*This World and the Beyond*, p. 149).
[16] *Glauben und Verstehen*, 4, p. 140. The T. S. Eliot passage comes from 'Burnt Norton', *Four Quartets*, p. 14.
[17] *Theologie*, p. 318 (*Theology*, I, p. 318).

grace which comes into contact with it. The man of faith knows that he is *chosen* through the encounter with grace.'[18] When we said that the saving event was the condition for the possibility of faith, that did not mean that man knew about the saving event *before* his faith, so that he could accept it or reject it on the basis of this knowledge. If that were the case, he could still always understand his existential attitude towards the saving event as his own contribution, of which he might be proud. But the saving event is the presupposition of faith and faith is impossible without the action of God *in so far as* the reality of God's saving action only discloses itself *in* faith, because this saving action of God only becomes event in faith. Of course, man can know what a saving action is. He can also understand the assertion that God has acted. But *that* it is a saving event, *that* God has acted, cannot be known outside faith, for faith is simply the *experience* of this saving act; with his salvation God does not give man this or that, to be appropriated in faith, but gives man his authenticity as human salvation: he gives him himself as a believer. That means that faith is only possible where it is experienced as a gift, as a concrete gift now received, as the realization of the saving act itself. Otherwise man would objectivize God's saving act and understand his faith as a work in which he brought himself into a relationship with this object. This would make faith and saving event nothing; for as *God's* action, God's saving event can never become an object. Rather, the saving event takes place as salvation here and now, in faith, so that faith itself belongs to the saving event just as the saving event belongs to faith. Any possibility of regarding faith as a *work on the basis of* the saving event is thus excluded.

That faith in its very nature cannot be a human contribution, and that man, were he to understand his faith as a work, would only attest his lack of faith, does not of course mean that faith is not an *act*. On the contrary! 'Indeed, the less faith is a

[18] *Glauben und Verstehen*, 2, p. 157 (*Essays*, p. 177).

work, the more it is an act; and it will now perhaps be clear in what the difference consists. In the case of the work I remain the man I am; I place it outside myself, I go along beside it, I can assess it, condemn it or be proud of it. But in the act I *become* something for the first time; I find my being in it, live in it and do not stand alongside it. If I were to seek to look at myself and my act, I *would destroy* the act as an act, and degrade it into a work.'[19] This relationship of work and act can be clarified from human relationships: '*Works* of love are fundamentally easy even when I extort them from myself in certain circumstances with an effort: for in them I remain my old self. The real *act* of love is fundamentally difficult and is not to be extorted by any violence, as I give myself away in it, and attain my being only by losing it in this act.'[20] Faith is act, 'it is never something that has been done, never a work that man produces or accomplishes. Rather it is the momentary act in which he lays hold of himself in his God-given freedom.'[21]

In stressing the character of faith as act, Bultmann shows the great value he attaches to the assertion that faith is 'not a mysterious supernatural quality',[22] which is passed on to man, or a 'propensity of the soul', 'the soul's perfect state',[23] but an occurrence known to man existentially. If 'faith' is man's concrete act, then man can give information about the 'content' of his faith, and the believer can understand himself in his faith. Bultmann has learnt from Wilhelm Herrmann that faith has a content of consciousness which makes it possible for it to be made comprehensible, and in stressing this character of faith as act, he brings this recognition home decisively—differing to some degree here from Karl Barth.

Faith as act is an *act of decision*: for in faith man surrenders

---

[19] ibid., p. 156 (ibid., p. 175).   [20] ibid. (ibid., p. 176).
[21] *Glauben und Verstehen*, 3, p. 30 (*Existence and Faith*, p. 87).
[22] *Kerygma und Mythos*, I, p. 34 (*Kerygma and Myth*, p. 26).
[23] *Theologie*, p. 317 (*Theology*, I, p. 316).

his previous self-understanding, and his previous direction of will is reversed. 'Faith is the abandonment of man's own security and the readiness to find security only in the unseen beyond, in God. This means that faith is security where no security can be seen; it is, as Luther said, the readiness to enter confidently into the darkness of the future. Faith in God who has power over time and eternity, and who calls me and who has acted and now is acting on me.'[24] The true, authentic life of man, grasped in the act of obedience, is that 'which is lived from what cannot be seen, what is not at man's disposal. Such a life means the abandonment of all self-contrived security.'[25] Faith is surrender to God who is man's future. It is living from God as the indisposable ground of life and, together with this, man's affirmation of the fact that he is not at his own disposal.

Bultmann is fond of describing the act of faith as an *act of obedience*, referring above all to Paul, who also has the phrase 'obedience to the faith' (*hypakoē pisteōs*) (Rom. 1.5). Faith is obedience to the word that proclaims the saving event. For God's saving action, with which the possibility of faith comes into the world, bids man surrender himself and receive himself ever anew from God. It bids him give up all his own security and all reliance on his own efforts: 'Faith is obedience, because in it man's pride is broken. What is actually a foregone conclusion becomes for man in his pride what is most difficult. . . . He thinks he will be lost if he surrenders himself —if he surrenders himself as the man he has made of himself, but he is *supposed* to lose himself in order really to find himself for the first time. He is supposed to bow, to humble himself, to let his pride go, in order to come to himself in this way. . . . Obedience is faith because it is the abandonment of pride, and man's tearing himself free from himself—because it is surrender in pure trust, a trust without a guarantee, trust in God, "who gives life to the dead, and calls into existence the

[24] *Jesus Christ and Mythology*, pp. 40 f.
[25] *Kerygma und Mythos*, I, p. 29 (*Kerygma and Myth*, p. 19).

things that do not exist" (Rom. 4.17).'[26] In obedience to the word of salvation, man chooses himself as a gift of God. Such obedient choice is 'an act in the true sense: in a true act the doer himself is inseparable from it, while in a "work" he stands side by side with what he does'.[27]

The act of obedient faith is at the same time an act of *confession*; for the believer turns away from himself, 'confessing that all he is and has, he is and has through what God has done. Faith does not appeal to whatever it itself may be as act or attitude, but to God's prevenient act of grace which preceded faith.'[28]

So much for the structure of faith in so far as it is directly determined though the fact that faith is always faith in . . . How does Bultmann develop the New Testament concept of faith apart from this?

Faith is *hope*, i.e. faith is 'no self-contained condition of man's soul, but points towards the future'.[29] Faith is no new quality of man, but act, which is only real when it is accomplished at any time. Salvation is never the possession of the believer, but an experience which always comes to him each time from the future and is meant to be grasped in the realization of faith. The present character of salvation is therefore grounded in the perpetual futurity of God and would obviously be misunderstood if it were regarded as a '*temporal* and therefore a *temporary* state'.[30] 'Life is a possibility that *can* be laid hold of, but it is also a possibility that always *must* be laid hold of.'[31]

In the light of this Bultmann understands, for example, how Paul can call the believers 'the saved' (I Cor. 1.18) and *at the same time* can say that we are saved 'in hope' (Rom. 8.24).

[26] *Glauben und Verstehen*, 2, pp. 154 f. (*Essays*, p. 174).
[27] *Theologie*, p. 317 (*Theology*, I, p. 316).
[28] ibid., p. 319 (ibid., p. 319).   [29] ibid., p. 320 (ibid.).   [30] ibid.
[31] *Glauben und Verstehen*, 3, p. 28 (*Existence and Faith*, p. 84).

Paul writes to the community in Corinth: 'But you were washed, you were sanctified, you were justified in the name of the Lord Jesus Christ and in the spirit of our God' (I Cor. 6.11), because he sees them standing in faith, whereas he had addressed a group in Corinth a little earlier in the same letter with despairing bitterness and accused them: 'Already you are filled! Already you have become rich! Without us you have become kings!' (I Cor. 4.8), because the members of this group had forgotten that faith is always a gift and never a possession, that it never exists as a condition, but only 'from hope to hope' (Rom. 4.18).

Because faith is life from the future, it is necessarily characterized by confident openness for the future. It knows no anxiety about the future; for the future which encounters it is its life. 'In the world you have tribulation, but be of good cheer, I have overcome the world', runs a well-known saying from the Gospel of John on the lips of Jesus, 'that in me you may have peace' (John 16.33); the comfort of this saying lies in the fact that the believer has left the world behind him in the midst of the world with all its anxiety, 'because he has turned over his anxiety about himself and his future to God in obedience. For the sin of unbelief is just this: the man without faith insists upon living out of his own resources and so is anxious about his own future in the illusion of being able to have control over it. Though he naturally has his hopes, too—just as those "who have no hope" (I Thess. 4.13), of course, also live with certain hopes—still they are no real hopes. The man who is concerned for himself in fact lives in fear, shutting himself up against the future, which is not at his disposal. The man of faith is relieved of this fear because in faith he has let anxiety about himself go. He hopes where humanly there is nothing to hope, following the example of Abraham, who "hoping against hope believed" (Rom. 4.18). He lives, that is, in the true hope "which does not disappoint" (Rom. 5.5)';[32]

[32] *Theologie*, pp. 320 f. (*Theology*, I, p. 320).

for he does not hope for *something*—his life simply is hope, because God is his future and therefore his life always stands before him. Accordingly, the New Testament constantly stresses that patient waiting is characteristic of the believer, and Bultmann, too, points this out frequently.

Like hope in the sense described above, *fear* 'is an indispensable constitutive element in faith'.[33] That does not mean 'that Christian existence is a wavering between hope and fear; rather, hope and fear belong together as correlatives: just because faith is "hope", it is also "fear" and vice versa'.[34] How is that to be understood? Bultmann explains the dialectical relationship between hope and fear by means of the characteristics Paul displayed on arriving at Corinth (I Cor. 2.1–5): 'He came to Corinth "in weakness and in much fear and trembling"—so far, that is, as he looked to himself. But since he waived any eloquence or wisdom of his own and determined to know the one thing only, "Jesus Christ and him crucified", he was effective with a "demonstration of spirit and power", having as its purpose and result: "that your faith might not rest in the wisdom of men but in the power of God".'[35] That means that viewed from the believer's side faith must always contain fear 'as the knowledge of man's own insignificance and his constant dependence upon God's grace'; for 'faith would be cheated of its purpose if the believer were to consider himself secured by it'.[36] Not by chance is the grace of God, which frees man from his anxiety about the future, the grace of the judge who decides whether we have surrendered our life in anxiety for the future or whether we have gained it in that fear which teaches us 'to destroy false security and to direct the believer's attention away from himself towards God's grace which alone supports him'.[37]

[33] ibid., p. 321 (ibid.).　　　[34] ibid., p. 322 (ibid., p. 322).
[35] ibid., p. 321 (ibid., pp. 321 f.).
[36] ibid., pp. 321 f. (ibid., p. 321).
[37] ibid., p. 322 (ibid.).

The movement of faith between '*now already*' or 'no longer' and 'not yet' has the same dialectical character as the relationship between hope and fear. Bultmann is particularly fond of describing the character of faith in these logically exclusive definitions. Here it is important to note that faith is not on the way between 'now already' and 'not yet' in such a fashion that it finds itself in either the one *or* the other condition. Rather, the 'state' of faith is rightly described only when it bears the character of 'now already' and 'not yet' *at the same time*. This is particularly clearly expressed, according to Bultmann, in Phil. 3.12: 'Not that I have already obtained this or am already perfect; but I press on to make it my own, because Jesus Christ has made me his own.'

'Now already': in being grasped by Jesus Christ, the past is settled and there is freedom from the world of anxiety and the reality of death, true life as life from God's present.

'Not yet': 'surrendering a possession which had given a supposed security precludes taking a new possession in exchange for it.' The decision of faith must 'be maintained as true decision, that is, made again and again anew'. When Paul 'forgets what lies behind him' (Phil. 3.13), this 'forgetting' is not 'putting the past out of mind, but does mean constant holding it down, not letting oneself be caught by it again'.[38]

In short: 'viewed from man's side no one can say, "I have made it my own"; and yet in view of the fact that "Jesus Christ has made me his own", it can be said, "Nevertheless the hoped-for has already occurred".'[39] It is therefore part of the structure of faith, as Bultmann understands it, that man is constantly on the way between the 'now already' and the 'not yet'; where this being-on-the-way ceases, faith finds, not its consummation, but its end. 'The "not yet" motif applies to all our weakness and half-heartedness. But the "no longer" theme is heard when we look upwards to Christ and to his grace which frees us and comes to redeem us in all our joy and bitter

[38] ibid., p. 323 (ibid., p. 322).   [39] ibid.

sorrow. And then the "not yet" theme merges into a triumph-ant "yet already". "Yet already!" for divine grace accepts us as those whom we are not in our own strength, but whom we are to be and would wish to be; it accepts us as those who have been justified by faith. It fills our poverty with its riches, it helps our weakness with its power, it stills our anxiety with its comfort, it forgives our guilt with its love.'[40]

It might be pointed out in passing that the dialectical con-nection of the 'now already' with the 'not yet', which deter-mines the structure of faith, is also expressed in the central Pauline concept 'righteousness of God', to which Bultmann often refers. The righteousness of God is the gracious pardon of the sinner which is expressed in God's eschatological judgment; as such it is future by nature. According to Paul, the righteousness of God has, however, already been promised to the believer who is the one who has been 'rightwised'; it is thus present. In other words, it is present as God's future righteousness; it is there in hope and fear, it is 'not yet' possessed and 'yet already' received.

There is, finally, the same relationship in the dialectical connection of *the indicative and the imperative*, with which we shall be concerned later. This dialectic is developed particu-larly vividly in the discourse about the vine in John 15.1 ff. In this parable, on the one hand, the fruitfulness of the branch is made the condition of its remaining on the vine, and on the other hand, that the branch remains on the vine is made the condition for its fruitfulness. In other words, the indicative, the 'now already' of salvation is granted to the one who remains in the salvation offered in Christ; the imperative which makes remaining in salvation dependent on the yielding of good fruit, at the same time determines this remaining as the 'not yet', i.e. as the remaining in Christ which must

[40] *Marburger Predigten*, pp. 45 f. (*This World and the Beyond*, pp. 55 f.).

constantly be accomplished afresh. Within the framework of this dialectic we can also find in the New Testament that the believer does not sin (I John 3.9), a sentence which does not 'describe the empirical condition of believers, but what it means to believe';[41] for it is dialectically supplemented by another statement: 'If we say that we have no sin, we deceive ourselves and the truth is not in us' (I John 1.8). The confession of sinlessness and the confession of sin thus form a 'paradoxical unity',[42] which as such constitutes faith as living from the indisposable future of God. 'That "he cannot sin" does not lead to false security, but does the very opposite; it makes radical the consciousness of the believer.'[43]

Now in this way we have already come up against a new element in the structure of faith: faith is freedom, *freedom from sin*. It will therefore be a good thing to clarify this latest theme of the sinlessness of the believer under the heading of the freedom of faith.

According to Bultmann, sin is, as we saw, the self-understanding of the 'old' man, who lives 'for himself'. who wants to gain life from his own power and is in this very way carried into the slavery of sin, given over to sins, falls victim to death, and loses himself. If in faith man receives himself back again as a gift, then the freedom of faith is freedom from sin and from everything that is included in the concept of 'sin'. As freedom from the old man it is the freedom of man from his past; for his deeds, good or evil, no longer determine his life. The important thing is the future, after which he strives. In understanding himself from the future in which God encounters him, man is 'free from care, free from anxiety about death, free from legal prescriptions and human conventions and standards of value. In short, he is free from himself, as he actually is as he comes out of his past; he is a new creation

---

[41] *Theologie*, p. 432 (*Theology*, II, p. 79).
[42] ibid.   [43] ibid. (ibid., pp. 79 f.).

in Christ (II Cor. 5.17). As a man of faith, he has passed from death to life (John 5.24).'[44] Freedom from sin is forgiveness in the radical sense. 'The word of forgiveness does not simply mean that God forgives us this or that moral failing, as among ourselves we can and should forgive each other our lapses. It declares rather that God forgives and has forgiven the fundamental sin of our whole existence, the *one* sin, which is that we have separated ourselves from God and have as it were cut ourselves off from him in order to live independently in our own strength. In Christ he has created a new humanity: the humanity of those who allow Christ to lead them back to God, the omnipotent and omnipresent, from whom, to whom, and through whom are all things. *That* means, to believe in forgiveness: in the midst of care and responsibility to be free from care and the burden of responsibility, in the presence of fate to be free from the power of fate, and so free from the stresses of fear.'[45] Bultmann calls I Cor. 3.21–23 the 'most powerful expression' of this freedom: 'All things are yours, whether . . . the world or life or death or the present or the future, all are yours; and you are Christ's and Christ is God's.'

The end of this passage: 'You are Christ's', points to the dialectical character of such freedom from sin. It is no natural, magic security from sin, no liberation as a possession that is at one's disposal, but the freedom 'of the striving, willing self which is always after something and is always faced with its various possibilities, particularly the basic possibilities',[46] to live from the world or from God, to exist in freedom from sin or to lose it. As a result, freedom never loses the character of gift, but must be constantly grasped anew as gift, 'in that openness for what God demands and sends can never be taken for granted, but must always be realized anew.'[47]

[44] *Glauben und Verstehen*, 3, p. 42 (*Existence and Faith*, p. 255).
[45] *Marburger Predigten*, pp. 38 f. (*This World and the Beyond*, pp. 48 f.).
[46] *Theologie*, p. 333 (*Theology*, I, p. 331).
[47] *Glauben und Verstehen*, 3, p. 43 (*Existence and Faith*, p. 255).

After what has been said, 'freedom from sin' cannot be mis-understood as though it were freedom from concrete sinning. The man of faith is no way immune from the possibility of sin-ning; he has to be on his guard against temptation. He can constantly deny and lose his freedom from sin in everyday sins. But the freedom from sin is still freedom from the *com-pulsion to* sin. For apart from faith, *every* action is necessarily sin, in so far as even the good action serves consciously or unconsciously to confirm man's arbitrary self-understanding. Paul's very pride at his irreproachability before the law there-fore appears to him as an expression of his total fallenness in sin. In freedom from sin, on the other hand, he can do the good which remains demanded as before, as an act of life and not of death—and here we come up against the problem of acting from faith, the problem of ethics, which is to be treated separately in the penultimate chapter.

The description of freedom already given protects us, how-ever, from misunderstanding the biblical concept of faith in a libertarian way; for it is clear that when Paul asserts his freedom in the form of rhetorical question, 'Am I not free?' (I Cor. 9.1), he is not referring to the lack of ties, the freedom of subjective arbitrariness, but to freedom bound up with God, and only granted in this way. Nor does he mean the freedom of the Greek, who understands himself as part of the eternal spirit and as such sees through the nothingness of the world and frees himself from the world; for the believer knows that he is flesh and not spirit. As freedom from sin, the freedom of faith is rather being free from creation for a life from God in constant 'openness towards what encounters me in the "now", towards the future which will transform me'.[48]

As freedom from sin, man's faith is at the same time *freedom from the world* to which man himself has given the power of death over himself, by making it his god instead of using it as

[48] *Glauben und Verstehen*, 2, p. 71 (*Essays*, p. 81).

the creation of God. Bultmann is fond of describing this aspect of freedom as an element of the structure of belief as 'detachment from the world'. The obedience of faith 'means radical surrender to God in the expectation that everything will come from him and nothing from ourselves. Such a life spells deliverance from all that is worldly and under our control, and thus complete detachment from the world, freedom from the world.'[49] 'That is the victory that overcomes the world, even our faith' (I John 5.4).

At this point in our study it is no longer possible to misunderstand the concept of 'detachment from the world', say in the sense of a dualistic world-view. Such a dualistic world-view was widespread at the time and in the environment of the New Testament. It is not by chance that over wide areas the New Testament makes use of dualistic terminology, particularly gnostic language, in describing the character of faith as 'detachment from the world'. Gnosticism saw the world as a creation of evil powers which have also made the human body a prison for the immortal soul. This soul, the authentic inner man, is a lost piece of incorruptible divine substance. It languishes, watched carefully by the demonic powers of the world, in the prison of the flesh and longs to be freed from the world, in what seems to it to be a redemption. Where the New Testament, particularly Paul and John, sometimes makes use of gnostic terminology in a measured way, 'the gnostic dualism of fate has become a dualism of decision',[50] and faith is no longer, as in Gnosticism, knowledge of the imperishable divine substance whose deliverance is in God's own interest, but the conversion of the human will, 'the decision against the world for God'.[51] Thus in the concept of 'detachment from the world' the world does not represent a cosmic entity, but the historical force as which we have described it in the previous chapter: the force which promises man life so that he

[49] *Kerygma und Mythos*, I, p. 29 (*Kerygma and Myth*, p. 20).
[50] *Theologie*, p. 429 (*Theology*, II, p. 76).   [51] ibid.

tries to live from it, and which gives him death. From the world, understood in this sense, the believer is free. He is 'no longer "of the world" (John 15.19; 17.14, 16), i.e., since the world is no longer his determining origin he no longer belongs to it. That is why the world does not "recognize" the believers just as it did not recognize him (I John 3.1).'[52]

Asceticism is one of the consequences of a dualistic world-view. But detachment from the world through faith is 'something quite different from asceticism'.[53] Of course, for the person who has been detached from the world the world does not lose the character of creation. On the contrary, it receives back this characteristic of its nature for the man of faith, because he no longer allows the world to be the source of his life. To this event freedom from the world is freedom *for* the world and faith; far from making life in the world impossible, it is the presupposition of true worldliness.

So far we have not yet spoken of the responsibility of the believer for the world as Bultmann understands it, but only of the participation of the believer in everything worldly. If the believer does not live from the world, he at least lives in it; he is not torn away from his human contacts. In the Gospel of John, Jesus expressly asks the Father, *not* 'that thou shouldst take them out of the world, but that thou shouldst keep them from the evil one' (John 17.15). It is therefore a question of 'escaping into the world from the world', of the 'earthly still already being heavenly', as is also expressed in Paul's words in I Cor. 7.29–31, to which Bultmann refers untiringly and with special affection: 'Let those who have wives live as though they had none, and those who mourn as though they were not mourning, and those who rejoice as though they were not rejoicing, and those who buy as though they had no goods, and those who deal with the world as though they had no dealings with it.' To understand these

---

[52] ibid., p. 428 (ibid.).
[53] *Kerygma und Mythos*, I, p. 29 (*Kerygma and Myth*, p. 20).

words in an ascetic way, says Bultmann, is to misunderstand them. The detachment from the world expressed in them is 'preserving a distance from the world, and dealing with it in a spirit of "as if not" ';[54] for everything that is worldly and transitory has kept the character of transitoriness for the man of faith. True, the world is the place in which the man of faith has to live, but he no longer expects life from it:

> By nature they are all of Adam born,
> Their faces bear the mark of earthly breed;
> They suffer in the flesh the sinner's scorn;
> They eat and drink, according to their need.
> Awake, asleep, in all that life requires,
> One thing alone reveals the hidden fires:
> They mock the folly of the world's desires.
>
> They walk upon the earth, yet live in heaven;
> Though powerless, they still protect mankind.
> Amidst the tumult, peace to them is given;
> In poverty, enough is what they find;
> They suffer, but their joy remains immense.
> Though death is theirs to every outward sense,
> Within they lead a life of faith intense.
>
> *C. F. Richter*

Understandably, Bultmann can also quote I Cor. 6.12 in this context: 'All things are lawful for me, but not all things are helpful', a statement which expresses the Christian freedom from the world in a particularly pregnant way by using Stoic concepts; where the world loses its power for the believer, he gets back his place as lord of creation, while at the same time the world gets back its true place as the profane realm of human action. The distance from the world of the man detached from the world is not distance from what is not, but distance from 'what is insignificant in itself',[55] though it also happens to be the place in which the man of faith must prove his existence concretely; it is therefore the case that: 'The believer

[54] ibid.   [55] ibid.

may rejoice with those who rejoice, and weep with those who weep (Rom. 12.15), but he is no longer in bondage to anything in the world (I Cor. 7.17–24). Everything in the world has become indifferent and unimportant. "For though I am free from all men, I have made myself a slave to all" (I Cor. 9.19–23), "I know how to be abased, and I know how to abound; in any and all circumstances I have learned the secret of facing plenty and hunger, abundance and want" (Phil. 4.12). The world has been crucified to him and he to the world (Gal. 6.14). Moreover, the power of his new life is manifested even in weakness, suffering and death (I Cor. 4.7–11; 12.9 f.). Just when he realizes that he is nothing in himself, he can have and be all things through God (II Cor. 12.9 f.; 6.8–10).'[56]

Only briefly, because it is immediately clear after what has been said so far, we must note Bultmann's repeated remark that *joy* is also a necessary element in the structure of faith. Bultmann points, for example, to Rom. 12.12: 'Be joyful in hope', and Rom. 15.13: 'The God of hope fill you with all joy and peace in believing', and writes: 'When God is called "the God of hope" in this wish, it is clear that the joy of the present is based upon the reference of Christian existence to the future "rejoicing in hope" . . . Indeed, this joy, which is not a joy over anything within this world, is itself the Christian's relatedness to the future, in so far as it is consciously realized.'[57] That means that the man of faith can only be conscious of his faith with joy, because faith is true, future life. The Christian joy in faith has no object which faith can present to itself objectively; the man of faith rejoices that he may believe. His joy is joy in and from faith.

It is exactly the same with the *peace* which is mentioned in a saying of Jesus in John 14.27: 'My peace I give to you', a

[56] ibid.
[57] *Theologie*, p. 340 (*Theology*, I, p. 339).

promise which is expanded in a remarkable way by the remark: '. . . not as the world gives give I unto you.' In this way, Bultmann writes, peace is described as a possibility 'lying beyond all possibilities that are of this world. It is not something that can be realized in the external conditions of life or in some state of mind. On the contrary, it can be seized as a reality only by faith.'[58] It is thus clear that neither peace nor joy nor indeed even faith can become a condition. But with faith is given the true, the eternal peace in which man shares where he refuses the world with its lack of peace and puts his future into God's hand.

At the beginning of this chapter we said that it would be advisable to leave traditional ideas of faith on one side as far as possible—even (indeed, particularly) ideas of Christian faith— if we wanted to understand Bultmann's concept of faith. How far we have been successful in that remains to be seen. It may, however, have become clear that essential characteristics of our everyday concept of faith are lacking in the biblical concept of faith as it is interpreted by Bultmann. It is not surprising that for Bultmann faith is not a supernatural quality, a religious certainty of faith, a timeless attitude of the soul, or something similar. At the same time there was no question that the holding of certain objective things to be true was any part of faith. To what extent Christian faith is always 'faith in . . . ' must be developed later. But the character of faith as an existential trait of human existence is, as our analysis of its structure has made clear, so important for Bultmann, that it is impossible that the mere holding of certain facts, even if they are 'saving' facts, to be true, can affect Christian faith. Bultmann therefore explicitly stresses 'that to believe is something qualitatively different from accepting a greater or smaller number of statements'.[59] The demand of faith is rather 'the demand that the

[58] ibid., p. 435 (*Theology*, II, p. 83).
[59] *Kerygma und Mythos*, III, pp. 50 f.

world surrender the understanding it has had of itself hitherto—that it let the whole structure of its security which it has
erected in presumptuous independence of the Creator fall in
ruins. . . . Faith is turning away from the world, the act of
desecularization, the surrender of all seeming security and
every pretence, the willingness to live by the strength of the
invisible and the uncontrollable. It means accepting completely
different standards as to what is to be called death and what
life.'[60] Note that all this is faith *itself*, but that faith is not the
presupposition for authentic life in such a way that man
accepts the word which addresses him, holding it to be true,
'and subsequently arranges his life according to it in such a
way that it leads to "life".'[61] 'Holding to be true' does not in
any way form part of the structure of faith. Nor can faith
have, for example, 'trust' as a characteristic, even if this is trust
in God and his word as an *achievement* of man himself—
another widespread misunderstanding of Christian faith. Faith
is not brought about *on the basis of* trust; it *is* trust, trustful
self-surrender to God's future.

In order to avoid these and other misunderstandings, Bultmann, as we remarked at the beginning, is fond of using the
description 'self-understanding' as an alternative to 'faith'—or
even the synonymous 'understanding of existence'; for man is
himself as existence.

Faith is self-*understanding*, because it is far from being a
sacrificium intellectus, a surrender of rational thought. Faith is
rather based on understanding, on understanding the character of human nature, on understanding the concrete possibilities of existence, on understanding what it means to speak of
God's saving acts. As self-*understanding*, faith is, or can be
made, comprehensible to believer and unbeliever alike. 'Faith
is not blind faith, which accepts the incomprehensible on the
basis of external authority. For man can understand what the

[60] *Theologie*, pp. 427 f. (*Theology*, II, p. 75).
[61] *Glauben und Verstehen*, 1, p. 283.

word of revelation says, as it offers him the two possibilities of his self-understanding.'[62]

Faith is *self*-understanding, because it is concerned not with objective circumstances, of whatever kind, but with the man of faith himself, with man's understanding of himself as existence. Precisely in so far as Christian faith is essentially 'faith in . . .', it is self-understanding; for according to Bultmann, we only grasp God's saving action properly as an object of faith when it is itself grasped *in* a new understanding of man, when it leads to a new *self*-understanding.

Bultmann is fond of quoting a saying of Luther's on Romans 3.5, when he describes faith as self-understanding, in which God 'frees man from himself by teaching man at one and the same time to understand himself in his limitedness and God in his grace': 'By his outgoing, God thus causes us to enter into ourselves; and by making himself known, he causes us to know ourselves.'[63]

However, the concept 'self-understanding' is itself misleading as an elucidation of Bultmann's concept of faith. At any rate, Bultmann often has to deal with the misunderstanding that, 'All that happens is "consciousness"; the content of the self-understanding is a timeless truth, which once perceived remains true quite apart from the cause which set it in motion and "cranked it up"', i.e. without reference to the saving event.[64] To this, Bultmann replies: 'Existential self-understanding is here being confused with the existentialist understanding of human Being elaborated by philosophical analysis. The affirmations of the latter are certainly meant to be timeless truths, and in so far as they are adequate, they may pass as such. But existentialist analysis points so to speak beyond itself, by showing that existential self-understanding can be appropriated only existentially. In my existential self-

[62] Bultmann and Jaspers, *Die Frage der Entmythologisierung*, p. 71.
[63] *Kerygma und Mythos*, II, p. 200 (*Kerygma and Myth*, p. 202).
[64] ibid., p. 201 (ibid.).

understanding, I do not learn what existence means in the abstract (that would be existentialist understanding), but I understand myself in my concrete here and now, in my concrete encounters.'[65] Or more simply: 'It is impossible to tell someone what death and life, sin and grace, are in the same way as one can tell him that there are flesh-eating plants or kinds of fish which bring living young into the world. Rather, if we speak to anyone about death and life, sin and grace, we speak to him about his own life, to which all this belongs, just as much as light and darkness, love and friendship belong to it. Only on the basis of this presupposition can he understand, and only on the basis of this presupposition can we understand what a text says. In that case, the text does not teach me remarkable things that I did not know before, or communicate a knowledge of processes of which I was ignorant; it discloses to me possibilities of myself which I can only understand in so far as I am open and ready to keep myself open for my possibilities. I cannot simply accept what is said to me as a communication; I understand it only in saying either "yes" or "no". It is not that I first understand and then adopt an attitude; my understanding comes about only in saying "yes" or "no". For it is a question of the disclosure of my own possibility, which I understand only by grasping it, or rejecting it as a perversion of myself. Thus understanding is always at the same time resolve, decision.'[66]

Thus Bultmann believes that the concept of self-understanding of itself excludes the false idea that faith is only a question of events of consciousness: 'for I am indeed myself only in each particular situation . . . I understand myself in each case only in concrete historical encounters.'[67] To overlook this would be to succumb to the fatal subject-object division and to flatter oneself that the 'I' which one regarded

[65] ibid. (ibid., p. 203).
[66] *Glauben und Verstehen*, I, pp. 126 f.
[67] *Kerygma und Mythos*, I, p. 222.

from a distance was one's authentic self. But *self*-understanding is 'never really anything but what *happens*, what is achieved on each particular occasion in the *self*'.[68] The 'self-understanding' of the lover, who understands himself anew with his loved one in his love is, as Bultmann remarks, not the understanding of a general truth or a mere act of consciousness, but an existential event which alters lover and loved one alike; exactly the same is true of faith as a 'self-understanding' which 'opens up his "way" to him, guides all his conduct, and gives him clarity and assurance',[69] not because he knows more than before, but because he understands himself anew in faith.

In so far as faith rests on the coming saving event as its basis, it is, as self-understanding, obedience and confession; not new knowledge, but *recognition*, in which something new *happens*. When Paul says, for example, that Jesus has been made known to him as Messiah through a revelation (Gal. 1.12–16), then in Bultmann's view this does not mean that Paul had some supernatural communication. 'One does not acquire knowledge about the Messiah; one either acknowledges him or rejects him. . . . The *acknowledgement* of Jesus as the Messiah is the material content of that revelation, but that means that Paul now *understands Jesus* as the Messiah—for without understanding there is no obedience. To understand someone else as Lord accordingly means to *have a new understanding of oneself*, as standing at the service of the Lord and finding one's authenticity in such service.'[70]

So far is faith as self-understanding from being a mere act of consciousness that Bultmann can say, 'this existential self-understanding need not even be conscious',[71] just as the lover does not only understand himself anew in his love when he brings his love to the level of consciousness. The believer can

---

[68] ibid., p. 223.
[69] *Theologie*, p. 370 (*Theology*, II, p. 18).
[70] *Glauben und Verstehen*, 1, p. 203.
[71] *Kerygma und Mythos*, II, p. 201 (*Kerygma and Myth*, p. 203).

exist completely in the new self-understanding of faith without being conscious with conceptual clarity of his new existence.

Self-understanding must therefore be clearly distinguished from self-consciousness. Whereas an exposition of faith as self-consciousness would destroy the character of faith as hope —its 'not yet'—and would thus destroy faith itself, this very character is brought to the fore in the interpretation of faith as self-understanding. For 'just as in human contacts the new self-understanding given one by encountering another in love and trust remains true only when it permanently retains its connection with the other who is encountered, so too the self-understanding granted by faith never becomes a possession, but remains true only as a repeated response to the repeated encounter of the Word of God. . . . "His compassions are new every morning." True, but I can only be genuinely aware of it when I perceive it anew every morning, for as a timeless truth it is meaningless. That means that I can know of it only as one who is renewed every morning—by allowing myself to be renewed by it.'[72]

Bultmann makes yet one more thing clear in this context. In understanding myself anew in my encounter with the other, say the loved one, I also understand the other and his conduct anew; that means that he encounters me as another and has in fact become another as far as I am concerned, even if he has remained the same. This is also true of the new self-understanding of faith. Not only do I gain a new self-understanding in the encounter with God's saving act in the sense described, which changes my existence, but I also understand God and his saving action anew, namely, God as the one who acts in me, who is known only by faith, and his action as *saving* action, as which it discloses itself only to faith.

Here at last is an indication of our new theme, which has

[72] ibid., p. 202 (ibid., p. 204).

constantly formed the background of the analysis of the structure of Christian faith as human self-understanding in this chapter; it is the saving event, which gives faith in such a way that it is only the saving event *with* faith. This is what we must look at in the following chapters.

6

The Saving Event: Cross
and Resurrection

THE WAY FROM inauthenticity to authenticity or, in biblical
terms, from sin to faith, from death to life, from damnation to
salvation is—in our understanding of Bultmann thus far—a
way which only God can re-open for man. Fallen man can see
his life, his salvation, only as a gift of God, only as grace. In
other words, faith is possible only as 'faith in . . .'; it presupposes a saving event, an act of God, which is the basis and
object of faith.

Bultmann explicitly stresses that 'if to speak of an act of
God is to have any meaning at all, it must denote an act in
a real, "objective" sense, and not just be a "symbolical" or
pictorial expression'.[1] This 'objective' is not, of course, to be
misunderstood as if it were 'objectivizing'. So Bultmann puts
it in inverted commas and explains his statement in a typical
way: 'On the other hand, if the action of God is not to be
conceived as a worldly phenomenon capable of being apprehended apart from its existential reference, it can only be
spoken of by speaking simultaneously of myself as the person
who is existentially concerned. To speak of the act of God
means to speak at the same time of my existence. Since human
life is lived out in time and space, man's encounter with God
can only be a specific event here and now. This event, our being

[1] *Kerygma und Mythos*, II, p. 196 (*Kerygma and Myth*, p. 196).

addressed by God here and now, our being questioned, judged and blessed by him, is what we mean when we speak of an act of God.'[2]

What is this *'objective'* saving event, which happens *to me here and now*? Anyone with even the most modest knowledge of the nature of Christianity knows not only that the proclamation of the action of God forms the centre of the New Testament but also that to speak in this sense of the action of God means to speak of Jesus Christ. And of course Bultmann does not mean it in any other way: 'At the very point where man can do nothing, God acts—indeed he has acted already—on man's behalf,' 'this is precisely the meaning of the *Christ event*.'[3] Christian 'faith in . . .', faith in the saving action of God, is thus faith in Jesus Christ, faith in him as a person, in him himself, in his work, and not in a general truth which is more or less fortuitously associated with him and which might therefore in principle be separable from him. The New Testament proclaims 'Jesus not primarily as the teacher, who certainly had extremely important things to say and will always be honoured for saying them, but whose person in the last analysis is immaterial for those who have assimilated his teaching. On the contrary, his person is just what the New Testament proclaims as the decisive saving event.'[4]

Paul expresses this state of affairs in the lapidary statement: 'God was in Christ' (II Cor. 5.19). When he continues: ' . . . and reconciled the world to himself, not counting their trespasses against them,' the statement leaves no doubt that God's action in Christ is a *saving* action, which takes place to deliver the world and not to destroy it. So Bultmann writes: 'The event of Jesus Christ is therefore the revelation of the *love* of God.'[5] He attaches importance to the assertion that when the New Testament speaks of the love of God it does not, or does not primarily, mean the *attitude* of love, but love as *action*, as

[2] ibid.   [3] *Kerygma und Mythos*, I, p. 39 (ibid., p. 31).
[4] ibid., p. 25 (ibid., p. 14).   [5] ibid., p. 39 (ibid., p. 32).

event, namely, as the saving event which the New Testament understands and proclaims to be the Christ event. Bultmann stresses this fact even more strongly in the case of the correlative of love, 'grace', a concept which occurs particularly frequently in Paul. 'God's "grace" is not a quality, not his timeless kindliness, and what the gospel brings is not enlightenment as to God's nature, hitherto misunderstood, as if till now he had been wrongly conceived as wrathful and ought henceforth to be regarded as gracious. On the contrary! Now, as then, "God's wrath" is poured out "against all ungodliness and wickedness of men" (Rom. 1.18). . . . God continues to be the judge, and Christian faith in the grace of God does not consist in the conviction that God's wrath does not exist or that there is no threateningly impending judgment (II Cor. 5.10), but in the conviction of being rescued from God's wrath.'[6] 'God's grace is not his hitherto unknown or misconceived graciousness, but his act of grace occurring now',[7] which is the gracious action of the *judge*.

In that case it becomes clear that 'God in his grace acts as the absolutely free God who has not been brought into debt by any human claim and who acts, therefore, as "the gracious One" in a *radical* sense.'[8] 'All this has its origin in God who through Christ reconciled us to himself', as Bultmann translates II Cor. 5.18; he also points to Rom. 5.10, according to which we were reconciled with God 'while we were enemies'.

These words of Paul show at the same time that 'the message of reconciliation' (II Cor. 5.19) is 'not the conciliatory and reconciling word but the proclamation of the already accomplished reconciliation',[9] that is, the message of the gracious saving act of God which comes before all human action and sets human action at nought. 'God's grace, therefore, is not his kindliness and goodness which cause him to take man's weak-

[6] *Theologie*, p. 287 (*Theology*, I, p. 288).
[7] ibid., p. 289 (ibid., p. 289).   [8] ibid., p. 284 (ibid., p. 284).
[9] ibid., p. 286 (ibid., p. 287).

ness into account and, in view of his endeavour towards the good, to excuse an occasional mistake, or even many, to forgive small sins, or even great ones. On the contrary, that endeavour is exactly what the grace of God repudiates—for it is just where man's sin of sins lurks, his arrogance, his fooling himself, that he can live on his own. And however much this man may be struggling, fighting with himself, near to despair, pleadingly looking for divine help and redemption, even so the grace of God comes to him, not as approval of his striving and a prop for his failing strength, but as the decisive question: Will you surrender, utterly surrender, to God's dealing—will you know yourself to be a sinner before God?'[10]

We have now shown sufficiently that Bultmann's understanding of the New Testament concept of faith is that God's act of love 'makes a man free from himself to be himself, free to live a life of surrender in faith . . .' that 'faith as man's freedom from himself, as openness for the future', is only possible as 'faith in the love of God', and that therefore the New Testament and faith know of Jesus Christ as an 'act of God which . . . first makes man's authentic life possible'.[11] Now, however, we must explain *in what degree* Jesus Christ is the act of God, in what way salvation occurs where he encounters us in preaching. The present chapter will closely follow the exegesis with which Bultmann attempts to make the proclamation of the saving event in *Paul* comprehensible. The following chapter will develop the same problem through the interpretation of the *Johannine writings* made by Bultmann.

What is Paul's view of the Christ event in his discussion of the saving event? Does he look at the whole of Jesus' appearance or at particular events in the life and destiny of Jesus? Are perhaps the words of Jesus, or particular actions important to him?

[10] ibid., pp. 284 f. (ibid., pp. 284 f.).
[11] *Kerygma und Mythos*, I, pp. 39 f. (*Kerygma and Myth*, p. 32).

Bultmann writes: 'The act of divine grace consists in the fact that God gave Christ up to die on the cross.'[12] So the Christ event as the saving act of God is the event of the cross of Christ. Paul declares that he preaches Christ, 'crucified' (I Cor. 1.23; 2.2). Even to the Galatians he publicly portrayed Christ 'as crucified' (Gal. 3.1). The gospel of the saving act of God is 'the word of the cross' (I Cor. 1.18), and the enemies of this gospel are 'enemies of the cross of Christ' (Phil. 3.18). That God's saving act took place on the cross of Christ was the content of Christian doctrinal tradition even before Paul. Paul himself says in I Cor. 15.1 ff., that he, too, received what he handed on to the Corinthians, namely 'that Christ died for our sins according to the Scriptures', and if according to I Cor. 11.26 the community proclaims the death of the Lord wherever it celebrates the Holy Communion, until he comes, then naturally this tradition of the Lord's Supper also comes from tradition.

But the saving event embraces not only the death but also at the same time the resurrection of Jesus. The crucified one is the risen one. Christ Jesus is 'dead, yes, but also raised from the dead' (Rom. 8.34); he 'died for all and was raised for all' (II Cor. 5.15); he was 'put to death for our trespasses and raised for our justification' (Rom. 4.25). Just as Paul can point to the cross by itself without mentioning the resurrection, so too occasionally he can speak only of the resurrection without mentioning the cross explicitly: Rom. 10.9. etc. Here, according to Bultmann, there are not two independent saving acts of God; on the contrary, for Paul cross and resurrection form a unity as the *one* saving act. 'The death and resurrection of Christ as saving event' is therefore a stereotyped formula of Bultmann's in his account of Pauline theology.

On the basis of these and other Pauline passages, then, Bultmann has no doubt that it is not Jesus' teaching or his life or his actions, but his death and resurrection which represent the saving event, as far as Paul is concerned.

[12] *Theologie*, p. 292 (*Theology*, I, p. 292).

But in what way does salvation *take place* in the cross and resurrection of Jesus? Bultmann writes: 'It is clear that the saving event, namely Christ's death and resurrection, is the act of the prevenient grace of God; and that the various expressions which describe this act intend to express its unprecedented nature and its might which so radically transformed the human situation. It is an event purely by God's initiative; for man, pure gift; by accepting it he is released from his perverse striving to achieve life or self-hood by his own efforts—only to be given it as a gift.'[13]

In these words we hear once again of the form of the salvation which takes place in the saving event for us and about which faith knows, as we saw in the last chapter. Here, according to Bultmann, the basic notion of the Pauline theology of the cross is as follows: 'In the cross of Christ God has pronounced judgment on the world and precisely by so doing has also opened up the way of salvation. Because a crucified one is proclaimed as Lord of the world, it is demanded of man that he subject himself to God's judgment, i.e. to the judgment that all of man's desires and strivings and standards of value are nothing before God, that they are all subject to death. If God has reconciled the world to himself through the cross, then this means that he has made himself visible in the cross and, as it were, says to man, "Here I am!" All of man's accomplishments and boasting are at an end; they are condemned as nothing by the cross.'[14] The significance of the confession of Christ's resurrection, indissolubly bound up with the confession of his cross, matches this exactly: 'Precisely he who accepts as valid for himself the judgment that is spoken in the cross, who, as Paul puts it, lets himself be crucified with Christ, experiences the cross as liberation and redemption, and is able to believe that, by giving Jesus up to the cross, God thereby led him into life—a life in which all share who let

[13] ibid., p. 294 (ibid., p. 294).
[14] 'Jesus und Paulus', p. 85 (*Existence and Faith*, p. 197).

131

themselves be crucified with him. It is precisely death that frees us for life. Therefore, Paul looks upon everything that was gain to him—namely, the national advantages of which he could boast and his irreproachable life and striving under the law—as loss, "so that," as he says, "I may know him (sc. Christ) and the power of his resurrection, and may share in his sufferings, becoming like him in his death, that if possible I may attain the resurrection of the dead" (Phil. 3.7 ff.).'[15]

'The question now is, how can this event be recognized and experienced by man as the act of grace? For only then can it take effect as a compelling and transforming power, when it can be understood as directed at man, reaching him, happening to him—i.e. when the challenge to accept it as saving event forces him into genuine decision.'[16] In other words: how can it be known that Jesus' death and resurrection have the saving significance for men which has been described and asserted? How does this event appear to man as a saving event?

In order to be able to answer this question, we must first try to understood how Paul describes the significance of the saving event in detail. Bultmann shows that to this end the apostle makes use of a series of concepts and ideas, which come from different fields and which are partly taken over by him from the Christian tradition with little reflection.

From ideas associated with the Jewish cult and determined by a juristic way of thinking comes the interpretation of Christ's death as an *expiatory sacrifice* through which the forgiveness of sins is achieved: the punishment caused by sin is borne by Jesus Christ and thus the guilt of man is atoned for. This idea occurs frequently in Paul, above all in stereotyped traditional phrases, but according to Bultmann it is not characteristic of Paul.

Closely related to the idea of an expiatory sacrifice which is

[15] ibid., pp. 85 f. (ibid., pp. 197 f.).
[16] *Theologie*, p. 294 (*Theology*, I, pp. 294 f.).

offered *for the benefit of* a man, is that of the *vicarious sacrifice* in which someone takes punishment on himself *in place of* another or all, and thus frees the guilty from condemnation. This idea, too, already present before Paul, is not, in Bultmann's view, characteristic of him. It cannot be, thinks Bultmann, because the idea of sacrifice does not say what it really would have to say for Paul. 'The most it can convey is that the cross effects the forgiveness of all the past and—even the future—sins of man, in the sense that the punishment they deserved has been remitted. But more than this ought to be said: the cross frees men from sin as a power over them, from sinning.'[17] Consequently the saving event does not find adequate expression in these ideas. In Bultmann's view, Paul was conscious of this. Bultmann points out that Paul hardly ever speaks of the 'forgiveness of sins', which 'elsewhere plays so considerable a role in primitive Christian preaching', and explains this striking and often overlooked fact in the remark that: ' "forgiveness of sins" is ambiguous in so far as it seems to declare only release from the guilt contracted by "former sins", whereas the important thing for Paul is release from *sinning*, release from the power of sin',[18] in other words, from 'sin' as Bultmann understands it on the basis of the New Testament and as we presented it in Chapter 4. Freedom from sin, understood in this radical way, cannot adequately be expressed in a theory of satisfaction.

Related to the interpretations of the cross already mentioned is the idea of the *'ransom'*, in which a 'payment' does away with the debt or penalty. 'Nevertheless, that is not the full extent of the thought,'[19] says Bultmann. He infers from passages like Gal. 1.4; 3.3 and 4.4 that for Paul the freedom purchased through the death of Christ is not only freedom from punishment but freedom from sin as a *power*: 'Christ's

[17] *Kerygma und Mythos*, I, p. 42 (*Kerygma and Myth*, pp. 35 f.).
[18] *Theologie*, p. 287 (*Theology*, I, p. 287).
[19] ibid., p. 296 (ibid., p. 297).

death is not merely a sacrifice which cancels the *guilt* of sin (i.e. the punishment contracted by sinning), but is also the means of release from the powers of this age: Law, Sin and Death.'[20]

According to Bultmann, *this* saving effect of the cross of Christ is more clearly expressed 'in the statement in which Paul describes Christ's death in analogy with the death of a divinity of the *mystery religions*'.[21] The original significance of this view is, as is well known, that the mystic shares in the destiny of the cult-god through participating in cultic ceremonies. Just as the cult-god finds the way to life through death, so too does the man initiated into his mystery and thus divinized. In Rom. 6.10 f., Paul expresses the saving significance of the cross and resurrection in the language of the mysteries: 'The death he died he died to sin, once for all, but the life he lives he lives for God. So *you also* must consider yourselves dead to sin and alive to God in Christ Jesus.' In speaking of sin and 'dying to sin', Paul precludes the misunderstanding that he is talking about the divinization of man. Even in these words, the saving event is understood to be *Christian*. According to Bultmann, the terminology of the mystery religions offers an adequate means of expressing such a Christian understanding in that it expresses the power of the saving event that transforms man; 'consider yourselves dead to sin and alive to God', in other words, that you have regained *authentic* life.

In Bultmann's view, the gnostic idea of redemption offered the apostle an equally appropriate form of expression. For *Gnosticism* there is no divinization of man. The gnostic's conviction is rather that the men who are to be redeemed have always been portions of the divine substance in their spiritual being, the *pneuma*; these fell under the power of darkness in primordial times and were fettered in the corporeal world by demonic powers. The redeemer forms a substantial, often indeed a physical, personal unity with the divine part of man

[20] ibid., p. 297 (ibid., pp. 297 f.).   [21] ibid. (ibid., p. 298).

that is to be redeemed. The work of the redeemer consists in disarming the evil powers of the world so that he, and with him the 'pneumatic', can discard their fetters and find a way to his heavenly home unmolested by the powers of darkness. For gnosticism, this process of redemption has cosmic dimensions; the disarming of the powers of the world means the end of the world itself, which is a work of the evil powers and is transitory, once the divine pneuma is taken from it. Paul quite often writes about the process of redemption in the categories of this gnostic thought. Thus: 'When the author of Colossians says, "He (God) . . . having forgiven us all our trespasses, having blotted out the bond written in ordinances that was against us, which was contrary to us; and he has taken it out of the way, nailing it to the cross," he hastens to add: "having put off from himself the principalities and powers, he made a show of them openly, triumphing over them in it" (Col. 2.13–15).'[22] Alongside the traditional language of the 'forgiveness of sins' there are statements which issue in gnostic conceptuality, which raise the historic event of the cross to cosmic dimension and mean to express the fact that 'forgiveness of sins' is a process which embraces our whole existence, because sin is not something in us, but we ourselves are utterly sinners. This form of expression thus says that in the cross of Christ 'the judgment of ourselves as fallen creatures enslaved to the powers of the "world" is accomplished.'[23] Here 'world' must be understood, of course, in the sense, described earlier, of a power which determines the whole of life. As this 'world' is disarmed, the new world dawns which has 'received its stamp from Christ'[24] because in his death and resurrection he has 'brought freedom from the annihilating powers'.[25]

Looking back at what has just been said, Bultmann writes: 'Clearly Paul found none of these thought-complexes and none

[22] *Kerygma und Mythos*, I, p. 42 (*Kerygma and Myth*, p. 36).
[23] ibid.   [24] *Theologie*, p. 299 (*Theology*, I, p. 300).   [25] ibid.

of their terminologies adequate to express his understanding of the saving event. Why did he not confine himself to presenting the significance of Jesus' death in the categories of Jewish cultic and juristic thinking? Because in them the meaning of the resurrection had no chance to come into its rightful place. Why did he, rather, also resort to the categories of the mysteries and the gnostic myth? He obviously did so because through them the saving event could be interpreted as happening actually to and for and in man':[26] 'Therefore, if any one is in Christ, he is a new creation; the old has passed away, behold, the new has come' (II Cor. 5.17).

But one question now remains. How does this event, which can be depicted in such different ways yet whose significance can clearly be indicated, *show* itself to men to be a saving event? It seems that only an answer to this question will permit us to go on to ask how this saving event *happens to us*. The fact that Paul develops the significance of the saving event with the terminology of different sets of ideas, which cannot always be harmonized, makes it impossible to make any one of these sets of ideas finally authoritative. But even if one does this, the question of the legitimacy of an interpretation of the saving event, made absolute in this way, still remains.

Is the cross legitimated as saving event by being the cross *of Christ*? 'In that case, we would first have to be convinced of the significance of Christ and believe in him before we could discern the real meaning of the cross.'[27] But what would be the concrete significance of believing in Christ before one can believe in the saving character of the cross? Would it, for instance, mean to resort to *the historical Jesus*? Bultmann feels that that is possible, that it was true in a way for those who first proclaimed the gospel. 'For them the cross was the cross of him with whom they had lived in personal intercourse. Out

[26] ibid., p. 300 (ibid.).
[27] *Kerygma und Mythos*, I, p. 43 (*Kerygma and Myth*, p. 38).

of this personal intercourse, in which it was an experience of their own lives, the cross presented them with a question and it disclosed to them its meaning.' But Bultmann continues: 'For us this personal connection cannot be reproduced. For us the cross cannot disclose its own meaning.' Moreover, 'the New Testament does not proclaim Jesus Christ in this way. The meaning of the cross is not disclosed from the life of Jesus as a figure of past history, a life which needs to be reproduced by historical research. On the contrary, Jesus is *proclaimed as* the crucified, who is also risen from the dead.'[28]

Does the *resurrection* of Jesus then represent the preliminary legitimation of the cross as the saving event, so that once I believe in Jesus Christ as the risen one I can believe in God's saving action in his cross? Bultmann emphatically denies that, too. Of course, he argues, one cannot deny 'that the resurrection of Jesus is often used in the New Testament as a miraculous proof. Take for instance Acts 17.31. Here we are actually told that God substantiated the claims of Jesus Christ by raising him from the dead. Then again the resurrection narratives: both the legend of the empty tomb and the appearances report demonstrations of the physical reality of the risen body of the Lord (see especially Luke 24.39-43). But these are most certainly later embellishments of the primitive tradition. Paul knows nothing about them. There is, however, one passage where Paul tries to prove the miracle of the resurrection as a historical event by adducing a list of eye-witnesses (I Cor. 15.3-8).'[29] But Bultmann describes such a guarantee as 'fatal', and is fond of confirming this by pointing to Karl Barth, who sets out to explain away the way in which I Cor. 15.3-8 seems to provide legitimation for the resurrection, because it is incomprehensible how any *historical* fact could be concerned with the resurrection from the dead. Bultmann agrees with these remarks of Barth: 'Yes, indeed: the resurrection of Jesus cannot be a miraculous proof by which the sceptic might be

[28] ibid., pp. 43 f. (ibid., p. 38).   [29] ibid., pp. 44 f. (ibid., p. 39).

compelled to believe in Christ.'[30] 'Resurrection' is never rightly understood as a historical event—and only as a historical event could it legitimate faith—but always as an event in which 'this world' finds its end.

According to Bultmann, 'only the Easter *faith* of the first disciples can be understood' as a historical event.[31] But of course this Easter faith is not a fact in which we might believe, taking away from us the venture of faith. Not only in this context, Bultmann warns against building one's faith on the faith of another. That is never possible. So even the Easter faith of the first disciples cannot interest us as the basis of our faith. And if we wanted to infer the resurrection of Jesus as a historical fact from the historical fact of the Easter faith, we would not only move on to ground which was not susceptible to historical investigation, we would also misunderstand the significance of the Easter event, which is not *as such* an event which can be demonstrated by the historian. For as soon as we objectivize it into an event of this kind, and take up the standpoint of an onlooker or an assessor over against it, it is no longer the event of the saving action of God. It is Bultmann's view that this saving action, in the light of which I understand sin and grace radically, i.e. existentially, cannot be controlled and verified by observation, even if the fact of the resurrection of Jesus were demonstrable as a historical fact. So the Christian Easter faith is not interested in the historical question because it is interested in the resurrection of Jesus as saving event, i.e. as an existential experience.

Moreover, 'resurrection' as a historical event which is objectively verifiable, i.e. as the return of a dead man to earthly life, is not only incredible, but a phenomenon that is by no means unusual in the history of religion. Furthermore, the resurrection, understood in this way, does not mean the annihilation of death at all. The resurrection cannot be established as this, i.e. as a saving fact understood in a Chris-

[30] ibid., p. 45 (ibid.).   [31] ibid., p. 47 (ibid., p. 42.)

tian way, as an event through which 'Christ abolished death and brought life and immortality to light' (II Tim. 1.10), 'no matter how many witnesses are cited, as though once it was established it might be believed beyond all question and faith might have its unimpeachable guarantee. No; the real difficulty is that the resurrection is itself an object of faith, and you cannot secure one faith (in the saving significance of the cross) through another (that in the resurrection).'[32] So, as we have already seen, cross and resurrection always represent a unity in the New Testament. It is not the case that 'the cross could be seen as an isolated event, as though it were the end of Jesus, which needed the resurrection subsequently to reverse it. The one who suffers death is already the Son of God, and his death by itself is the victory over the power of death';[33] put paradoxically, it is the risen one who dies on the cross. In that case it is impossible for the resurrection to legitimate the cross as saving event.

But what is the character of the preliminary faith in Jesus as the Christ which makes it possible to appropriate the cross to oneself as saving event? Is it faith in the incarnate and *pre-existent Son of God*, who makes it possible for men to share in the saving event of the cross? Bultmann objects to that, too, and occasionally refers to Martin Luther for support. 'Christ is not called Christ because he has two natures. What does that matter to me? He bears this glorious and comforting name by virtue of his office and work. Thus he takes his name from what he has taken upon himself' (WA 16, p. 217, lines 33 f.). In the same way, Bultmann thinks that the New Testament does not speak of the pre-existence of Christ and his incarnation in order to *authenticate* his cross as saving event; rather, faith in Jesus as the Son of God presupposes that his cross has been recognized as God's saving act. If this happens, then to talk of Jesus' pre-existence shows that 'the origin and significance of Jesus' person and his fate are not within earthly

[32] ibid., p. 45 (ibid., pp. 39 f.).   [33] ibid., p. 44 (ibid., pp. 38 f.).

occurrence, but God was acting in them'.[34] 'The fact of Christ's pre-existence, so understood, does not make faith in the crucified easier (as if the assertion of the cross's salvation-significance would be credible, once it were recognized that it was precisely the pre-existent Son of God who died on the cross) but itself becomes a scandalous and foolish matter of faith at one with the "word of the cross".'[35] What is true of Jesus' resurrection is true then of his pre-existence and incarnation, especially as the two phenomena are incapable of any objective demonstration: as objects of saving faith, they cannot provide the ground for such faith.

We asked whether the cross is the saving event because it is the cross *of Christ*, and saw that in Bultmann's view the significance of Christ is not disclosed if one neglects the fact that he is the bearer of the saving event. But that has the result of providing a negative answer to our question. The relationship enquired about is to be reversed: the cross is not the saving event because it is the cross of Christ, but it is the cross of Christ because it is the saving event. In other words, Jesus is acknowledged to be the Christ, the pre-existent, incarnate and risen Lord, because his cross has been experienced as saving event, and not vice versa. Confession of Christ is only meaningful and only possible in the light of the acknowledgment of the cross as God's sole saving act. This is in fact Bultmann's view. He writes: 'Hence you cannot first believe in Christ and then in the cross. To believe in Christ means to believe in the cross as the cross of Christ. The cross is not the saving event because it is the cross of Christ; it is the cross of Christ because it is the saving event. Otherwise it is the tragic end of a noble man.'[36] Or: 'Nor has God offered a proof of himself in "saving facts". For these, too, are objects of faith, and as saving facts are only visible to faith and to faith alone.

[34] *Theologie*, p. 304 (*Theology*, I, p. 304).   [35] ibid.
[36] *Kerygma und Mythos*, I, p. 46 (*Kerygma and Myth*, p. 41).

Our knowledge of them does not precede faith so as to provide a basis for it, as other convictions are based on proven facts. In a sense, of course, they do provide a basis for faith, but only as facts which are themselves apprehended in faith. It is just the same with human trust and love. These, too, are not based on any trustworthiness or lovableness in another which could be objectively ascertained, but upon the nature of the other apprehended *in* the love and *in* the trust.'[37]

In that case, we are thrown back on the question: 'How do we come to believe in the cross as the cross of Christ and as the saving event? How do we come to believe in the cross as the saving event?'[38] What is the preliminary faith which makes saving faith possible? Bultmann indicates that in this enquiry, which so far has only led us into a dilemma, two acts of faith and thus also two concepts of faith must be distinguished: first, a faith 'which consists in a willingness to consider true the facts reported of the pre-existent Son of God—incarnation, crucifixion, resurrection from the dead—and to see in them a demonstration of the grace of God'; and secondly, a faith 'which is self-surrender to the grace of God and which signifies the utter reversal of a man's previous understanding of himself—specifically, the radical surrender of his human "boasting." '[39] The first faith, then, is belief that God acts in Jesus Christ; with the second, man opens himself to this act of God and allows it to happen to him. In this way the possibility exists in principle that a man can remain in the first faith without believing 'existentially'.

Without question, for Bultmann this duality in the concept of faith and thus in faith itself is not acceptable; what it implies is nothing less than what he regards as the basic error of all theology, even of faith itself, as we demonstrated at length in Chapter 2: God's action is objectivized. Just as man cannot

[37] *Kerygma und Mythos*, II, p. 200 (ibid., pp. 210 f.).
[38] *Kerygma und Mythos*, I, p. 46 (ibid., p. 41).
[39] *Theologie*, p. 300 (*Theology*, I, p. 300).

make God his object if he really wants to have to do with *God*, so too he cannot consider and assess God's action as an objective *datum*; in that case he is no longer dealing with *God's* action. If God is the one who is simply not at man's disposal, then his action, his revelation, are not at man's disposal either. 'God as acting does not refer to an event which can be perceived by me without myself being drawn into the event as into God's action, without myself taking part in it as being acted upon. In other words, to speak of God as acting involves the events of personal existence.'[40] But in that case, 'the decision-question whether a man is willing to give up his old understanding of himself and henceforth understand himself only from the grace of God and the question whether he will acknowledge Jesus Christ as the Son of God and Lord should turn out to be one and the same question'.[41] Now according to Bultmann, this is in fact the case, and in his view that is 'the real intention of Paul'[42] and of the New Testament in general.

When it is objected that he must distinguish in theory 'between an act of faith which sees in the event of the cross the revelation of the love of God, and a second act of faith for which the first act sets us free . . . an act which consists in a radical change of self-understanding', he retorts: 'No, not at any price! For I cannot imagine how we can see and believe the revelation of God's love without being at the same time set free for a new self-understanding. I simply cannot understand how I can believe that I am really delivered from sin before I "change my self-understanding". I am afraid my answer to this must be: *"nondum considerasti quanti ponderis sit peccatum"*. The love of God is not a phenomenon whose apprehension leaves a man the same as he was before. Hence even the apprehension itself must be attributed to the opera-

[40] *Jesus Christus und die Mythologie*, p. 79 (*Jesus Christ and Mythology*, p. 68).
[41] *Theologie*, p. 300 (*Theology*, I, p. 301).   [42] ibid.

tion of the Holy Spirit. No proclamation which possesses "the character of a simple biblical *report* of what has *happened*" can tell a man "that this liberation is a reality antecedent to and transcending all his understanding". For the reality of the deliverance is not something which a report of a happening can display.'[43]

As we have already said, it is Bultmann's conviction that this is also the real intention of the apostle Paul, when he proclaims the cross of Christ as God's decisive saving act: for it is clear that, 'Paul can speak of Christ as "the Son of God who loved me and gave himself up for me" only as the Paul who has waived his own righteousness and given up his self (his *ego*) to die (Gal. 2.19 f.; Phil. 3.4–11). He knows of that Christ only by knowing himself anew in the same act of recognition.'[44] 'It accords with this that in Romans, where Paul is connectedly presenting the main ideas of his message to a hitherto unknown congregation in order to legitimate himself as a genuine apostle, he . . . does not first present the saving event, the credibility of which would first have to be acknowledged. Instead he begins by exposing the plight of mankind, so that then the proclamation of God's saving act becomes a decision-question.'[45] So according to Paul, as Bultmann understands him, one cannot regard the cross as an objectively visible, comprehensible event which convinces us of its saving significance, without ourselves being in salvation or at least without finding salvation at the same moment. To believe in the cross of Christ is only possible for one who takes the cross as his own, who allows himself to be crucified with Christ, just as Paul speaks of the 'cross of our Lord Jesus Christ, by which the world has been crucified to me, and I to the world' (Gal. 6.14), and strives 'to know "the fellowship of his sufferings", as one who is "conformed to his death" (Phil. 3.10).'[46]

[43] *Kerygma und Mythos*, II, p. 202 (*Kerygma and Myth*, pp. 204 f.).
[44] *Theologie*, p. 301 (*Theology*, I, p. 301).   [45] ibid.
[46] *Kerygma und Mythos*, I, p. 43 (*Kerygma and Myth*, p. 37).

So we have the answer to the question how, in Bultmann's view, the cross of Christ is to be known as saving event: 'Not by preparatory instruction about the crucified. He cannot first be recognized in his divine quality in order that one may then advance to faith in the significance of the cross.' Rather: 'Such recognition takes place only as acknowledgment. This is the decision-question which the word of the cross thrusts upon the hearer: whether he will acknowledge that God has made a crucified one Lord; whether he will thereby acknowledge the demand to take up the cross by the surrender of his previous understanding of himself, making the cross the determining power of his life, letting himself be crucified with Christ',[47] and living from God as the one who encounters him and is not at his disposal.

Were it otherwise, were the cross recognizable without the acknowledgment that makes men new, 'that would rob the word of the cross of its character as scandal and folly'[48] of which Paul speaks at the beginning of I Corinthians. For the word of the cross receives this character 'by the fact that a crucified one is proclaimed as Lord',[49] i.e. by the fact that I am bidden to allow myself to be crucified with the Lord, and not by the fact that the Lord, who would be my Lord even without the cross, is crucified. The cross can be recognized as saving event, Bultmann argues, only when the crucified one is recognized as Lord.

Christian faith is therefore 'venture', as Bultmann unwearyingly describes it, seeking to give it point. Just as there is no real trust and no true love without risk, so, too, there can be faith only as decision without assurance. If faith is robbed of this character of being a venture, then it is obviously not Christian. Faith cannot defend itself against the charge of being an illusion, 'yet there is no need for faith, in the sense of an existential encounter, to refute that charge, and indeed it could not do so without misunderstanding its own mean-

[47] *Theologie*, p. 303 (*Theology*, I, p. 303). [48] ibid. [49] ibid.

ing'.[50] Furthermore, Bultmann feels that the impossibility of demonstrating faith is, 'as Herrmann taught us long ago, its strength. For if it were susceptible to proof it would mean that we could know and establish God apart from faith, and that would be placing him on a level with the world of tangible, objective reality. In that realm we are certainly justified in demanding proof.'[51]

As we have already seen in passing, Bultmann understands even statements about the pre-existence of Christ and his incarnation in the light of the fact that knowledge of the saving event takes place only as acknowledgment. Taken by themselves they have manifestly nothing to do with Christian faith. But as statements about the crucified one—far from legitimizing the saving event as such and thus making faith possible— they serve to express, 'that Jesus' person and his fate are not within earthly occurrence, but God was acting in them . . . for the salvation of men, for whose sake he delivered Christ up (Rom. 8.32).'[52] The fact that the pre-existent one is even ascribed the role of mediator of creation, as happens in I Cor. 8.6, merely expresses, in Bultmann's view, the faith 'that creation and redemption constitute a unity: the love of God . . . originated before all time'.[53]

In the same way, even the resurrection, regarded as a miracle, is a concern which does not affect me decisively. According to Bultmann, in that it is proclaimed as the resurrection of the *crucified one*, rightly understood it has *no* miraculous character. It neither represents the return of a dead man to the life of this world nor is it understood as translation to the beyond. For Bultmann it has rather the significance of the elevation of the crucified one to Lordship, so that faith in the risen one is simply faith in the cross itself as saving event.

[50] *Kerygma und Mythos*, II, p. 199 (*Kerygma and Myth*, p. 200).
[51] ibid., pp. 199 f. (ibid., p. 201).
[52] *Theologie*, p. 304 (*Theology*, I, p. 304).
[53] ibid., p. 305 (ibid., p. 305).

Has Bultmann then given sufficient answer to the question with which we began, how the cross of Jesus can be recognized as saving event? Yes and no! *Yes*, in so far as Bultmann rejects this question if it looks for a legitimation of faith; there is no such legitimation, if faith is real faith. *No*, because we now have the problem how it is the cross of Christ, which does not reveal itself to be saving event to objectivizing views, which is in particular this saving event. In other words: what distinguishes this event from others? What makes it, more than any other worldly events, the saving event? What marks out Jesus' dying from other dying? Can I not existentially experience any other action, any other death, in just the same way as God's saving act? In that case, what has become of the 'once for all' of Rom. 6.10?

Of course Bultmann himself also raises these questions. They still remain to be answered, so that we must carry this problem forward to the next chapter.

7

The Saving Event: Revelation

THE PREVIOUS chapter was concerned with the saving event in Paul as Bultmann understands it: God has acted in the cross and resurrection of Jesus for the salvation of the world. If man grasps this saving act in obedience, it gives him true life from God, which is a life of resurrection from the dead, namely, the death of man's own, self-assertive ego; man allows himself to be crucified with Christ in order to live with him. According to Bultmann, this saving event is not accessible as such, i.e. as *saving* event, to the objectivizing, curious look of the spectator. This look perceives only the tragic death of a noble man and the incredible assertion that the crucified one is risen. The event of *salvation* discloses itself only to the eye of faith, i.e. to the concrete achievement of the obedience of faith in which a man lets himself be crucified with Christ in order to live from God and the future which is not at his disposal. The Jesus event is a *saving* event only where it *does* saving work.

Because that is so, the previous chapter raised the question how the cross of Christ, which shows itself to be a saving event only to faith, but is in other respects an ordinary event in the world, is distinguished from other earthly events. If the objectivizing look shows only a profane, causally determined, everyday event, then cannot any profane event become a saving event? What distinguishes the Christ event from all other history? How is it recognizable as a special event at all?

We shall be keeping this special question in mind as we once again take a comprehensive look at the problem of the saving event as Bultmann understands it. This time, however, it will not, of course, be through his development of Pauline theology as in the previous chapter, but on the basis of his account of the theology of the Gospel of John.

Bultmann has always had a special affection for the Gospel of John and he has paid special attention to it. After a number of preliminary works, his commentary on the Gospel of John appeared in 1941. Even the most emphatic opponents of Bultmann's theology could not fail to recognize that here there was not only a remarkable, but even a unique piece of exposition. No scholarly commentary on any book of the New Testament has ever sold as many copies as this commentary on John by Bultmann; in the past twenty-five years it has dominated the discussion of Johannine theology in Germany, and even today dominates it in such a way that the commentary must still be seen on each occasion as the newest and most topical work to have been written on the Gospel. The fact that, as friend and foe know and concede, one can preach from this commentary, that because it is a consistently theological commentary it is also an eminently practical one, may have done something more to assure this book (which can be read only by those with a knowledge of Greek) a unique position in the literature on the New Testament. Bultmann has summed up the results of his exegesis in his *Theology of the New Testament*, and in brief in a Lexicon article in *Die Religion in Geschichte und Gegenwart* (third edition). At present he is working on a commentary on the Epistles of John, and it is not a coincidence that the eighty-year-old is devoting the creative power still granted him to the Johannine writings.

We shall now ask, quite briefly, how the saving event is presented by John in Bultmann's exegesis of the Johannine literature.

According to Bultmann, the characteristic terminology of the Gospel of John consists in the antithetical concepts which above all permeate the discourses of Jesus: light-darkness; truth-lie; above-below; heavenly-earthly; freedom-slavery; life-death. All these pairs of concepts are variants of the one difference between God and the world which determines human existence. This difference, as we saw in Chapter 4, is not that of a metaphysical contrast as in Gnosticism, from which the dualistic conceptuality of the Johannine writings derives (the world is and remains for John the creation of God); rather it describes the two mutually exclusive *powers* from which man rightly and wrongly expects his life. It is as clear for John as for Paul that man has always already chosen the *world* as the source of his life and each time chooses it again in his fallenness, in other words that, seeking for life, he brings death on himself. For John, too, 'everything earthly is falsehood and seeming'[1] if it promises life. Only God has life, so life out of death, freedom from the slavery of sin, light in the midst of the darkness of the man fallen into the world can come only from God. Fallen man is directed to God's saving act, if he wants to find the way back to the authenticity of his life from his lostness in the world.

According to Bultmann, John's view of the saving event, like his view of sin, is not basically different from Paul's. God *has done* his saving work; this is the way the assertion which determines the Gospel runs, giving evidence of the *fact* of salvation. God has sent his Son, his 'revealer', namely, Jesus, as the Christ. Jesus is 'the light of the world, the good shepherd, the true vine; he dispenses the water of life, the true bread from heaven. What he is and what he gives is true; in fact, he can simply be called "the truth" (John 14.6). . . . All that man seeks in the world and all that he thinks he finds is, in the Revealer, "truth", i.e. reality. In all that man seeks he is seeking life—in the Revealer it is present. As he is "the

[1] *Theologie*, p. 363 (*Theology*, II, p. 11).

truth", he is also "life" (John 14.6).'[2] This fact, that salvation has taken place, and has taken place in Jesus Christ, is made particularly clear by the well-known 'I am' sentences of the Johannine Jesus. According to Bultmann, the 'I' is the predicate in these statements. They therefore do not answer the question of the curious, 'Who is Jesus?' or, 'Who are you, Jesus?'; in that case, the 'I' would be the subject in the answer: 'I am the life', 'I am the truth', 'I am the good shepherd', etc. They rather answer the question of those who are looking consciously or unconsciously for salvation: 'What is life?', 'What is truth?', and Jesus' answer runs: the life that you are looking for, it is I; the truth that you are looking for, it is I; the good shepherd whom you are seeking, I am he. Thus man is on the way to salvation—whatever he may understand by that—and the answer which John gives runs: Jesus is salvation, and therefore salvation is available here and now. God has performed his saving act.

The work of salvation, the sending of the Son into the world, is for John—as for Paul—the '*act of the love of God*'.[3] 'In this is the love of God made manifest among us, that God sent his only Son into the world, so that we might live through him' (I John 4.9). 'For God so loved the world that he gave his only Son, that whoever believes in him should not perish, but have eternal life' (John 3.16). Jesus is sent to *deliver* the world; he brings its salvation (John 3.17; 4.42; I John 4.14). 'The intent of this sending is therefore fulfilled in those who believe in Jesus as the Son sent from God; they receive the love of God— "we have come to know and to believe the love God has for us" (I John 4.16), while he who loves the world is not embraced by the love of God (I John 2.15).'[4]

The saving act of God in Christ is the decisive, *once for all*, unrepeatable and unchangeable *act* of the love of God. That is expressed particularly clearly for Bultmann in the fact that Jesus' coming is described in the Gospel of John as 'judgment

[2] ibid.   [3] ibid., p. 387 (ibid., p. 35).   [4] ibid., p. 388 (ibid.).

on the world'. The Johannine idea of judgment does not restrict the character of love in the saving-event. It is rather true, as far as the concept of 'judgment' can suggest it, that 'God sent his Son into the world, not to condemn the world, but that the world might be saved through him' (John 3.17). But the *saving* act of God that is accomplished in the sending of the Son is the act of God which brings the final division between men, and for the very reason that it brings salvation is at the same time the final judgment upon those who reject salvation. God's *love* is the origin of the judgment. 'Of course against its intention; for it does not mean to judge the world, but to save it (John 3.17). But unbelief makes the love of God into judgment by shutting itself up against it; for that is the very meaning of judgment, shutting oneself up against the love of God. There is therefore judgment only because there is God's love in the process of becoming event. And with the sending of the Son this judgment has become present: 'He who believes in him is not condemned; he who does not believe is condemned already (John 3.18).'[5] But if judgment is achieved in this way in God's saving act, there can be no doubt about the uniqueness and finality, the 'once for all-ness' of this saving event; 'Revelation has taken place once for all in the full historical appearance of a man, so that death and life for all are decided for ever in men's attitude to him.'[6]

From what has just been said it emerges with sufficient clarity that the *significance* of the Christ event in Johannine theology is assessed in the same comprehensive way as by the apostle Paul. But to what extent is the Christ event, as the Gospel of John understands it, the divine saving act? What in particular does John have in mind, when he looks on Jesus as the Christ of God? Whereas Paul proclaims the death and resurrection of Jesus as saving event, for John, Bultmann replies, the saving event consists simply in the *sending of the Son*. The Gospel of

[5] *Johannesevangelium*, p. 111.   [6] ibid., p. 189.

John declares again and again that God sent his Son, that Jesus has come from God (and goes back to God), that he is dwelling on earth for a short time, that he comes from above and not from below. Significantly enough, Jesus often calls God 'the (Father) who sent me'. Thus the saving event is the incarnation as such and as a whole, not particular works or experiences of the incarnate one. These, say Jesus' miracles or his crucifixion, are merely a concrete expression of the incarnation of the Son of God. One can therefore almost say that Good Friday and Easter are the Pauline feasts, Christmas and Epiphany the Johannine ones.

But to what extent does the *sending* of the Son have *saving* significance? Bultmann replies that the saving significance of the sending of Jesus consists for John in the fact that 'in the person of Jesus the transcendent divine reality became audible, visible, and tangible in the realm of the earthly world'.[7] In that God sent his Son, life has appeared in this world of death. Among men who have fallen victim to the lies of the world, the truth of their own existence has become present. In this way judgment has dawned on the world and has made possible for men the act of decision against the world and for God. These statements must be clarified in detail, but it is already clear that *salvation itself* is seen and assessed by John in exactly the same way as by Paul: salvation is the life given to the sinner from the God who is constantly future and not at his disposal, yet who encounters him in the present.

Of course, in Bultmann's understanding of the Gospel of John the coming of the Son does not mean that something completely new has come into the world. The light of truth had not been completely inaccessible to men in the world. The life which the Son is and which he means to grant to men has not only been from eternity with God, but has also shone in the darkness from the beginning, as the Prologue of the

[7] *Theologie*, p. 386 (*Theology*, II, p. 33).

Gospel of John explicitly states: for 'everything was made by him' (John 1.3). This assertion makes it clear that 'in the *origin* of existence was given the possibility of the *illumination* of existence, and salvation, which is the definitive understanding of itself. The creation is at the same time revelation in so far as the created had the possibility of knowing about its creator and thus understanding itself. Man's decisive understanding of himself would thus have been his knowledge of his creatureliness; only in such knowledge would he have been "in the light", and would have had life in the sense in which created man (as opposed to the creator) can have life.'[8]

But man, situated in the possibility of life that is his *authentic* possibility, in fact chooses death. The light was in the world—but at the same time there was also the possibility of closing oneself to it, in other words, darkness—and the world was made through the light, but the world did not recognize it. It came into its own, but its own did not receive it (John 1.5, 10 f.). Men fell victim to the world.

This is the same idea as Paul develops in Rom. 1–3, when he declares that God's Godhead has always been manifest in the works of creation and in the law written in men's hearts, but that men's hearts have become darkened since they turned to the created instead of the Creator, i.e. fell victim to the world, 'so that they have no excuse' (Rom. 1.20). If in view of these statements in Paul and John one wants to talk of 'natural revelation'—and Bultmann holds this to be quite permissible—one must establish at the same time that this revelation did not in fact fulfil its function as *revelation*, and was therefore no open source of revelation.

So when the time had come, God sent his Son: 'And the word became flesh and dwelt among us, and we beheld his glory, the glory as of the only begotten of the Father, full of grace and truth' (John 1.14). In Jesus Christ, the glory of life appears in the midst of the flesh. The bright divine light falls

[8] *Johannesevangelium*, p. 25.

on the darkness. The revealer leads men from sin into the authenticity of their existence.

But how does this salvation take place? In what way does God 'reveal' life in Jesus? Bultmann always develops the Johannine understanding of the saving event under the heading of 'revelation', in which the motif of Jesus' 'being sent', so central for John, is given a definite interpretation; Jesus is sent to reveal the authentic life of men.

Anyone who speaks of revelation must be able to indicate *what* is revealed. At any rate, one usually expects that 'revelation' is the transmission of some otherwise hidden fact. So without question the Christian revelation, too, must in some way uncover what is concealed. The characteristic element of the Johannine understanding of revelation is, according to Bultmann, that Jesus hands down no teaching. 'He has not imparted any information about God at all, any more than he has brought instruction about the origin of the world or the fate of the self. He does not *communicate anything*, but *calls* men to *himself*. Or when he promises a gift, he is, himself, that gift; he himself is the bread of life that he bestows (6.35); he himself is the light (8.12); he himself is life (11.25; 14.6).'[9] That means that he reveals himself, and by revealing himself he raises the claim to reveal the hidden life of man, to bring light into his darkness, to speak the truth about him.

How is that to be understood? Is not *God* the light, life and truth of men? Must not *God* be manifest for the sinner as his salvation? Yes, indeed! The paradox of the Johannine understanding of revelation consists precisely in the fact that God himself is present in the incarnate one. 'In the person of the man Jesus—and only in him—God himself is to be met, for: "No one comes to the Father, but by me" (John 14.6). In constantly varying expressions this unity of Jesus the Son with God the Father is insisted upon: "I and the Father are one"

[9] *Theologie*, pp. 393 f. (*Theology*, II, p. 41).

(10.30).'[10] Thus the Gospel begins with the assertion: 'In the beginning was the Word, and the Word was with God, and the Word was God' (John 1.1). In other words, what Jesus, who is called 'the Word', says and does is the word and act of God; in that he reveals himself, God himself is revealed; anyone who encounters him encounters God.

It sounds extraordinarily paradoxical that God should be manifest with his glory in the form of the flesh, in the person of Jesus, but nevertheless in this paradoxical way the *claim* of revelation sounds loud and clear; *God is present*, and thus 'life and truth as the reality out of which man can exist, light as the complete transparence of existence in which questions and riddles, are at an end'.[11] The world is robbed of the possibility of presenting itself as the only reality; it is even unmasked as a determined, transitory reality. The claim of the world to be able to give life is disputed, in that life is proclaimed from beyond the world, and for the believers the world has lost its power. They have encountered God—not teaching about God, but the reality of the gracious turning of God to man—and in this encounter have found their life in truth. 'And this is eternal life, that they know thee the only true God, and Jesus Christ whom thou hast sent' (John 17.3); that is, God is recognized in Jesus Christ, the one whom he has sent. It is clear that 'recognize' here has the sense of 'acknowledge'. Eternal life lies in the acknowledgment of God as the Creator of life in whom all true life is based. Such a recognition, 'faith', removes man from that circle of sin in which he always encounters only himself and therefore death, puts him before God, and thus gives him the future which places every moment of his life in the light of eternity.

'What, then, has been revealed? Nothing at all, so far as the question about revelation asks for doctrines—doctrines, say, that no man could have discovered for himself—or for mysteries that become known once and for all as soon as they are

[10] ibid., p. 402 (ibid., pp. 49 f.).   [11] ibid., p. 418 (ibid., p. 66).

communicated. On the other hand, however, *everything* has been revealed, in so far as man's eyes are opened to his own existence and he is once again able to understand himself.'[12] What has been revealed? Only one thing: that God is the authentic life of man. But this one thing cannot by its very nature be revealed or understood as an interesting novelty, but only as an existential truth which transforms man's existence. Otherwise it is a question of an 'objective' truth which as such would no longer be *God's* truth, because God does not let himself be objectified.

But as existential truth, the one truth, that God is the life of man, is the truth of all truths. 'Therefore, the Johannine Jesus, at the conclusion of the farewell discourses, can say that the fulfilment of revelation is that no one needs any longer to ask questions (John 16.23 f.). Man always asks questions because he does not understand himself; if he does understand himself, however, all questioning ceases. He is then transparent to himself; he has become "light". For if Jesus is the "light" that enlightens every man, this does not mean that he gives them a capacity for knowledge (or strengthens such a capacity), by means of which the things of the world may be illumined, but rather that he gives them the light through which they may understand themselves.'[13] Were knowledge of anything communicated to me in revelation, I would remain someone who asked; for I would never know *everything*. The revelation which Jesus Christ is, as the act of God, lets me know that I am freed from what is transitory and past and that the future, which is God himself, is given me. This knowledge, in which I grasp myself, which is realized in love and faith, in fact allows all questions to be answered.

To sum up: however it is understood, the concept of 'revelation' implies a knowledge of the limitation of man who in such limitation is directed to revelation. Revelation offers to do

[12] *Glauben und Verstehen*, 3, p. 29 (*Existence and Faith*, p. 85).
[13] ibid., pp. 29 f. (ibid., p. 86).

away with this limitation. In that the revelation in Jesus Christ claims to reveal *God* himself as life, it is clear that it does not see the real limitation of man in any ignorance, but in his godlessness; everywhere, without knowing it, man comes up against sin as his limit, which he cannot pass. God's revelation does away with this boundary in that God shows himself to be the boundary of man and in so doing gives man back his authentic existence, namely, the existence in which he is without limitation and without question *man*. This revelation has taken place and takes place in Jesus Christ, and above all in his incarnation. 'Thus revelation consists in nothing other than the fact of Jesus Christ. His coming as such is designated as the revelation. Because he was sent, life was revealed;'[14] because God himself was present in the man Jesus.

But is all this more than a mere, indeed a meaningless, assertion? What does a man see when he looks at Jesus Christ? Surely, he sees only an ordinary man! And how could the paradoxical assertion that God is present in this man ever be understood? Of course, the phrase 'the word became *flesh*' is 'extremely strongly stressed'[15] in the programmatic statement of the Gospel of John which we have already quoted (1.14). But in that case, how can the glory of this event be recognized as that of the saving act of God? Surely the flesh above all has the character of the transitory? God's revelation, God's act must 'in some way distinguish themselves'[16]—at any rate, that is what man expects. Revelation must unmistakably present itself as such. 'Though he must appear in human form, the revealer must nevertheless have something glittering, mysterious or fascinating about him, as a hero or a "divine man", as a performer of miracles or a mystagogue. His humanity must really be only his garb, it must be transparent.'[17]

Bultmann feels: '*Despite* such a desire we hear, "The word

[14] ibid., p. 18 (ibid., p. 75).   [15] *Johannesevangelium*, p. 40.
[16] ibid.   [17] ibid.

was made flesh". He is the revealer in pure humanity. True, his own also see his glory, and if it were not to be seen then there could be no talk of revelation. But that is the paradox which runs through the whole Gospel, that the glory is not to be seen *alongside* the flesh or *through* it, as though it were transparent, but nowhere else than in the flesh, and that the gaze must bear being directed towards the flesh without letting itself be led astray—if it means to see the *glory*. Thus revelation is there in a strange form of concealment.'[18]

In this way, as in Paul, the question how the Christ event, as John understands it, is shown to be or legitimated as the divine saving act is explicitly rejected, and at the same time is given an answer: as God's saving act the Christ event is concealed from the gaze of the 'natural' man and manifest only to faith. Bultmann sees this situation, which is familiar to us through his treatment of Pauline theology, expressed and developed with special intensity in the Gospel of John. 'John emphatically expresses this paradox.'[19]

Because he understands revelation strictly as *God's* revelation, for John it is not revelation of a truth which can be objectively examined and then affirmed or denied. Revelation is rather understood strictly as *God's act*, and as such—to repeat Bultmann's basic thesis once again—is quite hidden from the detached inspection of the beholder. The claim of the Johannine Jesus to be the revealer sent by God is therefore to all outward appearances senseless, and indeed is meant to be. 'The Jews' think that Jesus blasphemes, or is mad. And rightly, from their standpoint, for 'outside faith revelation is not visible; there is nothing revealed *on the basis of which* one believes. It is only *in* faith that the object of faith is disclosed; therefore, faith itself belongs to revelation.'[20] 'Why do "the Jews", who know him and his home town, nevertheless not know who he is nor where he comes from? Because they do not

---

[18] ibid., pp. 40 f. [19] *Theologie*, p. 403 (*Theology*, II, p. 50).
[20] *Glauben und Verstehen*, 3, p. 23 (*Existence and Faith*, p. 79).

know God!'[21] Only the obedience of faith can make it clear
that Jesus is the revealer. The world, on the other hand, does
not see him with seeing eyes (John 12.40), and the fact that the
revealer has come makes all who reject him ultimately blind
(John 9.39).

According to John, as Bultmann understands him, revelation cannot be demonstrated, but what could be regarded as
the weakness of faith is for Bultmann in fact its strength, 'as
my teacher Wilhelm Herrmann insisted. For if the relation
between faith and God could be proved as the relation between
subject and object in worldly situations can be proved, then
God would be placed on the same level as the world, within
which the demand for proof is legitimate.'[22] The invisibility of
God in his action—'one cannot see him, but only hear him'[23]—
is thus his divinity, and his revelation can be experienced only
as an act that is taking place 'and is never made manifest'.[24]
Because God's saving act only can and only should be recognized in the obedience of faith, i.e. *authentically*, the introductory words of the Gospel of John are radically true: 'The
Word became flesh' *and*—as a confession of faith—their
continuation 'We saw his glory'.

The scandal which lies in this impossibility of demonstrating the divine act of revelation is a stumbling-block, not to the
intellect but to the will of the 'old' man, who will not surrender
his self-understanding but wants to go on living from what is
at his disposal. This stumbling-block must be kept for the
sake of the truth of revelation. The revealer *may* not identify
himself. 'For the revelation is judgment upon the world and
is necessarily felt as an attack upon it and an offence to it,
so long as the world refuses to give up its norms.'[25] The
stumbling-block can and should be overcome only in the

[21] *Theologie*, p. 399 (*Theology*, II, p. 46).
[22] *Jesus Christ and Mythology*, p. 72.
[23] *Glauben und Verstehen*, 3, p. 120.
[24] ibid., pp. 120 f.   [25] *Theologie*, p. 399 (*Theology*, II, p. 46).

confession of faith in which man recognizes his sin, grasps his authentic life from God and thus no longer sees the claim of the incarnate one to be the revealer as nonsense, but understands himself anew in it and therefore recognizes it in a paradoxical way to be meaningful. 'Only *in* faith is the attested matter seen, only *in* faith is the witness recognized as legitimate. In other words, the object of faith makes itself accessible to nothing but faith. But anyone who, having such faith, "has the testimony in himself", thereby has life itself: "And this is the confirmation; the fact that God gave us eternal life" (I John 5.11).'[26] This is the only testimony that the self-witness of faith can and may give for the revealer; 'But there is a testimony which consists of his claim to be the revealer, a claim which denies the world's competence to judge; in the world's opinion this cannot be considered true testimony (8.13). But this testimony he must bear.'[27] Bultmann is also fond of quoting John 7.16 f.: 'My teaching is not mine, but his who sent me; if any man's will is to do his will, he shall know whether the teaching is from God or whether I am speaking on my own authority': the revelation is manifest as such only *in* faith.

But is not Jesus, according to the Gospel of John, *the all-knowing one*, who sees through those who encounter him? Is his human form not therefore simply a transparent curtain through which the divine being shines in a way that is generally recognizable? Bultmann answers, No! That Jesus sees through those who encounter him means for John 'that the believer feels himself searched and known by God',[28] in so far as his own existence is revealed to him in his encounter with the revealer. Thus Jesus knows of the previous sinful life of the Samaritan woman whom he asks for water at Jacob's well at Sychar, because for man the revelation is constantly the disclosure of his own situation. Where man finds life, the past

[26] ibid., p. 421 (ibid., pp. 68 f.).   [27] ibid., p. 399 (ibid., p. 47).
[28] ibid., p. 394 (ibid., p. 42).

is transparent to him as a desire for the transitory, as being filled with only phantom fulfilment, as sin. Jesus' 'omniscience', too, is 'not understood to be his superhuman ability, but his knowledge which is transmitted to the believer: the one who has recognized him as the revealer by knowing that one thing knows everything'.[29] So the disciples recognize and confess, 'that you know everything and do not need that men should ask you' (John 16.30). In this statement omniscience is not understood as an abstract characteristic. The 'you know everything' means 'you are the revealer', and that men need not ask this question means that 'the answer to every question which can oppress the believer is already contained beforehand in the revelation. The believers know that nothing unforeseen can happen to them, and their questioning can come to silence.'[30]

But does not Jesus act as a *miracle worker*? Indeed, but his miracles do not serve as an identification, as a legitimation of his saving significance. They are signs, and can be misunderstood as much as Jesus' mere word. 'They are remarkable occurrences, but that only makes them indicators that the activity of the revealer is a disturbance of what is familiar to the world. They point to the fact that the revelation is no worldly occurrence, but an other-worldly one.'[31] But only faith understands the meaning of miracles. For the unbeliever they are so little a legitimation that the healing of the lame man and the blind man lead to enmity and persecution, and the raising of Lazarus brings Jesus to the cross.

John also tells *Easter stories*, 'following the tradition'.[32] The question is, however, 'what they mean to him'.[33] Bultmann thinks that John understood the resurrection of Jesus in the same way as his miracles: as a sign. 'They symbolize the victory of Jesus over the world',[34] but like the miracles are

[29] ibid., p. 385 (ibid., p. 43).   [30] *Johannesevangelium*, p. 455.
[31] *Theologie*, pp. 396 f. (*Theology*, II, p. 44).
[32] ibid., p. 409 (ibid., p. 56).   [33] ibid.   [34] ibid.

'ultimately not indispensable',[35] as John makes clear in the story of Thomas: 'His wish to see the risen Jesus in the body, even to touch him, is granted. But in the same moment he is reprimanded: "Because you have seen me have you come to faith? Blessed are those who, though they do not see me, yet believe" (John 20.29).'[36] With this critical saying the evangelist ends his Easter stories. Here, according to Bultmann, is 'a strange criticism in the evaluation of the Easter stories: they can claim only a relative value. The fact that Jesus' critical saying forms the conclusion of the Easter stories warns the hearer and reader to take them as more than they might be: neither as narratives of events which he could wish or hope to experience himself, nor as a substitute for such experiences of his own, so that the experiences of others could as it were guarantee the reality of the resurrection of Jesus—but rather as a word of proclamation in which the events narrated have become a symbolic picture for the communion of the one who has ascended to the Father with his own. This admonition is the appropriate and impressive conclusion of the Easter stories',[37] which warns against misunderstanding the Easter stories as a legitimation of Jesus' claim to be the revealer.

What has been said so far sufficiently expresses Bultmann's main concern in his discussion of the concept of revelation and which he develops by means of Johannine theology: revelation as saving event is recognizable only in the existential achievement of faith, as acknowledgment, and that must always be the case if God is my Lord and not the object of my knowledge. Of course I can understand what revelation means in general; I can even understand the assertion that there is revelation; but I only experience that revelation *is real* if the revelation works in me and frees me from my sins.

I hope that we have understood Bultmann's understanding of revelation better than Bultmann feels Karl Jaspers to have

[35] ibid.   [36] ibid. (ibid., p. 57).   [37] *Johannesevangelium*, pp. 539 f.

done; for in attacking Bultmann's concept of revelation Jaspers is guilty of ignoring his intention. Jaspers' criticism is: 'that God localizes himself in place and time, once for all . . . is a faith that makes God an object in the world.'[38] To this Bultmann retorts: 'Does he not know that I am struggling against this very thing—fixing God as an object, and understanding revelation wrongly, as that which has been revealed?'[39] 'For the ground and object of faith are identical. Security can be found only by abandoning all security, by being ready, as Luther put it, to plunge into the inner darkness',[40] in other words, by surrendering the security of assurance and exchanging it for the certainty of faith.

Of course the phenomenon of revelation occupies Bultmann in other respects, too, and from specific perspectives, but all his relatively numerous statements on this theme in the end lead to a specifically Christian understanding of revelation which recognizes revelation as God's saving act in the way which we have described.

We have already said all that is necessary about the relationship of *revelation and knowledge*. In a lecture on the theme 'The Concept of Revelation in the New Testament',[41] delivered in 1929, Bultmann describes in detail how, wherever revelation is spoken of, the idea is maintained that man in his limitation only comes to his authenticity through revelation; but this happens for the New Testament not—as widely in the history of religion and also in many perverse expressions of the Christian understanding of revelation—by the communication of facts which are otherwise hidden, but by the introduction, through revelation, of a new *knowledge about a man's self*, so that he authentically understands and grasps himself and only

[38] Bultmann and Jaspers, *Die Frage der Entmythologisierung*, p. 41.
[39] ibid., pp. 68 f.
[40] *Kerygma und Mythos*, II, p. 207 (*Kerygma and Myth*, p. 211).
[41] *Glauben und Verstehen*, 3, pp. 1 ff. (*Existence and Faith*, pp. 58 ff.).

thus sees the revelation as *God's* revelation. For Bultmann, therefore, the knowledge given with revelation always has a 'dialectical' character, 'in the sense that as a knowledge that is preserved it is always spurious, however "correct" it may be, and that it is only genuine when the act of faith is realized in it, when the resolve to exist in faith is carried through to the end'.[42] What faith knows 'authentically' can, of course, also be kept and communicated inauthentically, as knowledge. But that only shows that in the Christian understanding, revelation of the divine salvation never communicates something new—we know no more than the fathers in the faith—but ever and again creates man anew. The problem of the relationship between revelation and the secular sciences is sometimes discussed under the heading *revelation and knowledge*, but for Bultmann there is no real problem. For the sciences, with their necessarily objectifying approach, and the divine revelation, which can never be objectified, can never affect one another if they are rightly understood. Faith in revelation therefore has no specific relationship to the secular sciences in so far as these know of and affirm their own nature; the results of objective science do not affect faith, and revelation can never be the object of objective knowledge and objective investigation.

Bultmann has occupied himself with the question of so-called *natural revelation* on several occasions, among others in 1941, when for many Germans God revealed himself in the victories of Hitler's armies. Bultmann emphatically contradicted this view. His verdict was 'that man in the face of God is a sinner, and his history is a history of sinful men, and therefore in actual fact enshrouds God in a veil. So man can only look out towards God, as towards the power which frees man from himself, endowing him with purity, and putting an end to his sinful history.'[43] Any talk of 'natural revelation' manifestly acknowledges the need of some revelation and thus

[42] ibid., p. 32 (ibid., p. 88).
[43] *Glauben und Verstehen*, 2, p. 93 (Essays, p. 106).

knows of man's limitations in some sense. But given man's *sin*, Bultmann argues in the passage just quoted, one cannot speak of revelation in history, which is as such the history of sinful men and therefore at least ambivalent. Nor could one speak of the revelation of God's omnipotence in nature, in which his life is itself entangled, with which he finds himself in conflict, to which he himself belongs, over against which he is not free. Wherever there is talk of 'natural revelation', it is presupposed that man is *free* from himself as a creature fallen into the world and that in such freedom he can bring himself into relationship with God. But the believer knows that man is not free. Only an act of God, revelation in the authentic sense, can make him free from the world and thus identify itself as divine revelation. For faith, therefore, there is no natural revelation, that is, no revelation which is a natural, objective datum, God's being revealed, which man can confirm; for man is a sinner, fallen into the world, blind to God. Revelation can have for him only the form of a free *act* of God, 'in which God makes a gift of his grace and transforms us and the world'.[44] 'Christian belief knows that only God's grace which forgives sin can be designated as the revelation of God. Where, then, is this grace manifest in nature and history? And if this grace is to be not a mere idea but a real event, God's act, then we will have to leave it to *him* where he might wish to perform this act, and we are simply asked, "Do we believe in God's grace in Christ or not?".'[45]

Moreover, 'anyone who looks for other revelations *alongside* the revelation in Christ has not yet taken seriously the idea of God and has not yet grasped his own existence in all its profundity.' For he is searching in another revelation *more* than in the revelation of Christ and so he misunderstands the meaning of revelation altogether, believing that it brings knowledge which can be measured in a quantitative way; if he looks for something other than the revelation in Christ, he still stands

[44] ibid., p. 95 (ibid., p. 109).   [45] ibid., p. 100 (ibid., p. 100).

outside faith; if he looks elsewhere for what he has found in the revelation in Christ, he is no longer looking existentially for revelation, that is, he is no longer looking for real revelation; his search for revelation is dictated only by curiosity. Following Bultmann, one may well put the question in this way, 'whether say Augustine, Luther, Schleiermacher or even the Bhagavadgita must be interpreted in the same way as the New Testament. In so far as I reflect in principle, in other words, see myself in an abstract, traditionless situation, there is no difference here. But whether in such an interpretation hearing in faith becomes event cannot be established *in principle*.'[46] For faith, however, it is clear *in practice* that God has revealed himself in Christ.

What has just been said has raised the question of the *absoluteness of the Christian revelation* and in effect has already answered it. For it is clear that with his understanding of revelation Bultmann must reject this question, if it is put as the detached question of an observer. Rightly understood, the question of the absoluteness of revelation is, on the other hand, the question of revelation itself, i.e. of revelation as *God's* revelation, as real *revelation*, and this question has always already been answered in faith.

'If the intention of the question is to try to arrange in order the religions of the world—including the Christian religion—as world phenomena, then it is senseless from the start; for in the realm of this questioning there is only relativity, and no absolute.'[47] Bultmann does not regard this sort of enquiry as simply impermissible. How can it be prohibited? It is the question of the history of religion, which from a scientific point of view is without doubt an interesting one. But the question of religions, and sometimes of the 'absolute' as the highest developed religion, put in this way, is not the question of the

[46] 'Das Problem einer theologischen Exegese', p. 353.
[47] *Glauben und Verstehen*, 3, p. 33.

faith that asserts the absoluteness of revelation. Bultmann alleges that when Jaspers objects to the assertion of the absoluteness of the revelation in Christ, he understands it in the sense of an assertion about the absoluteness of the Christian *religion*, and argues that in view of this Jaspers cannot possibly understand it. For 'the Christian religion is a phenomenon of world history, like other religions, and like these it can be examined for its spiritual content and for the understanding of human existence which is alive in it. Certainly one can classify the religions of the earth in respect of their content and the depth of their insight into human existence. But even if one were to allot the Christian religion the highest rank in such an attempt at classification, if one were, say, to want to assert its irreplaceable value for human culture, this would mean something fundamentally different from the claim of Christian faith to absoluteness.'[48] This claim does not assert that Christianity is a particularly highly developed religion, but that God has *acted* in Christ. 'This claim can only—and must indeed—be made each time by the believer, and not on the basis of a comparison with other ways of believing'[49] but as an expression of faith itself; for faith is an answer to the revelation which it experiences as God's saving act, as God's revelation and *thus* as *absolute* revelation. In faith, then, the question of the absoluteness of revelation has already been decided, and so the question is as meaningless, as such, as the unbeliever's question about the highest religion is meaningless as a question about the Christian revelation. 'Is it clear to Jaspers,' Bultmann asks, 'that wherever the revelation faith speaks it asserts, and must assert, the absoluteness of the revelation which it believes, because it understands itself as the answer to the statement: "I am the Lord your God. You shall have no other gods but me"? Anyone may regard such revelation faith as absurd. But if he does so, he should not speak of revelation.

[48] Bultmann and Jaspers, *Die Frage der Entmythologisierung*, pp. 72 f.
[49] ibid., p. 73.

For at all events it is also absurd to want to find revelation here or there by a glance at the history of religion or the spirit. As a historian I can only establish revelation faith here or there, but never revelation. For revelation is revelation only *in actu* and *pro me*: it is only understood and acknowledged as such in personal decision.'[50]

Thus all aspects under which Bultmann discusses the problem of revelation lead in the end to the repeated recognition that just as there is no faith without revelation, so in the understanding of the Bible one can speak of revelation only *in* faith; that revelation, therefore, because it takes place 'in faith', cannot be legitimated *before* the event of faith, but only *in* it.

This recognition corresponds to the recognition that God's revealing act does not occur *between* worldly acts, breaking through the connection of worldly events in a way which can be detected objectively, but *in* the worldly events, only 'in the flesh' itself. This is the only way in which Bultmann can see a guarantee of the character of faith as obedience, as existential decision, thus maintaining the revelation as God's action; for as we know, one can only speak meaningfully of God's action, according to Bultmann, if it is an action that takes place in us, which simply withdraws itself from objectivizing approaches.

In this way—and only in this way—Bultmann believes that God's saving act is really understood as *miracle*, as which it clearly *must* be understood. For a miracle is an event which simply goes beyond happenings within the world. And that is what the act of God does in each case, in so far as it is really *God's* act.

Now by 'miracle' one usually understands an action which is 'an interference with the course of nature, history, or the life of the soul, tearing it asunder'.[51] But as such an action, God's action would be visible to objective investigation; and in that

[50] ibid., p. 69.
[51] *Kerygma und Mythos*, II, p. 196 (*Kerygma and Myth*, p. 197).

way it would cease to be *God's* action. A true miracle, that is, an act of *God*, 'is not visible or ascertainable like worldly events'.[52] Otherwise it would be a miracle in which God's action 'is conceived for good or ill as a worldly force and projected on to the plane of worldly events';[53] for in miracle God's power is imagined 'to be analogous to the powers of this world and superior to them only in incalculability and force'.[54] It would only be quantitatively, and not qualitatively, different from human ability and knowledge.

'The only way to preserve the unworldly, transcendent character of the divine activity'—i.e the truly miraculous element of revelation—'is to regard it not as an interference in worldly happenings, but as something accomplished *in* them in such a way that the closed weft of history as it presents itself to objective observation is left undisturbed. To every other eye than the eye of faith the action of God is hidden. Only the "natural" happening is generally visible and ascertainable. *In* it is accomplished the hidden act of God';[55] God's miraculous act, his revelation, takes place *in* the worldly event which is the incarnation of Jesus.

This 'identity' of the divine act with worldly events is, of course, not a *direct* one, as in pantheism, but a *paradoxical* one. All that can be seen is the natural and historical context, the birth and death of the man Jesus. That God acts towards me in this context can only be recognized in faith, existentially. 'But just this is the paradox of faith; it understands an ascertainable event in its context in nature and history as the act of God. Faith cannot dispense with its "nevertheless".'[56] Where there is faith, the world, of course, loses its character as a closed context. 'In other words, in faith the closed context presented or produced by objective observation is transcended, though not as in mythological thought,' in such a way that, 'I

[52] ibid.   [53] ibid., p. 184.   [54] ibid., p. 183.
[55] ibid., pp. 196 f. (*Kerygma and Myth*, p. 197).
[56] ibid., p. 198 (ibid., p. 199).

transcend it as a whole when I speak of an act of God';[57] for *in* this context God's revelation encounters me, leaving it intact in detail and yet at the same time simply transcending it.

Where I encounter this revelation, where I 'believe' in God's revelation, there is true belief in miracle, for then I believe the event of the love of God which is real only as event, and indeed as miraculous event. Anyone who thinks he can speak 'of miracles as ascertainable processes, clashes with the idea of the hidden act of God. He surrenders the act of God to objective observation, and thus makes belief in miracles (or rather superstition) susceptible to the justifiable criticisms of science.'[58] Anyone, on the other hand, who feels himself affected by faith in the revelation of God in Christ and believes that the whole reality of the world and of man does not present itself to objective observation will, in full recognition of the scientific picture of the world which rests on the clear connection of cause and effect, acknowledge the miraculous act of God and testify: 'the Word became *flesh and* we saw his *glory*'.

With all this, however, we are again confronted by the question with which the previous chapter also ended: in what way is the Jesus-event distinguished from other worldly events, i.e. precisely how can this event in time and space raise the claim that it is the saving event? If the man Jesus is the revelation, why not any other man? To answer this question is the task of the next chapter.

[57] ibid. (ibid., pp. 198 f.).   [58] ibid.

8

The Saving Event: The Word

EACH OF THE last two chapters ended with the question how for Bultmann the Jesus-event was marked out as saving event from other worldly events.

As we saw both in his treatment of the saving event according to *Paul*, who proclaims Christ as the crucified and risen one, and also according to *John*, for whom Jesus is sent by God, Bultmann lays great stress on the statement that the *saving* event shows itself to be such only *in* faith. For the objectivizing approach it is visible merely as a worldly event: the tragic death of a noble man; the abstruse assertion of a mere man that he is *the* revealer of God. It cannot be otherwise, Bultmann argues, if *God* really acts in Christ. For God's action can never be perceived at a distance, because God never becomes man's object, even in his action; otherwise he would no longer be God. The objectivizing of God, making him into an idol, has, in Bultmann's view, already begun where God's action is presented or demanded as a phenomenon which can be made clearly visible, even before faith, as *God's* action.

Thus the saving event does not take place *between* earthly events, breaking through these in a miraculous way in certain places; it *is* a particular *earthly* event, the Jesus-event, which, when it is recognized as the saving act of God, now breaks through *every* earthly event. Precisely this is its significance: in the midst of all that is earthly, God wills to encounter man as the transcendent one and in this way to be present to man as true life.

In that case, the burning question is how a particular earthly event, the Jesus-event, becomes the saving event. If Jesus in his pure humanity is *the* emissary of God, the all-embracing manifestation of the glory of God in the world, why not any other man?

Please note that this question is not identical with that of the absoluteness of Christianity. Bultmann has to reject this last question completely, as we saw towards the end of the last chapter: as a question about the highest religion it is not a question about God's saving act, but about a worldly phenomenon. The faith which has recognized God's act in Christ can put the question of the absoluteness of Christianity as a question about God's saving act only by surrendering itself; for with such a question it would put *the action of God which it has experienced* in jeopardy. Nor can unfaith put this question in a true way, because it does not really know about God's saving action, and must enquire in a detached way about what can only be answered in existential terms.

The question of what distinguishes the Jesus-event as God's sole saving action from other earthly events is, on the other hand, in Bultmann's view not only a legitimate, but also a necessary question; for its purpose is not to legitimate the saving event as such, but to describe it—and that is the task of theology. Writing about Paul, Bultmann puts this question in the following way: 'How do we come to regard the cross as the cross of Christ, as the (saving) event? How do we come to believe in the cross as the saving event?'[1] In other words, there have been many worldly events and many crosses and many men who have died the death of the cross. Why is this *cross*, and in particular the cross *of Jesus*, the saving event? Why not any other historical event? Why not, say, the cross of one of the criminals who died with Jesus? We saw that Bultmann refuses to allow the cross of Jesus to be the saving event because it is the cross of *Christ*; he insists that it is the cross

[1] *Kerygma und Mythos*, I, p. 46 (*Kerygma and Myth*, p. 41).

of Christ only when and because it is the saving event. Once again: how is the cross of Jesus to be seen to be the cross of Christ, i.e. to represent the divine saving act?

Bultmann replies: 'There seems to me to be only one answer: because it is proclaimed as such.'[2] In saying this he means that there is really only this one answer: 'Christ, the crucified and risen one, meets us in the word of proclamation and nowhere else.'[3] It is proclamation that gives the Jesus-event the character of the saving act of God, i.e. the mere fact that this earthly event is proclaimed as saving event, that it is present as the '*word* of reconciliation' (II Cor. 5.19). Only the phenomenon of proclamation marks out the event of Jesus in the years 1–30 of our reckoning of time, *this* birth in the flesh, *this* life, *this* dying, from all other worldly events. Without preaching (in the widest sense) God would not be to be found in this event, at any rate in his saving act, even if it had been transmitted in great detail: 'For of course it can be said that God encounters us at all times and in all places, but we cannot see him and hear him everywhere unless his Word comes as well . . . as Luther not infrequently observed.'[4] In other words, revelation occurs, the saving event takes place, only in proclamation.

Bultmann can therefore speak of the 'identity of the work and word' of Jesus,[5] as it is expressed above all in the Gospel of John, which introduces Jesus right at the beginning as "the Word" which was 'in the beginning' (John 1.1). For John, 'to believe in Jesus' and 'to believe in the word of Jesus' mean the same thing, and the 'Word' as the word of Jesus is also the same thing then and today: preaching is itself revelation, and revelation takes place only in the preaching which is given in any particular place at a particular time. Only in the Word is the Jesus-event present as saving event, but it *is* present in the

---

[2] ibid.   [3] ibid.
[4] *Kerygma und Mythos*, II, p. 204 (ibid., pp. 206 f.)
[5] *Theologie*, p. 413 (*Theology*, II, p. 60).

Word, so that the Word itself is part of the saving event, as Bultmann emphasizes unceasingly—indeed, not only he himself, but the whole of the dialectical theology which we mentioned in the first chapter, and which has for that very reason been called the 'Theology of the Word'. Even in his review of Karl Barth's *Epistle to the Romans* in 1922, Bultmann stated with satisfaction that at this point Karl Barth's work represented some progress beyond their Marburg teacher Wilhelm Herrmann: the question how I come to faith in the Jesus-event as the saving event finds its simple answer in the fact that I follow the demand for faith which evokes the Jesus-event as saving event.

It is the Word that makes the Jesus-event the saving event. This is true in so far as the Word does not speak of the saving event but is itself the saving event. Without the Word, which gives the Jesus-event its significance as saving event, only an ordinary earthly event is perceptible. Therefore the Word is never superfluous. For it does not communicate timeless truth to the hearer, 'for in that case it would only have a mediatorial role; it is itself part of the fact' of the saving event.[6] This assertion that there is no saving event without the Word to proclaim it as such, that God's saving act includes the 'Word' as divine, answers the question as to what characterizes the Jesus-event above all other earthly events as the Christ event. This answer must now be developed further.

The concept of the 'Word' must not be understood too narrowly. There are several ways in which the Jesus-event is proclaimed as saving event, 'whether in church proclamation or in the Bible in so far as this is mediated by the Church as the word of God which addresses me, or through the word of the Christian brother', or through the sacraments which for the New Testament, according to Bultmann, simply have the function and effect of 'the word heard and proclaimed in

[6] *Glauben und Verstehen*, 1, p. 208.

preaching',[7] but also make present the saving event 'in the same way as the word of proclamation'.[8] 'Baptism and the Lord's Supper are only a special means of re-presenting the saving event, which in general is re-presented in the word of preaching.' Their 'meaning is simply that it is precisely through them that the once for all saving-event in Christ's death and resurrection is made present and actual for the individual, so that it may be personally appropriated by him.'[9] 'Indeed, one may finally ask whether proclamation must always be limited to the spoken word, whether it cannot also occur through silent action. Certainly an action, too, can have the character of address. But we are concerned with an action which can be effective as Christian proclamation, that is, not with possible effects of the Christian religion in Western civilization but with the proof of the Christian love of man for man. Does not Albert Schweitzer's work show us proclamation through action? For the one who receives it, the act of love opens the way to freedom from himself, as he is drawn into the kingdom of the rule of love and is led to understand man's spoken word of proclamation, too, as the Word of God.'[10]

It would also be wrong, argues Bultmann, to think 'that only the official preacher can be a true proclaimer', and to this effect he quotes Luther's *Lectures on Romans*: 'It is necessary to believe in Christ, "wherever and through whomever he may speak. Therefore we must be seriously concerned not to be stubborn in our own fashion, so that we do not resist Christ in unbelief, of whom we do not know when, where and how and through whom he speaks to us. And it almost always happens somehow, in some way, through someone, at a time and place when we do not expect it." '[11]

If the Word in all its manifestations is itself the saving event,

[7] *Theologie*, p. 312 (*Theology*, I, p. 312).　　　　　[8] ibid.
[9] 'Jesus und Paulus', pp. 88 f. (*Existence and Faith*, p. 200).
[10] *Glauben und Verstehen*, 3, pp. 129 f. (*Religion and Culture*, p. 242).
[11] ibid.

then according to Bultmann one cannot and may not go back beyond the Word, as though one would *then* come up against the 'saving facts', 'but the proclamation, the being-proclaimed as event, is itself an integral part of the revelation'.[12] To enquire behind the Word does not lead to *saving* facts but to objective facts which can be established in secular fashion, which represent the saving act of God only through the word which is added to them and only *with* that word. Therefore, 'there is no way back behind the preaching to a saving fact which can be detached from it, whether this be a "historical Jesus" or a cosmic drama. Jesus Christ can be reached only in the preaching.'[13] He is thus immediately and directly accessible, but only in the paradoxical form of the Word. For this, one can point to Rom. 10.6–8: 'But the righteousness based on faith says, *Do not say in your heart, "Who will ascend into heaven?"* (that is, to bring Christ down) or *"Who will descend into the abyss?"* (that is, to bring Christ up from the dead). But what does it say? *The word is near you, on your lips and in your heart* (that is, the word of faith which we preach).'

From this standpoint, the lack of constraint with which Bultmann himself investigates the tradition by means of historical criticism and thus can enquire behind the primitive Christian preaching is understandable. In his view, such an enquiry, which excludes the phenomenon of proclamation and concerns certain historical facts of the past rather than the saving event, does not affect faith. For faith grows, not from supposed saving facts, but from the saving event of proclamation.

Bultmann is therefore consistent in disputing that historical science is in a position to produce a crisis for faith, if it 'deals critically with the New Testament and casts doubt on our knowledge of the historical Jesus': for in the Christian proclamation man is not 'given an historical account of a section of the past, which he might put to the test, or critically confirm or reject. He is told, on the contrary, that in what happened

[12] *Glauben und Verstehen*, 1, p. 179.   [13] ibid., p. 180.

then, whatever the circumstances, God has acted, and that through this action of his the Word of divine judgment and forgiveness which now confronts him is authenticated; this action of God's is to be interpreted as the actual establishment of this Word—as the proclamation of this Word itself. No science of history can verify this assertion—either to confirm or to reject it; for it is beyond the sphere of historical observation to say that this Word and its proclamation are God's act.'[14] Historical investigations of the saving event would obscure the fact that salvation happens each time now, from beyond all inner-worldly connections. An enquiry into the 'objective facticity' of saving acts may investigate what it may; but—according to Bultmann—it cannot investigate salvation for me.

For Bultmann, as we know, this association of saving event and Word is grounded in the very nature of the saving event; for the saving event is no objectively establishable fact of the past, which can be recognized as the saving event and then taught and known as such. All that can be recognized is a relatively insignificant human fate. That God's saving act takes place in this fate must be announced through the Word. Because the Word *announces* the Jesus-event as saving event, Bultmann is fond of calling the proclamation *kerygma*, which means *announcement*. The *keryx* is a messenger, an announcer, who passes on an authoritative word of his master. His word is '*kerygma* in the literal sense, authorized, plenipotent proclamation, an edict from a sovereign'.[15] So the Christian *kerygma* is not a report which communicates theoretical knowledge, timeless truths, but 'a word which has power (I Thess. 2.13), which is effective. It is essential for this word to be spoken; it is proclaimed and must be heard. It is an instruction, a command, and must be done, must be kept'[16]—otherwise it is an empty

[14] *Glauben und Verstehen*, 2, p. 16 (*Essays*, p. 18).
[15] *Theologie*, p. 308 (*Theology*, I, p. 307). [16] *G.u.V.*, I, p. 280.

word which does *not* announce the saving event. 'God's word is always *address*, and is understood as such only when the *address* is understood and heard, in the real sense of the word',[17] that is, when it is *obeyed*. The Christian *kerygma* is thus *kerygma* in so far as it summons to faith, to the obedience of faith towards the saving act of God which occurs in it.

Proclamation makes the Jesus-event of the past the saving event in the present. As *kerygma*, it does not do this (according to Bultmann) by bringing proof that this event is the saving event—that would not be *kerygma*, but an impossible and impermissible attempt to objectivize God's action—but by *proclaiming* the Jesus-event as saving event. Thus the proclamation does not prepare for the question of decision, but implies it. It is an announcement of the saving event *and* an appeal to man all in one; the announcement seems comprehensible only to the man who follows the appeal in obedience. The proclamation does not prove that some historical facts are saving facts, but is itself the saving act which identifies itself as such only to the obedience of faith.

The one condition for the possibility of faith is thus the *viva vox evangelii*, the perceptible voice of preaching. Faith is merely an answer to the Word thus received. Indeed, Bultmann can even ask whether faith is not simply *listening* to the word of Scripture itself. 'The answer is yes. But this answer is valid only if the Scriptures are understood neither as a manual of doctrine nor as a record of witnesses to a faith which I interpret by sympathy and empathy. On the contrary, to *hear* the Scriptures as Word of God means to hear them as a word which is addressed to me, as *kerygma*, as a proclamation. Then my understanding is not a neutral one, but rather my response to a call.'[18]

The claim of the *kerygma* to be God's word cannot be examined by science because it does not communicate knowledge, but demands faith. The sciences are a crisis for faith

[17] ibid., p. 282.   [18] *Jesus Christ and Mythology*, p. 71.

only because man wants to control the *kerygma*, 'because he claims to have criteria where in the very nature of the matter there can be none'.[19] So Bultmann regards the crises into which faith has been brought by natural and historical science as being welcome. 'They bring the constant and for the most part latent crisis of faith into the open; they compel reflection on the real nature of faith, throwing into relief the question which has to be decided for or against faith—one which is never a question of knowledge gained by research and preservable as a possession, but is always one of the will.'[20]

'But if it is true that the proclamation of the saving event is not a preparatory instruction which precedes the actual demand for faith, but is, in itself, the call for faith or the challenge to give up one's previous self understanding . . .—If that is so, then that means that *the saving event is nowhere present except in the proclaiming, accosting, demanding, and promising Word*. A merely "reminiscent" historical account referring to what happened in the past cannot make the saving event visible. It means that the saving event continues to take place in the proclamation of the word . . . Paul expresses this by saying that at the same time that God instituted reconciliation he also instituted the "ministry of reconciliation" (II Cor. 5.18 f.) which is the "message of reconciliation". Consequently, in the proclamation Christ himself, indeed God himself, encounters the hearer.'[21] '*The preaching is the saving event*, because it is no mere historical communication, but, as it occurs to Paul himself, the decisive question to man. For that reason it is itself revelation and spreads abroad death and life in the world because it is the basis for the decision for death and life (II Cor. 2.14–16; 4.1–6). It does not address itself to the curiosity or the "interest" of the hearer, but to his conscience (II Cor. 4.2; 5.11). Like the death and resurrection

[19] *G.u.V.*, 2, pp. 16 f. (*Essays*, p. 19).   [20] ibid., p. 17 (ibid., p. 19).
[21] *Theologie*, pp. 301 f. (*Theology*, I, pp. 301 f.).

179

of Jesus, preaching, the gospel, is "the power of God for salvation to every one who has faith"; for in the gospel the righteousness of God is made manifest (Rom. 1.16 f.). Thus the saving fact is the Word (Rom. 10.13–17), but not, of course, as the bearer of an idea or the mediator of historical knowledge, but as preaching',[22] i.e. as kerygmatic proclamation.

According to Bultmann, this is also where the difference in the understanding of the word of God in Old and New Testament lies. 'For in the Old Testament word and history at first part company. The history is that which the people has experienced, from which it keeps coming into its "Now", and the word of the prophet or the word of the law is addressed to this "Now". Unity with past history is provided by the word that occurs now, recalling past history and in that way presenting it and taking it further. The word of *Christian* proclamation and the history which it communicates coincide, are one. The history of Christ is not a history that is already past; it is accomplished in the proclamation of the Word. For the recollection of Jesus is not like the recollection of Moses, of what he did and what the people experienced at his hand, to which they had to remain faithful. He himself appears in the *present* Word, he begins history for the hearer at the *present* moment. *The recollection of what happened then is simply a call to the establishment of the Word.*'[23]

As *kerygma*, the 'Word' is necessarily an *understandable* word (for a *kerygma*, an announcement, must be understood); but it is understandable in the only sense in which God's saving act may be understood: 'not in the sense of a derivative explanation, so that what is proclaimed might be incorporated in an already existing picture of the world',[24] still less in the sense of objective insight into the Jesus-event as the saving event, but as a word, 'which shows man himself and teaches

[22] *Glauben und Verstehen*, 1, p. 209.   [23] ibid., pp. 292 f.
[24] ibid., p. 177.

him to understand himself. It is not theoretical instruction about him; the event of address discloses to him a situation of existential self-understanding which must be grasped in action. Address does not confront me with this or that to choose as I please; it forces a decision, it as it were presents me with myself to choose.'[25] The Word is thus understandable in so far as it confronts me with a decision, and it is really understood only in decision. Understanding the Word is thus connected with the possibility of a new self-understanding. This is what Bultmann means to express when he writes: 'The possibility of the Word being understood coincides with the possibility of man understanding himself. He is asked whether he *wants* to understand himself in the way he is shown in the Word. *That* he *can* understand himself thus is the only criterion for the truth of the Word, or rather: the man who asks for a criterion is thrown back on that alone, and the task of preaching is thus to offer the Word in such a way that the possibility of understanding is not a question of theory, of *Weltanschauung*, but is made clear as a possibility disclosed by the Word and to be grasped by the will.'[26]

Because the *kerygma* has the character of address, it is a 'definite word addressed at a particular occasion',[27] i.e. a concrete event, a divine act, just as the saving event itself represents a concrete act of God. The *kerygma* is no timeless truth, but a historical event. Its eternity is not 'its endless endurance but its actual presence at specific moments. It is the Word of God only in so far as it is a word which happens on specific occasions, and not in virtue of the ideas it contains—e.g. the mercy and grace of God (however true these things may be). It is the Word of God because it confronts me with his judgment or grace.'[28] Precisely because God's Word is an eternal Word, it is what it is as God's Word only in the moment in

[25] ibid., p. 283.   [26] ibid., p. 284.
[27] *Kerygma und Mythos*, II, p. 204 (*Kerygma and Myth*, p. 207).
[28] ibid.

which it is spoken. Its eternity is its presence being realized at each particular moment. Bultmann calls the *kerygma* a 'sacramental event'; for 'it makes present the event of the past in such a way that it renews it and thus becomes an encounter for me myself'.[29] This is in accord with Bultmann's remark which we quoted at the end of the second chapter, that one cannot 'improve' a sermon, even if it was a bad one, because it is *kerygma*. By its very nature it is new on each occasion.

From this, it follows for Bultmann that it can never be clearly and finally said 'what the *kerygma* is, how many and what statements it embraces'.[30] Theological investigations can be made in such a way as to provide a conscious elucidation of the self-understanding of faith. The theologian will give his answers each time in accordance with his understanding of Christianity; he will always be trying to give better answers and will therefore never withdraw his answers from the realm of critical discussion. With the *kerygma* it is different. It is of its nature that it can never be understood in scientific objectivity, but only in obedience, 'that the understanding must always be achieved anew'.[31] The *kerygma* can only be understood 'authentically', i.e. existentially. Understanding the *kerygma* is therefore never a matter of summing up what has been understood. It always takes the form of self-understanding. On each specific occasion it is total and new or it is nothing at all. It never has its object, the *kerygma*, at its disposal, but always experiences it anew. Anyone who claims to understand it finally or comprehensively simply betrays his fundamental misunderstanding of the nature of the *kerygma*. By its very nature, the *kerygma* is address. Address, however, can never be definitive; it can only be understood on each particular occasion; and it is never understood if I pass judgment on it, but only if I present myself to it in my decision.

Salvation and doom, life and death, are given in the Word,

[29] *Kerygma und Mythos*, I, p. 132.
[30] *Glauben und Verstehen*, 1, p. 186.   [31] ibid.

the *kerygma*, and only in the Word. In the Word, the judgment of God goes out constantly over this world—to some a judgment for life, for others a judgment for death. John 5.24 runs: 'He who hears my *word* and believes him who sent me, has eternal life; he does not come into judgment, but has passed from death to life.' Bultmann is particularly fond of quoting this saying. It expresses the fact that the mere Word brings the definitive decision upon man; for this Word is *kerygma*, which can only be heard in obedience or in disobedience. 'Where preaching resounds, the time of salvation dawns: "Behold, now is the acceptable time; behold, now is the day of salvation" (II Cor. 6.2).'[32] 'That is why the apostolic preaching brings judgment. For some the apostle is "a fragrance from death to death" and for others "a fragrance from life to life" (II Cor. 2.16).'[33]

In the Word, life has appeared and the world has been judged. So the Word is a stone of stumbling for the world. 'The Word resounds in the world and does not allow it to rest in its illusions. That Word is intolerable to it and disturbs and vexes it constantly. Although its eyes are sealed and it does not see the judgment which is invisibly being executed upon it, it has an uneasy and vexing suspicion that this is so. It desires that this Word, which assails its self-sufficiency and its claims, should cease to be heard and it attempts to suppress it. By the Word we do not mean only the word of the preacher which is heard in church; the witness to the Christ has taken many various forms, and whatever the form, it vexes the spirit of the world. It may take the form of works of Christian charity; such activity is a word which speaks and testifies to Jesus. But as such it is provoking to the world. Certainly the world admits the necessity of such works, but only in the guise of secular philanthropy. Or the word of Christ may have taken shape in art, poetry and music, in painting and sculpture. The world

[32] ibid., p. 180.
[33] *Kerygma und Mythos*, I, p. 47 (*Kerygma and Myth*, p. 43).

gladly admits the beauty of the artistic expression and claims that as its own. But the Word thus embodied is hateful to it. Nevetheless this Word, which so vexes and disturbs the world, gives to the Christian disciple the power to challenge the world; for he knows that by the mighty Word the sway of the prince of this world is shattered' (from a sermon of 1938).[34]

Bultmann believes that the *once-for-allness* of the saving act of God of which Paul speaks in Rom. 6.10 is only understood in its true meaning when it is recognized that the saving event is the event of proclamation on each several occasion. For this once-for-allness of the divine saving act, which expresses the fact that it is there before me and apart from me, does not mean 'the datable uniqueness and finality of an event of past history', 'an objectively demonstrable fact which can be dated "before me" ', but 'Christ *for me*, who encounters me as the Word'.[35] The reference to the unique event taking place in the years 1–30 is thus to be understood as a reference to the once-for-allness of the salvation which takes place for me in the Word on each particular occasion. For this Word 'tells me—as an event of address—that the prevenient grace of God has already acted on my behalf, though not in such a way that I can look back on this act of God as a datable event of the past, but in the sense that God's having acted is present as a Now', which ultimately concerns me.[36] Talk about the once-for-allness of the saving event thus means that the Word which goes out would not be the saving, healing word if it is not the word of Jesus Christ as the saving act of God, just as on the other hand Jesus Christ would not be God's saving act if this saving act were not 'each time event as the *viva vox* of the Gospel'.[37]

The fact that the saving event is present only as word-event clearly allows no distinction between the disciples 'at first

[34] *Marburger Predigten*, pp. 58 f. (*This World and the Beyond*, pp. 69 f.).

[35] *Kerygma und Mythos*, II, p. 206 (*Kerygma and Myth*, p. 208).

[36] ibid. (ibid., p. 209).   [37] ibid.

hand' and those 'at second hand', i.e. between the first Christian generation of eyewitnesses and all later generations. Bultmann often stresses this fact, which had already been pointed out by Kierkegaard. Even the first generation could only believe on the basis of the mere Word; they could only 'hear', i.e. obey, whatever they saw. The decision between faith and unbelief was therefore the same as it is today. Kierkegaard, whom Bultmann follows, can even say that the disciple at first hand must really have longed constantly for the end of immediate contemporaneity, 'so that he would not be tempted to run and want to see with his physical eyes and hear with his earthly ears; all of which is a lost labour of love and a sad, indeed dangerous, plague' (*Philosophical Fragments*). For revelation is by nature 'indirect', as we saw in the last chapter, and can be recognized only *in* faith. 'What was misleading for the first disciples was the illusion of a false security, in which they thought to have revelation in what was directly given, immediately granted and experienced, and therefore wanted it never to end. But that everything given and experienced in time is as such essentially transitory and affords no security is regularly stressed in the remark that the giver himself vanishes (John 16.7). Otherwise he and his gift would be misunderstood. He can only be the revealer as the one who constantly shatters what is given, who destroys all security and constantly breaks in from the beyond and summons to the future. Only in this way is the believer preserved from turning back on himself and dwelling on himself as he turns to the gift, instead of allowing himself to be torn from himself and to be shown what is constantly future, in accordance with the meaning of the gift. Revelation will indeed make the believer free; the security which it gives is not the permanence of the present—which in truth is always already past—but the eternity of the future.'[38]

These remarks have themselves shown, by means of a concrete example, that the question of legitimation, put to the

[38] *Johannesevangelium*, pp. 431 f.

Word, must be rejected just as it would be were it put to the saving event in any other way. The Word proclaims the Jesus-event as the saving event and in this way distinguishes it from other worldly events, but it cannot legitimate itself for such action. God's word has 'no credentials, but demands acknowledgement. It cannot be understood as God's word in neutrality (I Cor. 2.14)'.[39] Bultmann means something different when he says that the origin of the Word 'is an historical event which provides the credentials for its utterance on each specific occasion. This event is Jesus Christ,'[40] in other words, the unique saving event that is itself 'legitimated' as such only through proclamation, which makes it 'once for all'. That means that the unique historical origin of the Word 'authorizes' the proclamation to confront the hearer with the ever-repeated Word itself as God's saving act, whereas the very fact that this historical origin occurs in the *kerygma* makes it 'legitimate' to speak of the Jesus-event as God's saving act. In no way is the 'Word' here demonstrated to be God's word independently of faith. As saving event, the Word thus bears the same paradoxical character as the unique event of the incarnation and cross of Jesus. It is a human word, spoken to me in human language, just as the Bible is a human book, originating in a human way —and it is nevertheless God's unique saving act, 'not invented by the human spirit and by human sagacity'.[41]

If the question of *legitimation* put to the Word is to be rejected, so too, of course, is the corresponding question of its absoluteness. The Word is a human word and it is delivered in human language. Its uniqueness lies neither in linguistic perfection of language nor in its communication in 'heavenly tongues'. The absoluteness of the Word lies in its content, rather than in its form. But the divine quality of this content— and this very quality gives the Word its absoluteness—can be

[39] *Glauben und Verstehen*, I, p. 282.
[40] *Kerygma und Mythos*, II, p. 205 (*Kerygma and Myth*, p. 207).
[41] *Jesus Christ and Mythology*, p. 79.

perceived from outside faith only as an absurd assertion of a Word which is itself completely of this world. *In* faith, on the other hand, the truth of this assertion has already been perceived—for it is perceptible only in faith—and the question of its absoluteness has thus been answered. Faith can indeed understand the question of absoluteness, but it can pose it only where it is unsure of itself—which must and will happen again and again if faith wants to prove its authenticity. Yet the answer to this question on each specific occasion grows only out of the newly-won certainty of faith itself, and not from an objective demonstration prior to faith, because such a demonstration does not *authentically* focus on the word of revelation.

The constantly repeated reference to Jesus Christ as the saving event, which is *identical* with the Word of proclamation, makes us ask whether, if Bultmann can say that *revelation* takes place *in the Word*, he cannot also say that the *cross and resurrection* take place, or happen again, in the Word. He can in fact do this. His view of the cross is that 'it may no longer be considered as just the historical event of Jesus' crucifixion on Golgotha', for 'removed from all temporal limitation, it continues to take place in any present moment, both in the proclaiming word and in the sacraments. The apostle bears about in his body the dying of Jesus and is stamped with the "stigmata" of Jesus (II Cor. 4.10 f.; Gal. 6.17).'[42]

Bultmann can speak in a similar way of the Easter event. Christ is present in the *Word* as the living one. He encounters us nowhere else. His life is the living and life-giving voice of the Word. Therefore, 'the truth of the Easter faith is just this —faith in this Word',[43] as surely as the word of proclamation is derived from the Easter event. Asked whether he could not say that Jesus is risen in the *kerygma*, Bultmann replies: 'I accept this proposition. It is entirely correct, provided that it is

[42] *Theologie*, p. 303 (*Theology*, I, p. 303).
[43] *Kerygma und Mythos*, I, p. 46 (*Kerygma and Myth*, p. 41).

properly understood . . . It expresses the fact that Jesus is really present in the *kerygma*, that it is *his* word which involves the hearer in the *kerygma*. If that is the case, then all speculations about the modes of being of the risen Jesus, all the narratives of the empty tomb and all the Easter legends, whatever elements of historical fact they may contain, however true they may be in their symbolic form, are of no consequence. To believe in the Christ present in the *kerygma* is the meaning of the Easter faith.'[44]

Bultmann can speak in the same way about the *incarnation*. It is misunderstood if it is taken to be a 'miracle which happened about 1,950 years ago',[45] which is to be 'believed' today as an event of the past, framed in the conceptuality of Greek metaphysics. As God's saving act, the incarnation is 'not a datable event of the past; it is an event which is continually being re-enacted in the event of the proclamation'.[46] According to Bultmann, the incarnation, rightly understood, is an event 'which, beginning in the historical person of Jesus, is constantly present in the proclaimed Word of proclaiming men as action, speech and experience performed by men'.[47]

Perhaps we may end this chapter with some remarks which might not necessarily be expected among its themes. They are included here because Bultmann usually deals with them at this point.

If the *kerygma* is part of the saving event, then so, too, in Bultmann's understanding, is the *keryx*, the apostle, i.e. the preacher himself: 'But how are men to call upon him in whom they have not believed? And how are they to believe in him of whom they have never heard? And how are they to hear with-

[44] 'Das Verhältnis der urchristlichen Christusbotschaft', p. 27 (*The Historical Jesus and the Kerygmatic Christ*, p. 42).
[45] Bultmann and Jaspers, *Die Frage der Entmythologisierung*, p. 70.
[46] *Kerygma und Mythos*, II, p. 206 n. 1 (*Kerygma and Myth*, p. 209 n. 1).
[47] Bultmann and Jaspers, *Die Frage der Entmythologisierung*, p. 70.

out a preacher?' (Rom. 10.14). In so far as the saving event is present in the word of the preacher, the preacher represents Christ himself: 'So we are ambassadors for Christ, God making his appeal through us. We beseech you on behalf of Christ, be reconciled to God' (II Cor. 5.20)—a passage which Bultmann quotes particularly often and interprets to mean 'that in the preaching of the apostle, Christ himself, indeed God himself, speaks'.[48] Or even: 'Thus Paul has become Christ himself for his hearers—not because he is deified and gazed upon by them as a pneumatic, but because he preaches to them,' Christ preaches to them![49] For just as revelation takes place in a particular, historical man, Jesus of Nazareth, so it renews itself 'at any given time in the proclamation of concrete historical men'.[50] 'Thus the preaching apostle, whom God guides, using him to spread the fragrance of the knowledge of him everywhere, is "the aroma of Christ to God among those who are being saved and among those who are perishing" (II Cor. 2.15).'[51]

It is obvious that for Bultmann the connection of saving event and apostolate which can be seen in Paul does not relate to a particular apostolic authority but to the priesthood of all believers. No-one is in principle dispensed from the commission to speak the 'Word'; basically, each believer takes part in the continuing realization of the saving event. For each one who knows himself to be a believer has to look at the other 'conscious of his responsibility to make God's grace so plain by practice and precept that the question of faith is really put to this other man.'[52]

Not only the messenger, the *keryx*, the preacher, but also his specific word, i.e. 'Holy Scripture' as the apostolic word,

[48] *Glauben und Verstehen*, 1, p. 289.
[49] *Glauben und Verstehen*, 3, p. 19 (*Existence and Faith*, p. 76).
[50] *Glauben und Verstehen*, 2, p. 258 (*Essays*, p. 287).
[51] *Glauben und Verstehen*, 1, p. 289.
[52] *Glauben und Verstehen*, 2, p. 158 (ibid., p. 178).

also belongs to the saving event. It and its significance must, of course, be understood rightly if the saving character of the 'Word of God' is appropriately to be grasped. According to Bultmann, that happens 'when Scripture is understood neither as a compendium of doctrines nor as a document enshrining the beliefs of other people', but 'when Scripture is heard as a word addressed personally to myself, as *kerygma*', in other words, when my being addressed by the word of Scripture is the answer to God's *address*. 'That Scripture is the Word of God is something which happens only in the here and now of encounter; it is not a fact susceptible to objective proof. The Word of God is hidden in Scripture, just like any other act of his.'[53]

Above all the community, the 'Church' itself, belongs to the saving event. 'As it was called into existence by the proclaimed word, its existence in turn is the foundation of preaching.'[54] For, according to Bultmann, the Word is *kerygma*, authoritative address, and not the communication of timeless truths. Preaching is not interesting as a presentation of generally valid statements, just as the preacher is of no consequence to his hearers as a 'religious personality'. The preacher is a messenger, his message is a call to obedience. A messenger is always sent, authorized; the Christian messenger is sent and authorized by God, or Christ: 'As the Father has sent me, so send I you' (John 20.21); and 'How can men preach unless they have been sent?' (Rom. 10.15). In so far as such sending and authorization continually takes place in the Church, Bultmann can venture the dangerous statement that just as the Church lives from the Word, so, on the other hand, 'the Word is constituted by the Church'.[55] In connecting the Word with the Church in this way, Bultmann does not mean to describe any

[53] *Kerygma und Mythos*, II, p. 200 (*Kerygma and Myth*, p. 201).
[54] *Theologie*, p. 309 (*Theology*, I, p. 308).
[55] *Glauben und Verstehen*, 1, p. 181.

legal process of authorization but to demonstrate the continual kerygmatic character of the Word. By sending out preachers, the 'phenomenon' Church guarantees that the word which is uttered on any given occasion is understood as 'address'. It protects the Word from becoming a known and transmitted *doctrine*, which needs no sending and therefore no Church. On the other hand, this very Church is constituted only through the Word.

'We cannot, then, play off the Church against doubt about the Word, for the Church is itself constituted by the receiving and handing on of the Word. Nor, however, can we play off the Word against doubt about the Church, as though the Word intrinsically had a timeless character, as though the essential fact about it were not precisely that it is spoken here and now (i.e. the fact 'Church'). It is in fact address handed down under orders.'[56] The Church is as it were the 'place' of the Word. Without the Word there would be no Church as saving community, but without the Church there would no longer be the Word as *kerygma*.

Of course, everything depends on a right understanding of what Bultmann means by 'Church'. Bultmann's understanding of 'Church' should be distinguished from the usual ideas of an 'institution', although of course he can also speak of the 'Church' as a structured organization. But because the Church is part of the saving event, it also shares in its paradoxical character. 'The Church is just as ambiguous a phenomenon as the cross of Christ: visible as a worldly fact, invisible—yet to the eye of faith also visible—as a thing of the world to come.'[57] This paradoxical character of the Church is reflected for Bultmann, for example, in the fact that in the New Testament the Greek word '*ecclesia*' (= church, community) sometimes means the whole Church, not present in a particular institution, and sometimes describes the organized individual community: the Church is 'on the one hand no phenomenon of the

[56] ibid.   [57] *Theologie*, p. 309 (*Theology*, I, p. 308).

world, but belongs to the new aeon', and on the other hand, while 'being as such invisible', it 'takes visible form in the individual congregations within the world'.[58] In so far as the latter happens, it is easy for those outside to mistake the nature of the Church. They may see the Church as an association 'in which like-minded individuals have banded together'.[59] To others it may be an institution which has saving benefits to administer. In neither case is the other-worldly character of the Church understood; for the Church is true Church 'as an event which happens each time here and now', and is 'only in a paradoxical way identical with the ecclesiastical institutions which we observe as social phenomena of secular history'.[60]

For Bultmann the community is represented in its purest and most unmistakable form in its assembling for worship, in which Christ is acknowledged as the present Lord. The worship of the community is 'primarily proclamation of the Word and an answering confession of faith, faith which celebrates the saving act. Even when it is also performed in the sacraments, it still stands under the dominion of the Word.'[61]

The community is visibly and invisibly 'the community of those among whom God creates life—and rules'.[62] It knows that it is in the way of salvation, and removed from the world, just as 'this world's distinctions have lost their meaning';[63] for here, 'There is neither Jew nor Greek, there is neither slave nor free, there is neither male nor female, for you are all one in Christ Jesus' (Gal. 3.28), and at the same time it is true that 'each one should remain in the state in which the call of God encountered him' (I Cor. 7.17–24): 'i.e. the negation of worldly differentiations does not mean a sociological programme within this world; rather, it is an "eschatological" occurrence which

---

[58] ibid.
[59] ibid., p. 311 (ibid., p. 310).
[60] *Jesus Christ and Mythology*, p. 83.
[61] *Glauben und Verstehen*, 1, pp. 180 f.
[62] 'Jesus und Paulus', p. 89 (*Existence and Faith*, p. 201).
[63] *Theologie*, p. 309 (*Theology*, I, p. 309).

takes place only within the "eschatological" community'.[64] In other words, the community is a part of the saving event itself, which takes place only within the saving community.

It is further significant for Bultmann's understanding of the Church that he always develops it in the context of his discussion of the *saving event*. Catholic theologians have noted this fact with interest and have thought that Bultmann ought to be consistent and affirm the visible, legal institution of the Church and its ministry as a sign of the dialectical structure of the Church, which is both visible and invisible. There may be a misunderstanding here. The visible side of the Church needs no sign—only the invisible side does. But its sign is only the Word which is proclaimed in the Church and is in a paradoxical way itself the saving act. The Church lives only through the Word and for the Word, which is not of this world. That is why Bultmann deals with the Church in the immediate context of the saving event, so that the sheer transcendence of the ambivalent phenomenon 'Church' may be preserved and the 'from grace alone', the *solus Christus* from which it lives, may not be concealed *despite* law, ministry and other sociological manifestations.

We began the present chapter with the question of how the Jesus-event is characterized as saving event, and we heard Bultmann's answer: through the *Word*, i.e. by the Jesus-event being *proclaimed* as God's saving act, being encountered as *kerygma*. Apart from this proclamation the Jesus-event is just an ordinary earthly event.

We now go on to ask why the Jesus-event, rather than any other worldly event, is given the status of saving event by proclamation. For cannot every earthly event be characterized as saving event through the Word of the *kerygma*?

If one asks questions like this as a matter of principle, Bultmann feels, the answer cannot, of course, be in the negative.

[64] ibid., p. 310 (ibid.).

But *in* faith this sort of question of principle can no longer be asked; for faith believes on the basis of *this* event being proclaimed as the saving act of God. Anyone who has experienced the event of the love of God in the Word of Jesus Christ will not speculate about other possibilities which God might have had of instituting his 'word of life'. He will gratefully acknowledge *that* God has performed and still performs his gracious act in the Word of Jesus Christ. He will leave to God 'where he wills to perform this act'.[65]

[65] *Glauben und Verstehen*, 2, p. 100 (*Essays*, p. 113).

9

The Historical Jesus

WE NEED NO excuse for discussing the significance of the 'historical Jesus' in Bultmann's theology in connection with the development of the Christian saving event as Bultmann understands it; for we saw that Bultmann, in agreement with the whole of Christian tradition, regards Jesus Christ, and only him, as the event in which God has acted once and for all for the salvation of the world. On the other hand, we need to explain why we are looking at the historical Jesus *in connection with* the discussion of the saving event. For if Jesus Christ is the event of the saving act of God, is not the historical Jesus himself this saving act?

Bultmann replies to this question with an emphatic 'no'. This answer emerged, without any specific mention of the problem, in the previous chapters; for in outlining the sense in which for Bultmann Jesus Christ is the divine saving event, in practice we only come up against the 'fact' of the historical Jesus, i.e. the facticity of his manhood as such. *That* he was born, or 'made flesh', *that* he lived, *that* he was crucified, executed and buried—these were the historical data of the appearance of Jesus which were sufficient for Bultmann in his account of the significance and content of the Christian confession of Jesus as the sole saving event. The Word in which the saving event takes place on each particular occasion has no other content for Bultmann than this 'fact' of the historical existence of Jesus which is proclaimed as the saving act of God.

Kierkegaard, in his *Philosophical Fragments*, already regarded this as an appropriate standpoint when he wrote: 'Even if the contemporary generation had left behind nothing but the words: we have believed that in such and such a year God showed himself to us in the humble form of a servant, lived and taught among us, and then died—that is more than enough.'

To speak of the 'historical Jesus' means, on the other hand, in the usual theological terminology, to investigate the manner and substance of his historical appearance: his teaching, his conduct, his inner development, his personal faith, the effect he had on his contemporaries, in short, everything about the particular manhood of a significant figure which might be of interest. In his investigation of the saving event Bultmann examines none of this. His interest in Jesus as the saving event is directed at the mere fact of his coming, at his humanity. 'The historical Jesus is one phenomenon among others, and not an absolute,' like the saving event;[1] and '. . . what things seemed like in Jesus' heart I do not know and do not want to know'.[2] So we can examine the problem of the historical Jesus in Bultmann's theology only as an *appendix* to the account of his understanding of the saving event, and our most important task must be to make it clear why Bultmann, in his enquiry into Jesus as the saving act of God, is not interested in the 'historical Jesus'.

The problems surrounding the question of the historical Jesus have only become clear at a relatively late stage in theology. It therefore seems to me to be important to give a brief sketch of the recent history of this problem up to Bultmann's position by taking up certain themes from the first chapter. A historical survey of this kind may be the easiest way of clarifying Bultmann's position on the historical Jesus.

In 1835–6, David Friedrich Strauss's *The Life of Jesus*,

[1] *Glauben und Verstehen*, 1, p. 4.   [2] ibid., p. 101.

critically investigated, was published in two volumes. The criticism of the biblical tradition developed in this book, which caused controversy and scandal, was quite brilliant, in that David Friedrich Strauss succeeded in emphatically disrupting the historical reliability of the biblical picture of Jesus with *one* critical principle: he declared that the biblical stories of Jesus represent a *mythical* transformation of the reports of the real Jesus. Strauss saw in this destruction of the biblical tradition of Jesus the justification of his attempt to base religious belief on the history of the eternal Spirit instead of that of Jesus Christ, an undertaking which he made in the steps of his teacher, Hegel. The person of Jesus was replaced by the 'real idea', immanent throughout the world, by the absolute Spirit of Hegelian speculation bringing itself to realization. This was the real purpose of Strauss's work; his discussion of the Jesus tradition merely served as a means to this end.

David Friedrich Strauss thus produced a radical denial that Jesus had any significance for salvation. It is understandable that reaction against Strauss should have stressed the significance of *the history of Jesus Christ* as a unique event which could be established by the historian. Albrecht Ritschl, himself a former pupil of the theological Hegelians, was the leader on the way from the idea with its effect in history to the contingent historical event.

The influential 'Quest of the Historical Jesus' also moved in the same direction. It was determined by historistic as well as liberal ideas. The liberal element was its conviction that salvation lies in personalities and that therefore the question of Jesus was the question of his *personality*, which had to be reconstructed on the basis of his teaching, his conduct, his inner development, and the impression he made on his contemporaries. This liberal 'life-of-Jesus theology' was bound up with historicism to the extent that it was quite confident that such reconstructions could be engineered through undistorted historical judgment. Through a vast amount of literature, and

with great confidence in the results achieved, the personality of
Jesus, in whom God brought his fatherly goodness to bear and
revealed the infinite value of the human soul, was depicted in
the form of 'Lives' of Jesus. The question of the historical
Jesus thus presented itself as the question of the 'personality of
Jesus'.

Both in outline and in detail, this liberal theology based its
account of the personality of Jesus above all on the Gospel of
Mark, which had been demonstrated by historical-critical
scholarship to be the oldest Gospel, on which Matthew and Luke
were dependent. The tradition about Jesus in Mark was held
to be fundamentally reliable; in particular, writers were convinced that Mark's biographical outline gave a faithful picture
of the *development* of Jesus' personality. The liberal theologians
recognized the preaching of the kingdom of God to be the
central message of Jesus: it had dawned and come to consummation—according to the interpretation of this preaching—in
moral personalities.

There is no point in repeating what we said briefly in the
first chapter about the way in which the liberal picture of Jesus
was superseded within the liberal school itself. We simply
draw attention here once again to Bultmann's contribution to
the collapse of the Life of Jesus theology. His chief contribution was made in his *History of the Synoptic Tradition*, the first
edition of which appeared in 1921. This book thus appeared
before Bultmann's encounter with 'dialectical' theology, even
longer before his work with Martin Heidegger. It represents
the real scholarly fruit of his 'liberal' period, and has also been
generally accepted as an expression of liberal theology. Rightly
so, in so far as Bultmann makes a historical-critical investigation of the Jesus tradition without any dogmatic prejudices.
Wrongly so, in that this book destroys any possibility of writing
a 'Life of Jesus', the beginning and the end of liberal theology.
Moreover, Bultmann's *History of the Synoptic Tradition* was
one of the three most significant books about what is known as

form criticism, which appeared at roughly the same time quite independently of each other: in 1919 Karl Ludwig Schmidt wrote his book *Der Rahmen der Geschichte Jesu* and in the same year Martin Dibelius' *Die Formgeschichte des Evangeliums* appeared. Because of its comprehensive examination of the synoptic material, Bultmann's book became the most influential of the three.

What is form criticism?

Form criticism begins from the recognition that our synoptic Gospels (Matthew, Mark, Luke) represent collections of individual small units which were originally transmitted orally. These units took shape according to different forms, in each case characteristic ones. Form criticism, which ought really to be called the history of forms, analyses and classifies the synoptic material according to these pre-literary units of determined form. Bultmann here distinguishes between the tradition of sayings and narrative material. In his view, the sayings tradition falls into two large groups: the sayings of the Lord which were transmitted without a narrative framework, and the apophthegms, which, though containing a short historical scene, came to a climax in a saying of the Lord; Bultmann is convinced that in most cases the historical scene in the apophthegm was formed later, as a framework for the original saying of the Lord. In his view, the narrative material is divided into miracle stories and historical narratives; the latter are often of more or less legendary character. There are contemporary profane and religious parallels to all these forms which justify and support the form-critical analysis of the gospel tradition in general and in particular.

What is the significance of the work of form criticism?

The form critics dispute that its significance is limited to a particular expression of an aesthetic approach. On the contrary! In Bultmann's view, the significance of form criticism is not 'that it identifies the individual units of the tradition according to their characteristics—aesthetic or otherwise—and places them in their various categories'.[3] On the contrary, it should be noted that 'the literature in which the life of a given community, and therefore also the primitive Christian community, has taken shape, arises from quite definite needs and from expressions of the life of this community. The result is a quite definite style and quite specific forms and categories.'[4] Form criticism thus looks for the '*Sitz im Leben*' (life setting), i.e. the place of the individual pieces of tradition with definite form, in the life of the community which gave them shape and passed them on—in our case, the primitive Christian community.

This makes further developments possible. Knowledge of the fixed forms provides criteria for recognizing the development of an individual piece of the tradition and for reconstructing the original state of the tradition. This already raises the question of authenticity, which is touched on by form-critical methods even more closely when they investigate the place of individual passages in the life of a *particular* community. If it turns out, for example, that a tradition could have had its *Sitz im Leben* only in the life of the *Hellenistic* community, then the question of authenticity must be answered in the negative. Here we have a passage constructed by the community.

It was Bultmann who, among the form-critics, placed particular emphasis on the question of the setting of individual traditions in the life of a particular community. In so doing he reached fairly negative verdicts about the historical reliability of the Jesus tradition. We shall have something to say about this later.

First of all, however, we should note that the recognition that the synoptic tradition is composed of individual traditions which were inserted into a gospel framework created for the purpose only at a later date, finally brought the construction of

[3] *Die Geschichte der synoptischen Tradition*, p. 4 (*History of the Synoptic Tradition*, p. 4).
[4] ibid.

the Life-of-Jesus theology crashing to the ground. This construction was, as we have already remarked, built on the *framework* of the Gospel of Mark, in other words, on the latest part of the tradition, which already belonged to the *literary* stage of the tradition and comes from the hand of the evangelist himself. If this framework can lay no claim to historical reliability, it was no longer possible to reconstruct the inner development of the personality of 'Jesus' which formed the basis of all the liberal 'Lives' of Jesus.

At the very time when the above-mentioned investigations of the form-critical school were being published, Karl Barth's *Epistle to the Romans* also appeared. The first edition was published in 1919, the second, epoch-making edition, completely revised, in 1921. Against liberal theology, which wanted to express the divine in terms of the greatness of human personality, it set the recognition that God is the 'wholly other', and is separated from man by an infinite qualitative difference.

In the face of this two-pronged attack, the Life-of-Jesus theology, long since smitten and committed to the 'personality' of Jesus, left the field almost without a struggle. 'Dialectical' theology of all shades rejected the question of the historical Jesus as a theological question and based Christian faith on the word *of* Jesus as the Christ, the crucified and risen Lord. II Cor. 5.16 was quoted a good deal in connection with the historical Jesus: 'From now on, therefore, we know no one after the flesh; even though we once know Christ after the flesh, we know him thus no longer', and Karl Barth could remark to the doyen of liberal theology, Adolf von Harnack: 'If anyone still does not know that we cannot any longer know Christ after the flesh, then he may as well let critical study of the Bible tell him so—and the more frightened he is, the better for him and the cause.'

Was this unconditional and notorious 'no' to any theologically legitimate quest of the historical Jesus, which Rudolf Bultmann

and Karl Barth have maintained unswervingly up to the
present day, sufficiently grounded by the demonstration that
the question of the 'personality of Jesus' was, as Bultmann
showed, impossible for the historian and, as Barth affirmed,
wrong for the theologian to answer? Obviously not! For the
question of the 'historical Jesus' is clearly not identical with
the question of the 'personality of Jesus'. If this latter question
is thought to be irrelevant, the question of Jesus' teaching,
his preaching, his conduct, his self-understanding remains.
Furthermore: is not the tradition, the New Testament itself,
interested in the historical Jesus in at least some of the above-
mentioned respects? Otherwise, whatever would be the significance of the gospel tradition? And in that case, how can one
regard as theologically inadmissible *any* interest in Jesus which
goes beyond the establishment of the fact of his historical
existence?

Is it perhaps the case that Bultmann's *historical scepticism*
towards the Jesus tradition prevents him from raising the
question of the historical Jesus at all? We saw that his form-
critical work led him to the recognition that the Jesus tradition
as it is presented to us in the synoptic Gospels has been largely
shaped by the needs and problems of the later community.
Does Bultmann then make a virtue out of necessity by excluding any theological interest in the historical Jesus? In 1926 he
wrote: 'I do indeed think that we can now know almost nothing
about the life and personality of Jesus, since the early Christian
sources show no interest in either, are moreover fragmentary
and often legendary; and other sources about Jesus do not
exist. Except for the purely critical research, what has been
written in the last hundred and fifty years on the life of Jesus,
his personality and the development of his inner life, is
fantastic and romantic.'[5]

It is, however, a grotesque misunderstanding when one finds
Bultmann's statement that we 'can now know almost nothing

[5] *Jesus*, p. 10 (*Jesus and the Word*, p. 14).

about the life and personality of Jesus' quoted as an expression of the fact that in Bultmann's view one can know nothing about *Jesus*. While Bultmann is of the opinion that we can now know nothing about the 'personality' of Jesus, because the primitive Christian community was not interested in Jesus as a 'personality', he has never doubted that it is possible for us to gain a sufficiently clear picture of Jesus' *teaching*, which represents his real work. 'Little as we know of his life and personality, we know enough of his message to make a consistent picture for ourselves.'[6] Of course, 'Here, too, great caution is demanded by the nature of our sources. What the sources offer us is first of all the message of the early Christian community, which for the most part the Church freely attributed to Jesus. This naturally gives no proof that all the words which are put into his mouth were actually spoken by him. As can easily be proved, many sayings originated in the Church itself; others were modified by the Church.'[7] In agreement with other scholars, Bultmann excludes the Gospel of John as a source of descriptions of the proclamation of the historical Jesus. In the synoptic Gospels he distinguishes three strata of tradition 'which can on the whole be fairly clearly distinguished'.[8] The latest stratum belongs to the Hellenistic, Greek speaking communities; it is often clearly recognizable and is not relevant—at least directly—to the reconstruction of the proclamation of Jesus. According to Bultmann, the essential material of the sayings traditions of the three earliest Gospels comes from the Aramaic tradition of the earliest communities of Palestine. In this material there is a further stratum which 'betrays the specific interests of the church or reveals characteristics of later development'.[9] After excluding this stratum we come to the earliest material from which Bultmann is convinced we can distinguish the basic features of Jesus' teaching.

[6] ibid., p. 13 (ibid., pp. 16 f.).
[7] ibid. (ibid., p. 17).   [8] ibid.
[9] ibid.

He himself undertakes the attempt to reconstruct the preaching of Jesus in his famous book *Jesus and the Word*, which appeared in 1926 in the *Deutsche Bibliothek* of the Jewish publisher Wertheim, who also had a second edition, with a few additions, printed in 1929. The book was soon translated into other languages and is also available today in English, Danish, Swedish and Japanese translations. (It is most easily accessible to the English reader in the Fontana paperback edition.) Anyone who wants to tackle Bultmann's own publications is strongly urged to read this Jesus book first, as it is regarded by many who know Bultmann's theological work as his most brilliant achievement. In its first and second editions, it appeared as the first volume in a series intended for interested readers of all backgrounds entitled 'Heroes'; the series continued with the lives of great personalities. This curious fact makes it clear to what extent the book represented a turning point. Whereas the publisher regarded it as obvious that a meaningful account of the historical career of Jesus could depict him simply as a religious hero, Bultmann with his whole book expressly attacked the dominant view that the divine revealed itself in great personalities.

Bultmann's account of the preaching of Jesus has been called 'the portrait of Jesus by dialectical theology', and surely this is right; of course, the phrase simply means that it is Bultmann's own picture of Jesus, produced by a historical enquiry into sources in and from 'the concrete situation of a man living in time'.[10] Bultmann's Jesus book is thus a work which was written by him at a particular time, written at this time only by *him*, and which could have been written by him only *in that way* at that time. Bultmann does not mean to give the reader of his book a dispassionate account of historical facts but to lead him to an existential encounter with the historic phenomenon of the 'historical Jesus'. It is not by chance that his book ends with the sentence: 'Whether his word is

[10] ibid., p. 12 (ibid., p. 16).

truth, whether he is sent from God—that is the decision to which the hearer is constrained, and the word of Jesus remains: "Blessed is he who finds no cause of offence with me." [11] In this sense, Bultmann's Jesus book is not meant to give an objective account, and is not meant to be read 'objectively'. It bears witness to *his* encounter with the history of Jesus and is meant to guide the reader to 'a highly personal encounter'[12] with this history. This was the very way in which Jesus saw and regarded his own work and his own task: 'Therefore, when I speak of the teaching or thought of Jesus, I base the discussion on no underlying conception of a universally valid, ideal system of thought which through this study can be made enlightening to all. Rather the ideas are understood in the light of the concrete situation of a man living in time; as his interpretation of his own existence in the midst of change, uncertainty, decision; as the expression of a possibility of comprehending this life; as the effort to gain clear insight into the contingencies and necessities of his own existence. When we encounter the words of Jesus in history, we do not judge them by a philosophical system with reference to their rational validity; they meet us with the question of how we are to interpret our own existence. That we be ourselves deeply disturbed by the problem of our own life is therefore the indispensable condition of our enquiry. Then the examination of history will lead not to the enrichment of timeless wisdom, but to an encounter with history which itself is an event in time.'[13]

If Bultmann's Jesus book, as *his* highly personal encounter with the preaching of the historical Jesus, is thus itself a 'temporal event', the historical reliability of this picture of Jesus and the reliability of its sources may be questioned in general or in detail; but the more one doubted the historicity of the picture of Jesus' proclamation offered here, the clearer

[11] ibid., p. 148 (ibid., p. 154).   [12] ibid., p. 9 (ibid., p. 13).
[13] ibid., p. 12 (ibid., p. 16).

it would be that this Jesus book is a significant document of Bultmann's thought.

It would go beyond the compass of this chapter to examine the details of Bultmann's picture of Jesus, but it is worth making a few necessary observations. First of all, the most interesting point is that Bultmann feels it possible to give an account of what Jesus purposed, and of such a kind that on the basis of this account, 'the demand of his historical existence can be made present'.[14] Thus, while he is convinced that the *faith* which 'believes' the divine saving act is not interested in the question of the historical Jesus, this is not because according to Bultmann one no longer knows anything or no longer knows enough about Jesus, but is *despite* a tradition of Jesus which he has shown to be sufficiently comprehensive and reliable.

Logically, this means that for Bultmann the proclamation of the historical Jesus is still not gospel, or, as he is fond of putting it, *kerygma*. It is therefore not yet the sole saving event; otherwise he could not regard the question of the preaching of the historical Jesus to be illegitimate in the search for the basis and object of the Christian faith. Bultmann leaves no doubt that this is the case. He describes this situation quite pertinently: 'The historical Jesus does not appear in the *kerygma*, any more than my Jesus book is *kerygma*.'[15] The *kerygma* is concerned solely with the fact of the historical appearance of Jesus, not with its manner and content, in other words, not with Jesus as the 'teacher'. The *kerygma* is not preaching of Jesus, but preaching *about* Jesus as the incarnate, crucified and risen one. This is the background against which Bultmann's often misunderstood remark in the introduction of his Jesus book is to be understood: 'Anyone who prefers always to put the name of "Jesus" in quotation marks and to let it stand as an abbreviation for the historical phenomenon

[14] ibid., p. 10 (ibid., p. 14).
[15] *Kerygma und Mythos*, I, p. 133.

with which we are concerned is free to do so.'[16] Because, according to Bultmann, we have still to encounter the sole saving act of God in Jesus when we are concerned with the *historical* Jesus, it is unimportant whether the person behind the thoughts which he outlines, on the basis of his critical analysis of the Jesus tradition, in his Jesus book, really was Jesus—though Bultmann does not doubt this!—or not.

Precisely in view of Bultmann's emphatic assertion that to a considerable degree we possess authentic Jesus material— above all in the sayings of Jesus—the problem whether and why it is permissible to distinguish so strictly between the question of the historical Jesus and the question of the Christian *kerygma* (i.e. the question of Jesus as the proclaimer and the question of Jesus as the proclaimed) becomes all the more acute. Is he making a virtue out of necessity in so far as his historical investigation of Jesus has led him to the recognition that there is a considerable discrepancy or discontinuity between the preaching of Jesus and the community's preaching about Jesus, which makes it necessary to decide for one or the other?

It has in fact been asserted by liberal theologians, and in particular by William Wrede, that Paul is to be regarded as the second founder of Christianity, namely as the founder of a second Christianity. When it was thought that there was a certain and unassailable foundation for faith in the 'personality of Jesus', such a verdict could be allowed, and the proclaimed could be rejected in favour of the proclaimer. Does Bultmann perhaps turn the spit and decide for the 'second' Christianity as the legitimate *kerygma*?

Not at all! He expressly attacks the assertion that there is no continuity of content between Jesus and Paul. 'My assertion that it is the Christ of the *kerygma* and not the person of the historical Jesus who is the object of faith . . . is often improperly interpreted to mean that I destroy continuity between

[16] *Jesus*, p. 14 (*Jesus and the Word*, p. 18).

the historical Jesus and the *kerygma*. . . . To this I can simply reply that from the discrepancy which I emphasize between the historical Jesus and the Christ of the *kerygma* it does not at all follow that I destroy continuity between the historical Jesus and the primitive Christian proclamation.'[17]

In an article on 'The Significance of the Historical Jesus for the Theology of Paul' (1929),[18] and again in a lecture on 'Jesus and Paul' (1936),[19] Bultmann shows that the situation of man as a sinner before God, who acts towards him in his Word, is seen in exactly the same way by Jesus and Paul, despite all the differences in the way in which it is expressed.

The first article takes up the problem of the relationship between Jesus and Paul because Bultmann, as he himself writes (in a letter of 1926), neglected this question in his Jesus book: 'Thus we come face to face with the *problem* which consists in the relationship of the proclaimer to what he proclaimed; here the proclaimer must first be seen clearly—seen clearly by his proclamation and only by his proclamation.' The second article betrays its concern in its opening sentences: 'According to Alfred Rosenberg, the "great personality of Jesus" has "been misused" by ecclesiastical Christianity. "Whatever its original form, the great personality of Jesus Christ was immediately after his departure burdened and amalgamated with all the rubbish of Near Eastern, of Jewish and African life." Specifically, the teachings of Paul constitute "the Jewish spiritual matrix, so to say, the Talmudic-Oriental side of both the Roman and the Lutheran Church";'[20] Bultmann opens up a critical discussion of Rosenburg's thesis by demonstrating the continuity between Paul and Jesus.

Of course, anyone who has read Bultmann's Jesus book hardly needs to read one of these articles to recognize that for

[17] 'Das Verhältnis der urchristlichen Christusbotschaft', pp. 7 f. (*The Historical Jesus and the Kerygmatic Christ*, pp. 17 f.).

[18] *Glauben und Verstehen*, 1, pp. 188 ff.

[19] 'Jesus und Paulus', pp. 68 ff. (*Existence and Faith*, pp. 183 ff.).

[20] ibid., p. 68 (ibid., p. 183).

Bultmann, Jesus and Paul do not represent two Christianities, but that each expresses the same self-understanding in his own words. It is not by chance that we have so far been able to base our account of Bultmann's theology either on his interpretation of Jesus' preaching or on his exposition of Pauline or Johannine theology in exactly the same way. We shall be repeating some points in order to make clear the widespread agreement between Jesus' preaching and the *kerygma* about him.

According to Bultmann, Jesus' *concept of God* implies that one can only speak meaningfully of God by speaking at the same time of man: 'Jesus speaks of God only to affirm that man is claimed by the will of God and determined in his present existence through God's demand, his judgment, his grace. The distant God is at the same time the God near at hand, whose reality is not to be grasped when a man seeks to escape from his own concrete existence, but precisely when he holds it fast. Jesus speaks of God not in terms of general truths, in dogmas, but only in terms of what God is for man, how he deals with man. . . . He speaks of God by speaking of man.'[21]

For Jesus, too, the *nature of man* is his 'being-able-to-be': 'the worth of a man for Jesus is not determined by any given human quality or the character of his spiritual life, but simply by the decision the man makes in the here-and-now of his existence. Jesus sees man as standing here and now under the necessity of decision, with the possibility of decision through his own free act. Only what a man does now gives him his value.'[22]

Jesus' call to repentance presupposes that man is a *sinner*, in the totality of his existence. 'Sin is not a sort of appendage to man; it is the characteristic of sinful humanity. . . . Sin is the character which belongs inevitably to the man remote from God who denies the claim of God.'[23] For Jesus, too, *faith* is obedient decision at any given time in face of the manifest

[21] *Jesus*, pp. 104 f. (*Jesus and the Word*, p. 110).
[22] ibid., p. 40 (ibid., p. 46).   [23] ibid., p. 135 (ibid., p. 140).

God, for this God and thus for the authentic existence of man himself: 'Faith is for Jesus the power, in particular moments of life, to take seriously the conviction of the omnipotence of God; it is the certainty that in such particular moments God's activity is really experienced; it is the conviction that the distant God is really the God near at hand, if man will only relinquish his usual attitude and be ready to see the nearness of God. In the sense of Jesus it is possible to have faith only if one is obedient.'[24]

In Jesus' proclamation, the obedience of faith presupposes 'faith in ...', namely in *God's saving action*: 'It is clear that belief in forgiveness presupposes a God who acts as a person and whose act of mercy is an event in time.'[25] According to Bultmann, it is true of this event as Jesus understands it that: 'the event is nothing else than his Word, as it confronts the hearer'.[26] Jesus is the 'bearer of the Word, and in the Word he assures man of the forgiveness of God'.[27] 'Man is constrained to decision by the Word which as address brings a new element into his situation; in this way the Word becomes event for him. For it to become an event, the hearer is essential. ... In the Word and not otherwise, Jesus brings forgiveness. Whether his Word is truth, whether he is sent by God—that is the decision to which the hearer is constrained, and the word of Jesus remains: "Blessed is he who finds no cause of offence in me".'[28] Like the *kerygma*, the proclamation of Jesus is not interested in any features or characteristics of the person of Jesus but only in the 'fact' of the Word. In so far as Jesus points to his person, he points to an ambiguous fact, 'the character of which is understood only as it is heard'.[29]

Is that not the *kerygma*, as Bultmann understands it? In his last programmatic statement on the problem of the historical

[24] ibid., p. 130 (ibid., p. 135).   [25] ibid., p. 142 (ibid., p. 147).
[26] ibid., p. 146 (ibid., p. 151).   [27] ibid., p. 147 (ibid., p. 153).
[28] ibid., p. 148 (ibid., pp. 153 f.).
[29] *Glauben und Verstehen*, 1, p. 174.

Jesus, a discussion with his pupils, Bultmann at any rate acknowledges that they have demonstrated the formal and material unity of the Christ-kergyma with the proclamation of Jesus: 'Viewed in a formal way, this identity consists in the fact that Jesus' activity in word and deed confronts man with a decision in the same way as does the Christ-kerygma.'[30] Materially, the unity is no less: 'The message of Jesus, like the *kerygma*, requires a break with the old aeon and readiness for the new aeon which is already appearing, submission to the judgment of God and the acceptance of his grace.'[31]

Nevertheless, Bultmann will not accept that the Christ-kerygma and the preaching of Jesus coincide, and makes a clear-cut distinction between the two. Indeed, he expressly says: 'The historical Jesus does not appear in the *kerygma*, any more than my Jesus book is *kerygma*';[32] or, 'Only the preaching of the community, in which the person of Jesus belongs, is "gospel" (= *kerygma*); not the preaching of the historical Jesus which I have described in my book' (in a letter of 1926).

What is the difference? Is it that Jesus claimed none of the messianic titles, 'Christ', 'Son of Man', 'Son of God', 'Saviour', 'Son of David', 'Lord', for himself? It is in fact Bultmann's view that Jesus claimed none of these titles for himself. But he does not think that this fact is significant: 'While it is true that Jesus did not demand faith in his own person, he did demand faith in his Word. That is, he made his appearance in the consciousness that God had sent him in the last hour of the world. But this means that the decision to which he summons men by his proclamation is the definitive decision; that precisely the fact that he now summons men to repentance is the final proof of God's grace; that his coming is God's grace in the last hour; that in so far as anyone hears his Word, God's salvation is now freely offered to him. Indeed, Jesus demands

---

[30] 'Das Verhältnis der urchristlichen Christusbotschaft', p. 22 (*The Historical Jesus and the Kerygmatic Christ*, p. 37).
[31] ibid., p. 23 (ibid.). [32] *Kerygma und Mythos*, I, p. 133.

decision with reference to his ministry (Matt. 11.4–6; Luke 12.8 f.; 11.31 f.). If Paul, like the earliest community, saw the Messiah in Jesus, he did nothing other than affirm Jesus' own claim that man's destiny is decided with reference to his person.'[33] According to Bultmann, one can therefore say 'that Jesus' appearance and his proclamation imply a christology in so far as he called for a decision over against his person as the bearer of the Word of God, a decision determining salvation or destruction. The community's confession as given in the *kerygma* would then have to be understood as the explication of the answer to the question of decision, of the obedience which recognizes God's revelation in Jesus.'[34]

But here the last distinction seems to disappear; for the fact that Jesus said nothing about his death and resurrection as the saving event—as Bultmann is convinced—does not mean anything, if with Bultmann one does not see the cross and Easter event as 'objective saving facts', but as the origin of the event of proclamation.

In that case, how can Bultmann's attitude to the problem of the historical Jesus still be justified?

We must remember that Bultmann, as we saw, is against any objective guarantee for the saving event. God's saving act occurs only as Word and is recognized as saving act only in answer to the Word; to enquire behind the Word, especially if it serves to guarantee the saving event, puts the saving event itself in question, because the saving event does not lie behind the Word, but takes place in the Word. According to Bultmann, then, any search for the historical Jesus behind the biblical *kerygma* is illegitimate *theology*. I have not to ask what happened then, but the Word which took its origin then—in whatever way it did!—asks me today how things are with me now.

[33] 'Jesus und Paulus', pp. 82 f. (*Existence and Faith*, pp. 195 f.).
[34] 'Das Verhältnis der urchristlichen Christusbotschaft', p. 16 (*The Historical Jesus and the Kerygmatic Christ*, p. 28).

This verdict would hold even if there were no problems in the investigation of the historical Jesus as a historical question and it led to objectively assured results; for the basis and object of beliefs are not objective facts, but the address of the *kerygma*. As it happens, of course, the historical investigation of Jesus does not lead to historically indisputable results, as experience shows. Bultmann remonstrates with the liberal Life-of-Jesus theology, and this objection applies to any quest of the historical Jesus: 'Historical investigation cannot lead to any result which might serve as a foundation for faith, for all its results have only relative validity. How different are all the liberal pictures of Jesus, how uncertain his features really are! Can we still recognize him? Research ends here with a question mark—and that is where it *ought to* end!';[35] namely, because this would grasp the nature of the saving event more appropriately. Historical scholarship can lead only to a *historical* encounter with the man Jesus, but the 'salvation of the world', 'the *Kyrios Christos* occurs only in the *kerygma* of the church'[36] which preaches Jesus Christ crucified and risen.

Even if a historical investigation were to show that the *kerygma* is in complete continuity with the preaching of the historical Jesus, this investigation would remain *theologically* unproductive because as a step back behind the *kerygma* it already puts the saving event in question as such. Furthermore, *any* result achieved is involved in historical relativity which cannot and may not appropriate the saving event, and is in any case inappropriate to it as word-event.

These notions are completely convincing in the total structure of Bultmann's theology. But are they also based on the Bible? Bultmann claims to do theology on the basis of the New Testament. His theology is meant to be biblical theology. Its standard cannot be inner consistency; it must be congruent with Scripture. What does the New Testament say? Is the

---

[35] *Glauben und Verstehen*, I, p. 3.
[36] *Kerygma und Mythos*, I, p. 134.

New Testament also interested only in the *kerygma* of Jesus as the Christ? Does it refrain—at least in practice—from enquiring after the historical Jesus? Bultmann raises this question, and replies: in fact, the New Testament, too, is not interested in the historical Jesus. 'Paul and John, each in his own way, indicate that we do not *need* to go beyond the "that". *Paul* proclaims the incarnate, crucified and risen Lord; that is, his *kerygma* requires only the "that" of the life of Jesus and the fact of his crucifixion. He does not hold before his hearer's eyes a portrait of Jesus, the human person, apart from the cross (Gal. 3.1), and the cross is not regarded from a biographical standpoint but as saving event. The obedience and self-emptying of Christ of which he speaks (Phil. 2.6–9; Rom. 15.3; II Cor. 8.9) are attitudes of the pre-existent and not of the historical Jesus. The eschatological and ethical preaching of the historical Jesus plays no role in Paul. *John* gives all due emphasis to the humanity of Jesus, but presents none of the characteristics of Jesus' humanity which could be gleaned, for example, from the synoptic Gospels. The decisive thing is simply the "that".'[37] Thus: 'Neither Paul nor John communicate a historic encounter with the historic Jesus.'[38] Jesus' authentic preaching is irrelevant to both.

But what about *the synoptic Gospels*? As is well known, Bultmann draws the material for his Jesus book from them. Do they not then communicate an encounter with the historical Jesus? They do so, Bultmann thinks, 'if they are read with a view to historical inquiry, *but not in their original intention*'.[39] True, Bultmann's Jesus book is written on the basis of the synoptic Gospels, but it does not accord with their intention; for the Gosepls are meant to be *kerygma*, whereas Bultmann's Jesus book is not *kerygma*, according to the stated intention of its author. In his verdict on the self-understanding of the

[37] 'Das Verhältnis der urchristlichen Christusbotschaft', p. 9 (*The Historical Jesus and the Kerygmatic Christ*, p. 20).
[38] *Kerygma und Mythos*, I, p. 133.   [39] ibid.

synoptic Gospels, Bultmann follows Martin Kähler, who attacked the liberal picture of Jesus as long ago as 1892 in an article entitled 'The so-called historical Jesus and the historic, biblical Christ', which was long forgotten, but noticed again a great deal after the breakthrough of dialectical theology. Its basic theme is that we do not possess sufficient sources for a life of Jesus, because the Bible itself and as a whole was not interested in the historical Jesus; for—as Kähler writes—'the real Christ is the preached Christ'. The intention of the Gospels, too, is simply to proclaim the Lord of faith in the garb of the historical Jesus. The traditions of the historical Jesus were only significant for early Christianity in so far as they could be the ingredients of the *kerygma*. They were selected, shaped and formed in the light of faith in the crucified and risen one. Words of the exalted one, testimonies of the spirit, confessions of faith as well as authentic Jesus-material determine the picture of Jesus given by the first three evangelists. The apparently historical Jesus of the Gospel tradition is in fact the exalted Lord experienced as present in early Christianity. After his work on the *History of the Synoptic Tradition*, Bultmann had no further doubts about this position, which is widely recognized today. The historical enquiry into Jesus thus reveals itself as contrary to the intention of the synoptic Gospels in the very light of their self-understanding.

Bultmann is thus convinced that he is on the same ground as the New Testament when he turns away from encounter with the historical Jesus 'towards encounter only with the proclaimed Christ, who encounters me in the *kerygma*'.[40] In his investigation of *Primitive Christianity in its Contemporary Setting*,[41] Bultmann does not therefore deal with the preaching of Jesus in the section on primitive Christianity but in that on late Judaism, and in his *Theology of the New Testament*,[42] the

[40] ibid., p. 134.
[41] *Das Urchristentum*, pp. 67 ff. (*Primitive Christianity*, pp. 84 ff.).
[42] *Theologie*, pp. 1 ff. (*Theology*, I, pp. 3 ff.).

preaching of Jesus is discussed among the *presuppositions* of New Testament theology. 'For New Testament theology consists in the unfolding of those ideas by means of which Christian faith makes sure of its own object, basis and consequences. But Christian faith did not exist until there was a Christian *kerygma*; i.e. a *kerygma* proclaiming Jesus Christ—specifically Jesus Christ the crucified and risen one—to be God's eschatological act of salvation. He was first so proclaimed in the *kerygma* of the earliest church, not in the message of the historical Jesus, even though that Church frequently introduced into its account of Jesus' message motifs of its own proclamation. Thus, theological thinking—the theology of the New Testament—begins with the *kerygma* of the earliest church and not before. But the fact that Jesus had appeared and the message which he had proclaimed were, of course, among its historical presuppositions; and for this reason Jesus' message cannot be omitted from the delineation of New Testament theology.'[43]

If this also answers the question why *Bultmann* does not look for the historical Jesus behind the *kerygma*, and justifies this attitude on the basis of the Bible, there still remains the question how far a difference can be construed between the preaching of Jesus and the *kerygma* about him. But now this question is no longer to be put to Bultmann, but to the New Testament. Starting from the situation we have described, that the *kerygma* of Jesus is contained *in nuce* in Jesus' preaching, Bultmann himself formulates this question in the following way: 'If the proclamation (and activity) of Jesus confronts the hearer with a decision and discloses for him the possibility of a new existence, why cannot the apostolic preaching simply be limited to repeating the proclamation of Jesus? Why could the message about Christ in fact totally disregard any repetition,

[43] ibid., p. 1 (ibid., p. 3).

as Paul and John indicate? Furthermore, if a genuine interpretation of history makes the "now" of yesterday the "now" of today, if for that reason the historian, on the basis of his existential encounter with Jesus' history, can lead his hearers (or readers) to a situation where they must decide for or against him, then has not the Christ-kerygma lost its meaning, has it not become superfluous?'[44]

Bultmann answers his question: 'The solution to the problem lies in the fact that the *kerygma* has changed the "once" of the historical Jesus into the "once-for-all". In other words, the earliest community (with ever-greater clarity) understood the history of Jesus as the decisive eschatological event which as such can never become mere past but remains present, and does so, of course, in proclamation. . . . If the mere "repetition" of Jesus' preaching—whether it be through the tradition elaborated in the synoptic Gospels or through modern historiography—makes the past present in such a way that it confronts the hearers (or readers) with the decision for (or against) a possibility of self-understanding disclosed in the proclamation of the historical Jesus, then the Christ-kerygma demands faith in the Jesus who is present in it and who did not merely promise salvation, as the historical Jesus did, but actually brought it. All the attempts to indicate that the historical Jesus saw the appearance of the time of salvation in his activity cannot deceive us over the basic difference between his preaching and the Christ-kerygma, a difference which Paul and John have made clear. It is clear that we cannot retroject the "if anyone is in Christ, he is a new creation; the old has passed away, behold the new has come" (II Cor. 5.17) into the preaching of the historical Jesus any more than we can retroject the Johannine "now is the judgment of this world" (John 12.31; cf. 3.19) . . . into that preaching. . . . Only now is this faith present; only now can Jesus' death and

[44] 'Das Verhältnis der urchristlichen Christusbotschaft', pp. 23 f. (*The Historical Jesus and the Kerygmatic Christ*, pp. 38 f.).

resurrection be proclaimed as the saving events which inaugurate the new aeon.'[45]

That, then, according to Bultmann, is the real difference between the preaching of the historical Jesus and the *kerygma* about him, and makes it clear that the proclaimer became the proclaimed: 'Jesus looks to the future and points his hearers to the *coming* reign of God, which, to be sure, is coming even now, is already breaking in. Paul, on the other hand, looks back and points to what has already occurred. For him the turn of the age has already taken place, the day of salvation is already present! . . . God has already done the decisive thing, and even now the faithful have the possibility of being new creatures and belonging to the new world.'[46]

Bultmann warns against interpreting the new element in the *kerygma*, compared with the historical Jesus, wrongly, by means of the idea of development beloved of the history of religions school. For Paul is concerned 'not with the development of theological concepts and ideologies', 'but with providing the grounds for a judgment: the situation of the world is fundamentally different, is a new one, since Jesus came'. The important thing is not that Paul possibly developed the concept of the Messiah further; it is much more important that 'he asserts that the Messiah was here, that Jesus is the Messiah'.[47] Bultmann's 'negative' attitude to the question of the historical Jesus is thus significantly a piece of his often noticed (and occasionally criticized!) 'orthodoxy', which makes him emphatically assert the reality and once-for-allness of the saving act of God: God has acted once for all for man's salvation, that is the gospel. But the historical Jesus does not speak of this saving event as having taken place; he waits for it. It is the *kerygma* that speaks of Jesus as the incarnate, crucified and risen one.

[45] ibid., pp. 25 f. (ibid., p. 40).
[46] 'Jesus und Paulus', p. 84 (*Existence and Faith*, pp. 196 f.).
[47] *Glauben und Verstehen*, 1, p. 202.

After a long journey, we have now come to the goal of the present chapter. I hope that Bultmann's position within the discussion of the problem of the historical Jesus has become clear; whatever one may feel about it, it is consistent within the framework of Bultmann's theology. The reason for describing the present chapter as an *appendix* to the previous ones, which dealt with the saving event, has now been given: Bultmann's solution of the problem of the historical Jesus does not allow the 'historical Jesus' to be included in the saving event to which the *kerygma* bears witness; but this solution is only understandable when it is seen in its close connection with the question of the nature and right understanding of the saving act of God in Christ. At the same time, at the end of this chapter we have once again come up against the phenomenon of the saving event, so central for Bultmann, which occupied us in the previous chapters. God has acted; the time of salvation is the present; in faith the new creation takes place here and now.

We shall be devoting a whole chapter, the last, to this present reference of the *kerygma* and the way in which it makes salvation present in faith. There the relationship between the *kerygma* and the historical Jesus which we have just discussed will come up for discussion again in a more intensive way. But first it seems sensible to examine in some detail the 'hermeneutical problem', through which Bultmann has become known to a wider public—for the famous and notorious programme of demythologization is a special problem of hermeneutics.

IO

The Problem of Hermeneutics:
General Considerations

BULTMANN has become known beyond the circle of professional theologians above all through his demand for the demythologizing of the New Testament. The programme of demythologizing is, however, only a partial aspect of the wider problem of hermeneutics. In this chapter, therefore, we must look at the problem of hermeneutics in general, as it presents itself to Bultmann. The following chapter will then consider demythologizing, which represents for Bultmann a particularly characteristic side of hermeneutical concern for the New Testament.

Hermeneutics is the science of understanding. As a technical term, the word 'hermeneutics' is relatively recent; it only comes to the fore in the eighteenth century. The matter which it describes is, of course, older. Naturally, no clear limits can be set to hermeneutics as the science of understanding. Heidegger, for example, speaks of the hermeneutics of existence, by which he means the analysis of this existence, in other words, the characteristic human mode of being as existence. This is the approach which he has presented in *Being and Time*. Wilhelm Dilthey, on the other hand, occasionally described hermeneutics as 'the art of understanding expressions of life fixed in writing'. That is a very narrow definition. It limits hermeneutics to *expressions* of life, and more particularly, to those that are fixed in writing. It does not even include the understanding of works of pictorial art. Dilthey himself sees that with this definition he stands in the Christian tradition, for which hermeneutical concern—though not under this name—during the whole of the Middle Ages was directed towards the exegesis of biblical texts.

It is clear why such a narrow understanding of hermeneutics is generally to be found in Bultmann. As a New Testament scholar, he is concerned with the exegesis of texts, i.e. the texts of the New Testament, and he entertains no doubts at all about the principle of *sola scriptura*—scripture alone. Bultmann is a scriptural theologian. His theological work is strictly concerned with the exegesis of New Testament texts. That is a fact which this chapter cannot express sufficiently; it can only be indicated in particular instances. Otherwise we would go completely beyond the framework of this study. The present chapter cannot even explain how Bultmann's theological work is done as exegesis of the New Testament. Indeed, in view of its particular theme that is impossible, for the New Testament itself makes no reflections on hermeneutical questions and Bultmann, as we shall see later, is in any case convinced that there is not and cannot be a specifically theological hermeneutic. However, the mere fact that Bultmann is concerned in a particularly intensive way with the problem of hermeneutics is an impressive demonstration that his theology is meant to be textual interpretation, interpretation of the New Testament. That raises another question—as it were in parentheses: in Bultmann's view, what authority does the *text* have as a basis of proclamation? What is the significance of the canon of the New Testament for Bultmann's theology?

The historical problem of the origin of the canon is usually dealt with in an appendix to introductory work on the New Testament. Bultmann has paid no special attention to it. It is certain that he has found no occasion to make substantial corrections to the generally assured results of investigations into the history of the canon. We know that after a number of preliminary stages the formation of the canon began in the middle of the second century and was finished, in its essentials, a century later. In the selection of writings to be taken into the canon, the standard was their real or supposed apostolicity, based on the concept of the apostle in the later church, which included the twelve disciples of Jesus and Paul. The driving force towards the establishment of a normative canon of apostolic teaching was controversy with heretics, particularly the gnostics.

Later theology, not least Protestant orthodoxy, has sought to guarantee the authority of the canon by a more or less mechanical doctrine of inspiration. Such a theory of inspiration is no longer tenable today. Moreover, introductory work on the New Testament has shown that a large number of New Testament writings are not of apostolic origin. The scope and authority of the canon thus becomes questionable, or needs a new justification.

Why does Bultmann not think to question the canon as such and its binding authority as a text? The answer must be that for Bultmann the New Testament has the character of Word, that it is *kerygma*, the Word of God.

We have already dealt in some detail with Bultmann's understanding of the Word of God. For Bultmann, the word is not the vehicle of a content which could in principle be separated from its bearer; the biblical word is not a vessel for the saving event which has happened elsewhere. Word and saving event, rather, form a unity. Salvation takes place in the Word, which is itself the saving event. The Word does not communicate general truths; it is the decisive call to the man who, when he hears the call, is 'in the truth'.

'To hear the Scriptures as the Word of God means to hear them as a word which is addressed to me, as *kerygma*, as a proclamation.'[1] 'Proclamation is address, and authoritative

---

[1] *Jesus Christ and Mythology*, p. 71.

address at that, the address of the Word of God which is paradoxically spoken by a man, the preacher. He stands over against the community as the representative of God (cf. II Cor. 5.20). He does not speak as its mouthpiece and does not bring to consciousness or clarity whatever ideals or feelings, longings or even unexpressed certainties may slumber on in his hearers',[2] but directs a message to them which comes from beyond men. This state of affairs is produced by the *text* as the pre-existing basis of preaching, for 'the address of the Christian proclamation is something that a man cannot say to himself. He must always let it be said to him—said again and again.'[3] That the sermon 'has as its text a word of Scripture and consists in the interpretation of that word marks it out as proclamation'.[4] Of course, 'the mere fact that a sermon consists in the interpretation of Scripture provides no guarantee that it does not simply expound general truths',[5] but both text and sermon are misunderstood if they are taken to be 'general truths'. At the same time, the significance of the New Testament canon is also misunderstood; it is, or rather, in each several occasion of preaching becomes, binding only as a *text* and acquires its unconditional authority as *text*. It must be understood that 'the idea of the canon is intended to guarantee the contingent character of revelation and to guard against the misconception that revelation is merely a matter of generally evident truths or the faith of pious individuals.'[6] In Bultmann's view, then, the canon cannot be surrendered because its presence establishes and maintains the uniqueness of God's action apart from all possibilities of human reason or faith. As a product of history, the canon shows that 'the living word of God is never a word of human wisdom but an event encountered in history. The fact that it originates in a historical event

---

[2] *Glauben und Verstehen*, 3, p. 166.
[3] ibid., p. 170.
[4] ibid., p. 167.   [5] ibid.
[6] 'Das Problem einer theologischen Exegese', p. 356.

provides the credentials for its utterance on each specific occasion.'[7]

Such an understanding, of course, reverses the traditional orthodox understanding of the relationship of Word and canon. The canon is not the norm for the Word in that the Word receives its authority from the inspired canon. The canon has authority only because and in so far as it is Word. It receives its credentials from the Word and as a result it is sometimes also interpreted critically. According to Bultmann, this transposition is necessary because historical-critical investigation of the New Testament has shown that the canon is simply not in a position to be the *norm* of the Word as a Word of God; so many different voices are to be heard in the canon that it is the basis for a multiplicity of confessions rather than the unity of the Church. Above all, this transposition is appropriate because the Word cannot be legitimated by anything, even the canon; as the Word of God, the Word has its authority only through faith, and itself lends the canon *its* authority. That this transposition makes the relationship of Word and canon (or text) a dialectic one becomes clear as soon as one remembers that without the canon there is, in fact, no word.

All this, of course, is well said and stands in the Reformed tradition. Luther himself, to whom Bultmann appeals, was quite familiar with critical assessment of the canon in the light of the Word, that is, in the light of Christ. For example, in his preface to the Epistle of James, he writes: 'The true touchstone for testing every book is to discover whether it emphasizes the prominence of Christ or not. What does not teach Christ is not apostolic, not even if taught by Peter or Paul. On the other hand, what does preach Christ is apostolic, even if Judas, Annas, Pilate or Herod does it.' What for Luther 'emphasizes the prominence of Christ', Bultmann calls the 'saving event', the 'Word'. The New Testament canon is authoritative because and in so far as it 'emphasizes the prominence of Christ'.

[7] *Kerygma und Mythos*, II, pp. 204 f. (*Kerygma and Myth*, p. 207).

The question then, of course, arises whether it is not fortuitously authoritative. The Word was there before the canon. Nor, if we look at the problem in principle, is it even assigned to the canon, which is itself only a historically conditioned expression of the Word. There was already the Word when there was no canon. The individual writings of the canon, which are all older than the canon itself, are evidence of that. In principle, then, there can be Word without the canon, and no special authority can be attributed to the canon over and above other manifestations of the Word.

Indeed we can go further: does not the canon, and thus the text of the canon, in practice conceal the fact that the Word is the divine saving event only as the word which addresses me on each several occasion, the very fact which, according to Bultmann, the text and canon are meant to guarantee? For I meet the Bible first as a historical document, as an object for my consideration, which I approach at a distance of almost two thousand years. That means that I meet it as a book which cannot immediately become a word of address, because for contemporary man it is more or less incomprehensible. Who today, for example, can still read the original of a Pauline Epistle and understand it?

Writing about the first problem. Bultmann suggests that the Word—in principle—is not exclusively the word of the canon. It can encounter me in many ways, as we saw in the last chapter, 'either in the Church's proclamation, or in the Bible as this has been handed down to me through the Church as the Word of God addressed to me, or through the word of my fellow Christian',[8] in other words, through any direct 'pastoral' word, perhaps even through an act of love. Here the encounter by means of the Bible is obviously the most problematical; for this encounter must first, in Bultmann's words, be communicated to me through the Church which directs my attention to documents of the past as the Word of God which addresses me.

[8] ibid., p. 204 (ibid.).

In reality, however, the Word is present as the word of the Bible in *all* the encounters that have been mentioned. That, quite simply, is our historical situation, which we cannot and need not transcend. The Church is not only the Church of the Word but the Church of the word of the Bible, and the theologian who is directed to the Word of God which he is to interpret is in fact directed to the word of the Bible. The proclamation of the Church, too, is always renewed by this biblical word, and so is any pastoral word in the community. Thus in one way or another, faith grows 'out of encounter with the Holy Scriptures as the Word of God'.[9]

As far as Bultmann is concerned, this actual situation 'settles the question whether one should interpret Augustine, Luther, Schleiermacher or even the Bhagavadgita in the same way as the New Testament. If I am thinking theoretically, and thus see myself in an abstract situation without any tradition, it makes no difference which I choose. But whether hearing in faith can be realized in such interpretation is a question which cannot be decided in principle.'[10] Each person is thus free to ignore the Christian tradition, which points to the Bible in the expectation and with the promise that 'words of life' are to be heard there. But in the Church there is no occasion to deny the canon if one wants to preach the Word.

Now if the canon of the New Testament remains in practice the indispensable form of the Word, i.e. the saving event, the first problem still remains, too. In other words, there is still the difficulty of understanding this word spoken in a time long past; there is still the task of making such understanding possible; there is still the demand for concern about an appropriate hermeneutic.

What is referred to in the New Testament is not an 'everyday' matter but the once-for-allness of the divine saving act. Must there then not be a special, specifically theological her-

[9] *Jesus Christ and Mythology*, p. 71.
[10] 'Das Problem einer theologischen Exegese', p. 353.

meneutic to correspond with it? Or should not the theologian at least bring special *personal* presuppositions to the proper investigation of the New Testament? These questions, which are still quite controversial in theology today, are answered by Bultmann with a clear-cut 'no'. He writes: 'The work of the exegete is not theological by virtue of its presuppositions and its methods, but by virtue of its subject, the New Testament. Its character as theology consists in the fact that the church has directed it to the New Testament, which it is to explain. The work of the exegete is not made theological by what he can do on the basis of his presuppositions, his method, or even his inspiration. The scholarly investigation of the New Testament is as secular as the investigation of any other historical source. The New Testament itself bears the responsibility for the theological character of this work, and this work serves the New Testament alone. What the investigator contributes is secular—only the Word that is written there is sacred!'[11]

The Word itself and only the Word is holy. It does not obtain this holiness from some personal or material quality of the exegete. The exegete therefore merely has the task of disclosing the understanding of his text with the *best possible* method. But in order to discover the best hermeneutical method, the interpreter is thrown back on the results of general hermeneutical science: for 'the interpretation of biblical writings is not subject to conditions different from those applying to all other kinds of literature'.[12]

In 1950, in a celebrated article on 'The Problem of Hermeneutics', a theme with which Bultmann has concerned himself on a number of occasions,[13] Bultmann investigated the presuppositions and ways of understanding historical phenomena in general, and in particular the possibility of understanding texts as expressions of life fixed in writing. His view is that

---

[11] *Glauben und Verstehen*, 1, p. 133.
[12] *Glauben und Verstehen*, 2, p. 231 (*Essays*, p. 256).
[13] ibid., pp. 211 ff. (ibid., pp. 234 ff.).

it must be the aim of all attempts at understanding to achieve an 'objective' understanding of singular historical existence, that is, an understanding which can lay claim to being generally understood and can therefore be fixed and communicated.

'Philology is the science which has for its object the interpretation of literary texts, and which for this purpose makes use of hermeneutics.'[14] Since Aristotle, it has developed particular rules of hermeneutics, 'which have become traditional and are followed throughout as a foregone conclusion'.[15] Bultmann cites the following indispensable rules for understanding a text:

1. A literary work must be analysed in respect of its construction and style so that the details can be understood in the light of the whole work and the whole work in the light of the details.

2. In the interpretation of texts in a foreign language, the rules of grammar must be observed.

3. The individual terminology of an author must be noted if one is to understand what *he* has to say; for the interpreter will not necessarily attach the same meanings to concepts as does his text.

4. To obtain an adequate understanding of particular expressions, one must take into account the terminology of the period and the environment of the author.

5. As all literary documents are historically conditioned, and thus belong to their time, as wide a knowledge as possible of the relevant historical circumstances is a necessary presupposition for proper interpretation.

According to Bultmann, even the establishment of such hermeneutical rules does not clarify the process of understanding sufficiently. This was already seen by Friedrich Schleiermacher and Wilhelm Dilthey, whose contributions to the problem of hermeneutics are thought by Bultmann to be particularly important. Schleiermacher sets great store by the

[14] ibid., p. 213 (ibid., p. 236).   [15] ibid., p. 212 (ibid., p. 235).

view that a literary document is an expression of a particular moment in the life of a particular man. In his view, therefore, one can only understand such a document if one follows through the process of the production of this document in a sympathetic way. One must so to speak put oneself in the author's place in order to be his understanding interpreter. That is possible because 'the social life of men for purposes of speech and understanding' is formed 'on the basis of general human nature', as Schleiermacher asserts, following Winckelmann and Herder. Bultmann quotes Dilthey here, who takes up Schleiermacher's thought: 'Exegesis is a work of personal art, and its most consummate execution is conditioned by the originality of the exegete; yet it rests on affinity intensified by a thorough-going communion with the author—by constant study.'[16]

At this point Bultmann's own contribution to the clarification of the problem of hermeneutics, partly resulting from his encounter with Heidegger, begins. He agrees in principle with Schleiermacher and Dilthey. But he asks whether their 'psychological' method of interpretation is valid for *all* texts. Its validity for philosophical and poetical texts is clear. But are, for example, 'The inscriptions of the Egyptian kings, telling of their deeds of war . . . understandable only on the basis of their translation into the inner, creative process in which they arose?'[17] Obviously not. At any rate, not if one is investigating the texts for the historical facts reported in them, which is usually the case. But one *can* also ask what 'life feeling' or understanding of existence—whether of the king as inaugurator, or of the actual author, or of the whole epoch—is indirectly expressed in such inscriptions. From this standpoint, the hermeneutical rules of Schleiermacher and Dilthey are once again valid. It follows from this that any success in understanding 'is

[16] ibid., pp. 214 f. (ibid., p. 238).
[17] ibid., p. 215 (ibid., pp. 238 f.).

constantly orientated to a particular enquiry, a particular *objective*.[18] The question guiding the interpreter is part of the process of interpretation; it determines both the process of understanding and the text, in so far as it seeks to understand it in respect of a particular matter.

The manner of investigation, its 'objective', is largely guided by the text which is the object of the enquiry; the question is shaped by the intention of the text; the interpreter asks what the text is meant to communicate. However, the interpreter can also approach the text with a question which the text itself was not written to answer. A text which is meant to communicate details about particular historical events may also, for example, be investigated with a view to finding out how its author and his time approached historical events in general. The 'objective' of enquiry into a particular text is thus many-sided. It can be guided 'by interest in the reconstruction of the context of past history', or 'by psychological interest', or 'by aesthetic interest, which subjects the texts to a formal analysis'.[19] Religious, philosophical and poetical texts above all provoke from their own self-understanding the question of human Being as peculiar to each man. The 'objective' of interpretation can also be (and in the kind of texts just mentioned primarily indeed is) provided 'by interest in history as the sphere of life in which human existence moves, in which it attains its possibilities and develops them, and in reflection upon which it attains understanding of itself and of its own particular potentialities'.[20] Thus, as has already been said, this question of the possibilities of human existence can also be put to texts which themselves, for example, claim only to be historical documents.

The existentialist approach which we have just examined was largely suppressed in the period of 'historicism', when the texts were used primarily as sources for reconstructing past

---

[18] ibid., p. 216 (ibid., p. 239).
[19] ibid., pp. 227 f. (ibid., pp. 252 f.).
[20] ibid., p. 228 (ibid., pp. 252 f.).

times—a possible and legitimate approach, but obviously only a provisional one. Dilthey's efforts succeeded in regaining that understanding which reveals the possibilities of human existence displayed in the text and leads the interpreter to understand himself. Bultmann thinks that this is the sense in which Heidegger has shed decisive new light on the problem. In this context, he refers to *Being and Time*, paras. 31 f., but as early as 1925, on the basis of his collaboration with Heidegger, he had described this 'hermeneutical principle' in an article on 'The Problem of a Theological Exegesis of the New Testament': when the exegete puts to a text the question of the possibilities of human being expressed in it in an *authentic* way, he starts from the fact that his own existence is not assured and therefore is not at his disposal. Accordingly, he does not have control over the text to the extent that he would be in a position to assess at a distance the possibilities of the understanding of existence which are contained in it. Rather, the exegete who regards human existence as problematical, insecure and thus not at the disposal of man himself, goes to the text ready 'to hear questions which mean a decision to hear the claim of a text as an authority which has to be the basis of a decision'.[21]

From all that has been said so far it becomes clear how for Bultmann the questioning with which the exegete approaches his text is an essential part of the act of understanding (in which it goes without saying that 'the framing of the questions must not be allowed to prejudice the content of the object of the enquiry, that it should not anticipate particular results of exegesis'[22]). So wherever one sees Bultmann in hermeneutical reflection, one comes across the formula 'the objective of interpretation', which is also called 'the hermeneutical principle' or 'the perspective of the exegete'.

Immediately connected with this is another concept which occurs regularly and is significant for Bultmann's hermeneutic,

[21] 'Das Problem einer theologischen Exegese', p. 343.
[22] *Kerygma und Mythos*, II, p. 191 (*Kerygma and Myth*, p. 191).

that of *pre-understanding*, occasionally also described as 'unconscious knowledge'. If every interpretation is directed by a particular set of questions, an 'objective', it is always accompanied by a pre-understanding of the matter, which forms the basis of the enquiry into the text. Only 'on the basis of such a pre-understanding is the formulation of a set of questions and an interpretation at all possible';[23] for an 'objective' of the enquiry is inconceivable without a certain knowledge of the subject of the enquiry. Otherwise one could not ask at all! If, for instance, I want to learn something about 'love' as a possibility of human existence from a text, I must already have *some* understanding of love. That is a pre-understanding which can be confirmed, enlarged, modified, corrected, made more radical by an understanding of the text, so that the understanding achieved in the interpretation is not unrelated to the pre-understanding which is already present in the questioning.

If, therefore, we are looking for the possibilities of human existence which are expressed in a text, this question, too, 'is always guided by a preliminary understanding of "human being", by a particular understanding of existence, which may be very naïve, but which in the end is the only means of providing the categories that make an investigation possible—for example, the question of "salvation", of the "meaning" of personal life, or of the "meaning" of history, of the ethical norms of action, the order of human community life and suchlike. Without such a pre-understanding and the questions initiated by it, the texts are mute. It is of no value to eliminate the pre-understanding: on the contrary, it is to be brought into our consciousness and critically tested in our understanding of the text, it is to be put to the test. In short, it is valid in the investigation of the text to allow oneself to be examined by the text, and to hear the claim it makes.'[24]

[23] *Glauben und Verstehen*, 2, p. 216 (*Essays*, p. 239).
[24] ibid., p. 228 (ibid., pp. 253 f.).

It goes without saying that neither the pre-understanding nor the set of questions guiding the interpretation on any given occasion must be consciously grasped or explicated in conceptual terms. Unfortunately it also goes without saying that the pre-understanding is not always understood as such, and is often confused with a final understanding. Where this happens, *true* questioning is no longer possible; for anyone who has reached a final understanding can only ask as a spectator who measures his enquiry against the understanding that he already possesses, and no longer allows his own understanding to be put in question.

Though there may often be definitive understanding—why, for example, should not 'Caesar's murder or Luther's nailing up of his theses'[25] be clearly datable?—this is never possible with texts which do not impart information, but are intended to be addrooo or become address through the manner in which they are approached. In such texts a decision is demanded. Authentic understanding then takes place only in decision, 'because in the text the exegete encounters a claim, i.e. is there offered a self-understanding that he can accept . . . or reject, and therefore is faced with the demand for decision. Even in the case of a no, however, the understanding is a legitimate one, i.e. is a genuine answer to the question of the text, which is not to be refuted by argument because it is an existential decision.'[26] Such *authentic* understanding can never be final, because existential understanding must always be achieved anew. I can, of course, describe this existential understanding, or its object, the address of the text, in a conceptual way, and such exegesis of the text can, at any rate in a definite historical situation, also lay claim to general comprehensibility; but by the standards of the *authentic* understanding of a text that addresses me, any such objective exegesis is merely pre-understanding. I gain authentic understanding

25 *Glauben und Verstehen*, 3, p. 148 (*Existence and Faith*, p. 295).
26 ibid., p. 149 (ibid., p. 296).

only in the decision which is to be made on each particular
occasion.

Now for Bultmann it follows from the concept of pre-
understanding or from the necessary 'objective' of the enquiry,
that to point, with Schleiermacher and Dilthey, to the common
basis of all individual humanity is not a sufficient account of
the conditions for the possibility of understanding. Rather, the
possibility of understanding is only given when author and
interpreter have a *life-relationship to the matter* which is there
to an equal degree in the statement and in the questioning. It
is therefore necessary to 'consider the simple fact that the
presupposition for understanding is the interpreter's life-
relationship to the *matter* which is directly or indirectly
expressed in the text'.[27] If there is no life-relationship between
the matter expressed in a text and the interpreter, no hermeneutical method can disclose an understanding of the
matter. Anyone who is, say, tone deaf and has no kind of
acquaintance with music will not really be able to understand
a text dealing with music. A word in a text in a foreign language which describes something totally alien to the experience
of the translator cannot be translated, but must be left as a
foreign word. All exegesis is thus determined by the fact that
'interpreter and author live as men in the same historical
world, in which human Being occurs as Being in an environment, in understanding intercourse with objects and our fellow
men'.[28]

Everyone has a pre-understanding of the matter which is
expressed directly or indirectly in most *texts*—the reality of
human experience. 'I can evade this knowledge, conceal it from
myself, forget it; but I still have it;'[29] for 'we know—whether
consciously or unconsciously—our possibilities, because it is
part of our life to know what we are'.[30] Because that is so, I can

[27] *Glauben und Verstehen*, 2, p. 217 (*Essays*, p. 241).
[28] ibid., p. 219 (ibid., p. 243).
[29] *Glauben und Verstehen*, 1, p. 128.   [30] ibid., p. 126.

understand texts with reference to myself, that is, from time to time I can have disclosed possibilities of existence by texts which deal with human life.

If one considers the *matter* involved, one may say with Bultmann, as we have already seen, that there is 'objective' knowledge even of 'historical' phenomena, that is, of those which concern human existence. The concept of objectivity used here is not, of course, to be understood wrongly in a scientific sense ('in which, moreover, it may have become problematical today even in the traditional sense').[31] The intention of science is to grasp its objects as they are in themselves; the achievement of this knowledge is quite independent of the person of the scientist. But 'historical' phenomena, texts, for example, are fundamentally different from natural objects. They speak only for the subject who grasps them in a living way, who can understand them in this way only because he is bound up with them in his own historical life. Thus 'subjectivity' may not be excluded for 'objective' understanding, but must be developed to the highest degree. 'Historical' texts in the above-mentioned sense can *only* be understood 'subjectively', i.e. existentially, if they are to be understood *authentically*. Anyone who 'interrogates the texts with reference to the possibilities of human being as his own being', understands the text only if the basis of his enquiry is human existence lived to the fullest. 'The "most subjective" interpretation is in this case the "most objective", that is, only those who are stirred by the question of their own existence can hear the claim which the text makes.'[32] Only in existential encounter does the text disclose itself to authentic understanding and leave the realm of pre-understanding. It is therefore true that 'history precisely in its objective content can only be understood by a subject who is existentially moved and alive'.[33] For 'we do not stand

[31] *Glauben und Verstehen*, 2, p. 229 (*Essays*, p. 254).
[32] ibid., p. 230 (ibid., p. 256).
[33] *Glauben und Verstehen*, 3, p. 147 (*Existence and Faith*, p. 294).

outside historical forces as neutral observers; we are ourselves moved by them; and only when we are ready to listen to the demand which history makes on us do we understand at all what history is about.'[34]

The more 'authentic' the understanding is, the more 'objective' it is able to be. Understanding is 'objective' in being appropriate to the *matter* under investigation—a demand which obviously could not be made if all understanding of all human expressions of life rested only on the individual humanity which bound together author and interpreter—and all 'questioning leads, if the interpretation is methodically carried out, to unambiguous, objective understanding'.[35] The fact that the objective result of the interpretation remains open for correction and improvement, that it is gained in a dispute of opinions, that it is utterly bound up with the limitations of each exegete, still does not leave the possibility of objective understanding open to doubt.

The interpreter whose interrogation of a text is prompted by existential concern must reckon with hearing the text anew in each new situation. The old word will have a new meaning. 'Always anew it will tell him who he, man, is and he will always have to express this word in a new conceptuality.'[36] Objective existential understanding thus shares in the 'historicity' of existential understanding. It is not timeless, definitive, when it arises out of existential concern. This fact without question intensifies the clash of opinions, but it cannot in itself throw into doubt the possibility of objective understanding as such.

To sum up: according to Bultmann, all understanding of a text is guided by the '*objective*' of the enquiry. It thus presupposes a *pre-understanding* of the subject under investigation. It is—even as 'objective' understanding—possible, because (and if) author and interpreter have a *life-relationship to the*

[34] *Jesus*, p. 7 (*Jesus and the Word*, p. 11).
[35] *Glauben und Verstehen*, 2, p. 220 (*Essays*, p. 254).
[36] *Glauben und Verstehen*, 3, p. 150 (*Existence and Faith*, p. 296).

matter under investigation.

According to Bultmann, these hermeneutical principles are to be applied even to the interpretation of the New Testament.

First of all, that means that without a definite interrogation, an *'objective'*, even the Bible remains dumb. What sort of interrogation is appropriate for the Bible? Evidently not that of historical, psychological or aesthetic curiosity, though these may well be satisfied by the Bible and are justified within a limited framework. According to Bultmann, if it is true that 'our approach to and interpretation of all historical documents', is motivated by the possibility of using these documents 'to realize consciously the possibilities they afford for the understanding of human existence', then this applies even more strongly in the case of the Bible, because 'the Church's proclamation refers me to the scriptures as the place where I shall hear things about my own existence which vitally concern me'.[37] Or: 'I think our interest is really to hear what the Bible has to say for our actual present, to hear what is the truth about our life and about our soul.'[38] Anyone who interrogates the New Testament in an authentic way 'expects that from this source the questioner will hear something about himself—or, better, something that is said *to* himself.'[39]

Now if one follows the self-understanding of biblical texts, a more exact description of the questioning appropriate to the Bible would be to say that the 'objective' of interpretation is 'the question about God, about God's revelation'.[40] But is a *pre-understanding* of this particular matter possible at all? Can I have a preliminary life-relationship to God and God's action? Bultmann claims that God is quite hidden from sinners; must he not then really answer this question with a 'no'? Not at all.

[37] *Kerygma und Mythos*, II, p. 194 (*Kerygma and Myth*, p. 192).
[38] *Jesus Christ and Mythology*, p. 52.
[39] *Glauben und Verstehen*, 3, p. 5 (*Existence and Faith*, p. 62).
[40] *Glauben und Verstehen*, 2, p. 233 (*Essays*, p. 259).

For Bultmann, to put the question about God means to put the question about the truth of human existence. So because man is concerned with the question of his own existence, he has a pre-understanding of God. 'Man's life is moved by the search for God because it is always moved, consciously or unconsciously, by the question about his own personal existence. The question of God and the question of myself are identical.'[41] 'In human existence an existential knowledge about God is alive in the form of the question of "happiness", "salvation", the meaning of the world and of history, the authenticity of each person's particular being. If the right to designate such questions as the question of God is only granted by belief in God's revelation—the phenomenon as such is the relation of the matter to the revelation.'[42] Or, quite briefly: 'Even the natural man can talk of God, because he knows of God in his existence.'[43] Simply by knowing the limitations to his existence, man has a pre-understanding of God, of which Bultmann sometimes speaks under the heading of 'natural theology', a term which is, of course, used in an untraditional way.[44] Bultmann is fond of quoting 'Augustine's classical remark' as an indication that human life—consciously or unconsciously—is moved by the question of God: 'Thou hast made us for Thyself, and our heart is restless, until it rests in Thee.'[45] To have a pre-understanding of God therefore does not mean 'that the exegete must know everything possible about God, but rather that he is moved by the existential question of God—regardless of the form that this question actually takes in his consciousness (say, for example, as the question concerning "salvation", or escape from death, or certainty in the face of a constantly shifting destiny, or truth in the midst of a world that is a riddle to him)'.[46] In this sense, even the atheist has a

[41] *Jesus Christ and Mythology*, p. 53.
[42] *Glauben und Verstehen*, 2, p. 233 (*Essays*, pp. 257 f.).
[43] *Glauben und Verstehen*, 1, p. 304.   [44] ibid., p. 311.
[45] e.g. *Kerygma und Mythos*, II, p. 192 (*Kerygma and Myth*, p. 192).
[46] *Glauben und Verstehen*, 3, p. 149 (*Existence and Faith*, p. 296).

pre-understanding of God, though only the believer knows that it is a pre-understanding of *God*.

In the same way, there is a pre-understanding of God's *action* or revelation. Of course, I can only know what God's action *really* is when God *has* acted towards *me*. But we all know the term 'action', and we can also know what it may mean to talk of God's action—'as distinct from man's action, or from natural events'[47]—even without existential experience of divine action, even if we expressly deny such action; and doubtless every religion speaks in some way of the action of God. If anyone investigates the revelation of God in the New Testament, this 'question is guided by a certain understanding of the concept of revelation. . . . If one were to ask, for example, what the New Testament understands by marriage or the state, then some understanding of marriage and the state would be presupposed—i.e. an understanding that would guide the question and apart from which it could not be asked. Thus what the New Testament understands by revelation can only be asked if we ourselves have some idea of what we understand by it—if we already have a concept of revelation.'[48] The very knowledge of man's limitations which is awakened, or at least made comprehensible, by the question of the possibility of God's revelatory action would be such a pre-understanding.

The pre-understanding of God and his action is often corrected and made more radical by exegesis of the New Testament. If, for example, God appears in the pre-understanding as an object of human thought, say as the supreme entity, exposition of the New Testament concept of God makes it clear that God can never be object. Or if one understands God's action in his revelation to be the communication of doctrines otherwise unknown, the New Testament shows that God's action is rightly understood only when it *happens* to me and makes me a new creature. Once this last insight has been

[47] *Glauben und Verstehen*, 2, p. 234 (*Essays*, p. 257).
[48] *Glauben und Verstehen*, 3, p. 1 (*Existence and Faith*, p. 58).

achieved, it is immediately clear that *all* exegesis, 'all explication must remain in the realm of pre-understanding and that the radicalizing really takes place only when what is said in the New Testament is truly heard',[49] that means, when the understanding has become a self-understanding, which reveals itself to me only as I grasp the potentiality of myself disclosed in the proclamation, a knowledge 'that is only real in the act of faith and love'.[50] This 'existential' knowledge can, of course, be explained theologically, and it *is* explained theologically in the exposition of the text. So Bultmann can write: 'What "revelation" means in general cannot be any more exactly and completely specified by the man of faith than any man of unfaith.'[51] But correct though this explicit knowledge may be, it is still only a pre-understanding, as the *authentic* understanding of God can never be neutral or reserved to the consciousness. It is true only 'when the *act* of faith is realized in it, when the *resolve* to exist in faith is carried through to the end'.[52] An authentic understanding of the New Testament is always a matter of decision. The believer understands 'that revelation *has* encountered him, that he really lives, that he *is in fact* graced, that he *is* forgiven'.[53]

Authentic understanding of the New Testament, like pre-understanding—and indeed the pre-understanding based on authentic understanding and fashioned in the form of a theological expression—is possible if and because the hearers or interpreters have *a life-relationship to the matter* with which the New Testament is concerned. Without such a life-relationship there is no pre-understanding of the matter and therefore no 'objective' for the investigation of the text which makes it speak and makes its understanding possible.

[49] ibid., p. 35 (ibid., p. 90).   [50] ibid., p. 32 (ibid., p. 88).
[51] 'Die Geschichtlichkeit des Daseins', p. 351 (*Existence and Faith*, p. 100).   [52] *Glauben und Verstehen*, 3, p. 32 (ibid., p. 88).
[53] 'Die Geschichtlichkeit des Daseins', p. 352 (*Existence and Faith*, p. 100).

Now the *matter* of the Bible is revelation, God's action in such a way 'that the Bible not only *shows* me, like other historical documents, a possible way of understanding my own existence, a way which I am free to accept or reject; more than that, it becomes a word which addresses me personally, which *gives* me existence'.[54] If that is so, does not the uniqueness of the matter of the New Testament contradict Bultmann's assertion that the appropriate hermeneutical method for the exposition of the New Testament is the same as that which is also appropriate for profane texts? Not at all, for the uniqueness, the 'holiness' of the Word cannot be discovered by a particular method: but only through acknowledgement. I can, however, make that biblical claim understandable as such; I can demonstrate how the Bible regards human existence as totally fallen and proclaims God's saving action to be the freeing of men from this fallenness. I can understand the matter intended in the Bible and thus pre-understand the decision of faith.

Now such pre-understanding is again—at least in principle—possible as an objective scientific understanding, which must be achieved through exegetical discussion. This situation, on which the possibility of New Testament theology as a scientific discipline is based, and its significance for Bultmann are vividly expressed in the title which Bultmann has given to his systematic-theological articles, published in four volumes since 1933: *Faith and Understanding*. It is as significant here that faith is put in first place as it is that faith and understanding are connected. According to Bultmann, the mysterious character of faith does not lie in the fact that something mysterious, incomprehensible, is 'believed'—that is a quite absurd concept of faith as far as he is concerned—but that the existence of faith, which understands itself and its subject completely, is grounded from beyond itself. This is the very situation which New Testament theology elaborates in a scientific way.

[54] *Kerygma und Mythos*, II, p. 191 (*Kerygma and Myth*, p. 192).

Academic theological understanding needs a set of concepts appropriate to its subject matter, and a set of anthropological concepts at that; for it is only possible to speak of God if we speak of man. Consequently academic theology 'has to concern itself with the relevant concepts in which human existence may be spoken of'.[55] 'If it is true that the right questions are concerned with the possibilities of understanding human existence, then it is necessary to discover the adequate conceptions by which such understanding is to be expressed.'[56] We know that in Bultmann's view this is the task of philosophy, which makes human existence an object for contemplation and that Bultmann regards Heidegger's philosophy of existence as the 'right' philosophy, because in the present intellectual situation this 'offers the most adequate perspective and conceptions for understanding human existence'.[57] Of course, even for Bultmann there is never 'a right philosophy in the sense of an absolutely perfect system';[58] for 'objective' insights are not to be confused with a timeless system. But precisely because the question of the 'right' philosophy keeps being raised all over again, this question is answerable in principle on each particular occasion.

In all this it is taken for granted that not every Christian needs to be a theologian and to be able to fix his understanding of the word of God conceptually in objective form. Theology as such is not engaged in 'simply listening to what the New Testament says—which is directed towards an existential understanding of the self, and not towards an existentialist knowledge'.[59] The person engaged in this simple listening need not be directly conscious of an indirect connection with theological work. Such indirect dependence is, of course, there. Without continued theological work the Bible today

---

[55] *Glauben und Verstehen*, 2, p. 232 (*Essays*, p. 258).
[56] *Jesus Christ and Mythology*, p. 54.
[57] ibid., p. 63 (ibid., p. 55).   [58] ibid.
[59] *Glauben und Verstehen*, 2, p. 232 (*Essays*, p. 258).

would be a dumb, incomprehensible book and in a situation like ours, 'in which the understanding of Scripture has become uncertain and disputed, in which proclamation has become liable to misunderstanding and even incomprehensible, in which the reproduction of traditional statements of belief is thought to be the language of faith, there is need for reflection, attention to the conceptuality appropriate for exegesis, proclamation and confession. To accomplish this is the task of theology, and particularly of hermeneutics:'[60] for hermeneutics is the real work of theology.

This last remark explains why the central ideas of Bultmann's theology are concentrated and brought to a focal position in his reflections on hermeneutics.

The hermeneutical principle of the 'objective' of the investigation in principle represents the transcending of the subject-object pattern: the most subjective investigation of the text is the most objective. The fact that there can be a pre-understanding of God was a radical indication that if a man wants to speak of the transcendent God, he must speak of human existence. The concept of the *authentic* understanding of the New Testament presupposed the proclamation of a contingent act of God. The explanation of the theological undertaking to grasp conceptually the understanding of a text led to the problem of the relationship of theology and philosophy.

It is still necessary to clarify some particular problems in this context, because they are important for Bultmann's hermeneutics.

First of all, the concept of *the hermeneutical circle*. This circle results from the fact that all understanding presupposes a pre-understanding, i.e., that the answer is in a certain way determined by the question, but that on the other hand it corrects the question. Without pre-understanding there would be no understanding, and all understanding leads in turn to a new pre-understanding, makes

[60] *Kerygma und Mythos*, II, p. 188.

243

possible a new investigation of the text. Authentic, existential understanding rests on existential questioning and leads to new existentialist pre-understanding—possibly made more radical, corrected or extended. 'Thus in the end the question of the possibility of understanding a text depends on the openness of the exegete to his possibility of existence as a human possibility, on the interpretation the exegete has of himself *qua* man.'[61]

The hermeneutical circle is a presupposition of understanding. *All* 'historical' understanding moves in this circle. It would be otherwise only if I had finally understood myself and what encounters me and merely needed to understand everything new that came to me by measuring it against what I had definitively understood. But, as we have seen, there is no definitive understanding either in the sphere of existentialist understanding or in the sphere of existential understanding. For existential understanding is *per definitionem* always new understanding: it is never knowledge possessed, because it is a decision to be made on each several occasion. Existentialist knowledge also needs to be expressed afresh in each new situation, just as new enquiries must be made of the text as times change. The hermeneutical circle is therefore unavoidable, and Martin Heidegger rightly says: 'What is decisive is not to get out of the circle, but to come into it the right way.'[62]

This circle is drawn very provisionally, and even outside the existentialist pattern of questioning when—whatever the investigation may be—attempts are made to interpret a text from itself by attempting 'to understand the details from the whole work and the whole work from the details',[63] or when a question of authenticity is decided on the basis of the author's terminology, although this terminology must itself be discovered from the texts under investigation. It is also true, for example, that 'the individual phenomenon is on the one hand comprehensible on the basis of its age (and environment) and on the other hand is itself a precondition to making this comprehensible'.[64] We also move in a hermeneutical circle when the 'objective' of the interpretation is guided by the purpose of the text, although this purpose is really disclosed only during the course of the investigation. The hermeneutical circle is grasped radically only when one has understood that authentic understanding always moves in a

---

[61] 'Das Problem einer theologischen Exegese', p. 341.
[62] Heidegger, *Sein und Zeit*, p. 153 (*Being and Time*, p. 195).
[63] *Glauben und Verstehen*, 2, p. 213 (*Essays*, p. 236).
[64] ibid., p. 223 (ibid., pp. 247 f.).

circle with existentialist pre-understanding and that one can therefore say of theology: 'The demand to say once and for all and unambiguously what the Word of God is must be rejected because it rests on the idea that it is possible to designate a complex of statements that can be found and understood with respect to their "content". To be sure, what is meant by "Word of God" can be clarified in a formal way: but precisely this formal clarification tells us that no "content" of the Word of God can be conclusively exhibited, but rather can only be heard in the immediate moment.'[65]

The hermeneutical circle becomes particularly important for Bultmann in the *Sachkritik* which he practises on texts in general and even on the New Testament. This term, which introduces us to the second problem of detail, is often completely misunderstood. It is suggested that Bultmann's intention is to criticize the matter of the New Testament, the 'Word'. But Bultmann expressly attacks the kind of *Sachkritik* that pretends to have control over the truth before the critic encounters the text: 'Confronted with this, one can only be surprised why it bothers to interpret a text for other readers in anti-quarian terms. It knows everything better than the text, so why does it summon the reader to the New Testament at all?'[66]

For Bultmann, *Sachkritik* is rather a criticism 'which distinguishes between what is said and what is meant and measures what is said by what is meant'.[67] *Sachkritik* is therefore 'the consistent application of a basic principle which is held to be correct: understanding the text in the light of subject matter. The subject matter must be used as a standard for assessing how far this subject matter has been given adequate expression in all the words and sentences of the text. . . . It is impossible to presuppose that it must have been expressed adequately all through the text unless one wants to establish a modern dogma of inspiration. . . . In fact, I believe that such criticism can only serve to clarify the matter;'[68] for in Bultmann's opinion no man, not even Paul or John, 'always speaks only about the matter in hand'.[69]

In that case, this *Sachkritik* inevitably moves in a hermeneutical circle; for the '*Sachkritik* demanded by exegesis can take as its standard only what is disclosed through the text, over which it has no control'.[70] It comes to the subject matter only through what has been said and measures what has been said against the subject matter.

---

[65] *Glauben und Verstehen*, 3, p. 34 (*Existence and Faith*, p. 91).
[66] 'Das Problem einer theologischen Exegese', p. 340.   [67] ibid.
[68] 'Karl Barths *Römerbrief*', pp. 372 f.   [69] ibid., p. 373.
[70] 'Das Problem einer theologischen Exegese', p. 340.

'That means that it never arrives at generally valid principles as "results", but is constantly in living movement.'[71] Thus the same conditions apply to *Sachkritik* as to the criticism of the canon discussed at the beginning of this chapter. The latter is itself *Sachkritik* and as a hermeneutical principle already confronted Luther with the question of what 'emphasizes Christ'.

To conclude with, I should point out that Bultmann's hermeneutical method has been vigorously criticized by Karl Barth, i.e. from the standpoint of the dialectical theology which they have in common. This criticism is principally directed against the concept of 'pre-understanding', introduced by Bultmann, behind which Karl Barth and his pupils see the resurrection of central themes from liberal theology which they had once joined in overcoming. Liberal theology saw the immediate presence of the divine in human nature. Revelation could thus attach itself to the divine element in man, cleanse it, purify it and take it further. Dialectical theology countered this with the recognition that revelation is a contingent event from beyond all human nature, wholly different, miraculous, so that man can only experience the divine action as one who is overcome, who is presented with a gift. Is not this recognition, which presupposes the radical fallenness of man, denied by Bultmann's concept of pre-understanding?

In an article about 'Point of Contact and Conflict' (1946), Bultmann replies with an unmistakable 'no': 'God's action towards man through his word has no point of contact in man. . . . God's action first brings to nothing the man it seeks to make alive. God's action conflicts with man, particularly with man in his religion, in which he seeks to safeguard himself and to assert himself over against the world which oppresses him, and in which he wants to soothe his cares and fears. . . . For man, God's grace is grace in such a thoroughgoing sense that it supports the whole of man's existence, and can only be understood as grace by those who surrender their whole existence and let themselves fall into the unfathomable, dizzy depths without seeking any support. The revelation of God is God's conflict with man in his religion. Only such proclamation as allows this conflict to become known in all its acuteness can be authentic Christian proclamation.'[72]

But, Bultmann now feels, 'The conflict must actually be *understood*

[71] ibid.
[72] *Glauben und Verstehen*, 2, pp. 119 f. (*Essays*, pp. 135 f.).

as a conflict, and must not strike the ear as something incomprehensible.'[73] In that case, however, it would be senseless 'to proclaim the Word of God in the same form everywhere. Just as it must be proclaimed to peoples speaking foreign tongues in their own language, so it must in any case be translated into the language understandable at any given time to man—and basically to every individual man.'[74] Wherever I proclaim the word of God rightly, I proclaim it in the language of the hearer, and indeed, as the Christian proclamation is concerned with human existence, in the words in which any given hearer expresses his understanding of existence. As language always presupposes understanding, so language about human existence presupposes an understanding of human existence which reveals itself in the face of revelation as pre-understanding. This pre-understanding which expresses itself in human language 'is the point of contact for the word of God spoken by the human preacher',[75] and Bultmann feels that it is irresponsible for the preacher not to take account of this fact:

'It would be senseless and irresponsible if the preacher were to ignore the fact that man's understanding of himself can take very diverse forms; that it can be naïve or well considered, dogmatically rigid or unstable and agitated, frivolous or serious; that man may be unresponsive to the question of his existence or stimulated by it. Certain it is that God's conflict affects all men, and *God* has no points of contact in man. The serious-minded man stands no nearer to him than the frivolous man. He can make his Word accessible to the self-satisfied and the impenitent man in the same moment as to the man who strives and is simply a problem to himself. He can call the wanton man to himself today, and let the man who "ever striving takes great pains" wait. But *we* are not God and we do not have to perform miracles. We are men, and we have to inquire conscientiously and with an awareness of our responsibility into the possibilities which give scope for our work.'[76]

We therefore have to investigate the pre-understanding of human existence in each particular context so that our word may be as understandable as possible and we may create—humanly speaking—possibilities for God's word to prevail against men as a radical contradiction.

In the above-mentioned article, Bultmann demonstrates

[73] ibid., p. 121 (ibid., p. 137).
[74] ibid.   [75] ibid.
[76] ibid., pp. 121 f. (ibid., p. 138).

how the New Testament finds a point of contact in the interpretation of human existence current at the time of its writing, in popular philosophy, in the mystery religions and in Gnosticism. In this way he sets out to show how proclamation today, if it is really to be proclamation, must find a point of contact in current religious or secular interpretations of existence.

As a result of this, we can see quite clearly the interest which guides Bultmann throughout his discussion of the problem of hermeneutics: in looking for an appropriate understanding of the New Testament and pointing the way to such an understanding, it is his intention to serve preaching. Whether, or how far, he succeeds, is a question which we need not discuss here. But the intention of his work is unmistakable. It also governs the working out of the particular hermeneutical problem which, under the catchword 'demythologizing', has done more than all his other work to make Bultmann known.

I I

The Problem of Hermeneutics: Demythologizing

WE ENDED THE previous chapter with the statement that Bultmann is interested in the problem of hermeneutics, the problem of understanding in general, because he wants to understand the *New Testament* and make it understandable. It was clear from this that his discussion of hermeneutical questions was thus meant to serve proclamation, and that this was also true of 'demythologizing', that particular aspect of the problem of hermeneutics through which Bultmann gained a reputation reaching far beyond theological circles in the period after the second World War. I believe that an account of Bultmann's programme of demythologizing can leave no doubt about this intention.

An impressive indication of Bultmann's concern to serve the Church's proclamation with his demand for demythologizing can be seen in the audience before which he deliberately chose to deliver his famous remarks on demythologizing. He lectured on this theme on April 21, 1941, to pastors of the Confessing Church in Frankfurt. His article bore the title: 'New Testament and Mythology (The problem of demythologizing the New Testament proclamation)'. It was published in 1941 in the 'Beiträge zur Evangelischen Theologie' by Christian Kaiser Verlag in Munich, a press sympathetic to the Confessing Church; this series continued the work of the banned periodical

249

Evangelische Theologie. Discussion of Bultmann's theses, which was very vigorous even during the war, thus took place within the 'Confessing Church', of which Bultmann counted himself a member, as a conversation *within the church*, expressing a common concern to find the right form of preaching. This was in accord with Bultmann's intention; his desire was for a discussion *within* the church which was at the same time within the *church*.

It is not altogether surprising that this soon ceased to be the case, and that Bultmann was regularly branded as a heretic, once his article had become widely known and regular church authorities had again been constituted after 1945. The surprising thing is that it was only this particular article which involved Bultmann in a crossfire of conflicting views. For the article does not propose any new programme, but merely sums up in a systematic way what Bultmann had been teaching and publishing for twenty years. *All* his work had been 'demythologizing', even when this term did not occur. His theology had always been a consistently demythologizing theology. The 1941 article was therefore by no means a landmark in Bultmann's theological development.

We too have seen demythologizing in action in all the previous chapters, so in dealing with it systematically we shall not be discovering anything fundamentally new about Bultmann's theology.

First of all we must discover the sense in which Bultmann uses the word myth. In doing this we shall be ignoring the discussion which has been (and will continue to be) carried on over Bultmann's *concept* of myth. Bultmann has been accused of having an incorrect concept of myth, and it has even been argued that once this has been established the problem of demythologizing may be regarded as settled. Whether Bultmann's definition of what is 'mythological' is generally correct or universally convincing is, however, unimportant for our discussion. The only important thing is to know what Bultmann means by 'myth'. Anyone who finds the term 'myth' inappropriate for what Bultmann is talking about can introduce another term in its place. What Bultmann means is not affected. So Bultmann can concede: 'Anyone who regards my concept of myth as questionable and wants to understand something else by myth is at liberty to do so.'[1]

As a definition of his concept of myth, he writes: 'I use the term myth in the sense which is usual in the study of history and religion.'[2] 'Mythology is a way of representing the otherworldly in terms of this world, the divine in terms of human life, the "beyond" in terms of this side.'[3] Myth thus speaks 'of the other world in terms of this world and of the gods in terms derived from human life'.[4] This definition is not intended by Bultmann in a paradoxical way. It is not that the historical, worldly event of the cross of Christ is the action of the God 'beyond'. Myth sees a direct intervention of divine, supernatural and superhuman powers *between* historical events. The divine activity is thus imagined to be analogous to human, earthly activity.

An example may make the meaning clearer. For mythological thought, a 'miracle' is a divine action 'which intervenes in nature, in history or the life of the soul',[5] in such a way that on the one hand it becomes itself a natural event, open to direct observation and thus objectively perceptible, while on the other hand it breaks through the normal course of events, because the divine power is 'superior in incalculability and force'[6] to this-worldly powers. Thus for mythological thinking, God's power and activity can be perceived in inexplicable historical events. 'Other-worldly causality is introduced into the causal chain of worldly events, and a power which does miracles in this sense is for good or ill thought of as a worldly

[1] *Kerygma und Mythos*, II, p. 180.   [2] ibid.
[3] *Kerygma und Mythos*, I, p. 22 (*Kerygma and Myth*, p. 10).
[4] ibid.   [5] *Ibid.*, II, p. 196 (ibid., p. 197).   [6] ibid., p. 183.

power and projected on to the plane of worldly events. Myth speaks of gods in the same way as of men, of their actions as of human actions, with the difference that it imagines the gods to be endowed with superhuman power and their actions to be incalculable, capable of breaking through the natural course of things. It makes the gods (or God) into men of superior power, and it also does this when it speaks of God's omnipotence and omniscience, because it distinguishes this quantitatively rather than qualitatively, from human ability and knowledge.'[7] The supernatural is the natural to a superior degree.

Following the pattern of mythological thought, God's transcendence is conceived of as spatial distance. Thus the ancient world-picture is closely connected with myth: the world is a three-storied structure. Between heaven and the underworld lies the earth. Heaven is the abode of God, the underworld that of satanic powers. Divine and demonic forces make the earth the scene of their rule and activity. Thus the earth is 'more than the scene of natural, everyday events, of precautions and work which count on order and regularity';[8] the intervention of incalculable supernatural powers must always be reckoned with. Bultmann does not think that the ancient view of a three-storied world is necessarily mythological in itself. This was in fact the world-picture of ancient scientific cosmology. But in so far as it occurs in the context of mythical thought, it has to all intents and purposes been mythologized: 'for both the upper and the lower stories are thought of as "numinous" spheres',[9] that is, on the one hand as worldly and on the other hand as other-worldly.

That mythical thought is indeed connected with the old picture of the three-storied world is also clear from the fact that the replacement of mythological thinking by scientific understanding and the substitution of modern cosmology

[7] ibid., pp. 183 f.
[8] *Kerygma und Mythos*, I, p. 15 (*Kerygma and Myth*, p. 1).
[9] *Kerygma und Mythos*, II, p. 183, n. 2.

for the mediaeval world-picture took place at the same time.

For Bultmann, mythical thought stands in contrast to modern scientific thought. By setting the two ways of thinking over against each other he therefore attempts to clarify further the nature of myth. For scientific thought, and indeed for the natural sciences as well as history, the world and worldly events form a *closed* context set against the incalculable intervention of non-worldly forces. Scientific thought reckons with this 'closed context of cause and effect'.[10] It 'presupposes the unity of the world and the regular order of the make-up of the world and what takes place in it'.[11] Every hypothesis in scientific thought must be verified, and verified in a scientific way. Modern scientific thinking is convinced that all processes within the world can be verified on the basis of the world itself, at any rate in principle. Scientific thought is 'open' only in so far as 'its knowledge of the world and worldly events is always unfinished, incomplete'.[12] The world-picture of the natural sciences today is different from that of the nineteenth century; in some respects the causal law has been made relative. But that does not alter the method of scientific thought; it simply confirms it. 'Let us think simply of the newspapers. Have you read anywhere in them that political or social or economic events are performed by supernatural powers such as God, angels or demons? Such events are always ascribed to natural powers, or to good or bad will on the part of men, or to human wisdom and stupidity.'[13] For mythical thought, on the other hand, the world and world-events are open for, or, from the perspective of scientific thought, perforated by 'the intervention of powers from beyond'.[14]

'We are not only theoretically convinced that all happenings in the world take place according to certain norms, according to unalterable

[10] ibid., p. 180.   [11] ibid.   [12] ibid., p. 181.
[13] *Jesus Christ and Mythology*, p. 37.
[14] *Kerygma und Mythos*, II, p. 181.

laws, but in practice, too, in our work and affairs, we behave on the assumption that everything that happens has its natural cause and natural effect. In fact we could not carry on with our work, nor undertake responsibility for our doings, if it were otherwise, if we had to be prepared for the possibility that the continuity of cause and effect might suddenly and miraculously be broken. Naturally we are aware also that we have not always a comprehensive knowledge of the full scope of this continuity and cannot always securely calculate the effects of our deeds. We are aware that there are secret forces in the world of nature which we do not yet know and understand. That, however, does not mean that we believe in miracles; it means only that we reckon with the as yet unknown and uninvestigated. And science is constantly working at the investigation of the spheres of nature as yet unfathomed, at making known what is up to now unknown in order that our thinking and planning may be ever more securely based, that the world may pass ever more fully within our control.'[15]

The difference between mythical and scientific thought is, according to Bultmann, also clear in their respective assessments of personal human life. The 'modern' man, in so far as he has outgrown mythical thought, 'reckons his sensibility, thought and will his own'; he is conscious of 'his responsibility for himself and for his freedom'.[16] 'He can therefore only understand himself, even in his relationship to God, as a personal being who is addressed in his being as a person by God. In other words, he can only understand God's word and action as it approaches him and comes to meet him if it affects his personal existence, indeed if it becomes involved in it.'[17] Mythical thought is different. Here even man's personal life is open to the attack of powers from the beyond which ignore this personal existence. This happens, for example, in sacramentalism; for the basis of sacramentalism is the conception that man's spiritual life can be influenced by material means, which owe their effectiveness to substances not of this world.

[15] *Marburger Predigten*, p. 138 (*This World and the Beyond*, pp. 155 ff.).
[16] *Kerygma und Mythos*, II, p. 182.   [17] ibid.

The need for demythologizing stems from the fact that the New Testament was written at a time when mythical thought and the picture of a three-storied world associated with it still held sway, whereas modern man is dominated by scientific thought, to which we also owe the Copernican picture of the world. In Bultmann's view, our experience of the world and our ability to control it have advanced so far by means of science and technology that no-one can seriously maintain the mediaeval picture of the world and the mythological thought associated with it. 'Modern thought as we have inherited it through history provides us with a motive for criticizing the New Testament picture of the world.'[18] We cannot, he argues, ask men to acknowledge a different picture of the world from that given in their present historical situation. It is impossible 'to refurbish the mythical view of the world when all our thinking has been irrevocably shaped by modern science'.[19] Moreover, such a revival would be senseless, because mythological thought as such is not specifically Christian, but simply the thought of a past time which was still not dominated by the scientific way of thinking.

In view of this, Bultmann feels that it is quite arbitrary to accept New Testament mythology blindly, 'and to press for its acceptance as an article of faith would be to reduce Christian faith to the level of a human achievement. Wilhelm Hermann pointed this out many years ago, and one would have thought that his demonstration was conclusive. It would involve a sacrifice of the intellect which could have only one result—a curious form of schizophrenia and insincerity. It would mean accepting a view of the world in our faith and religion which we should deny in our everyday life. Modern thought as we have inherited it through history provides us with a motive for criticizing the New Testament view of the world.'[20]

The attitude of contemporary man to the mythological ideas

[18] *Kerygma und Mythos*, I, p. 17 (*Kerygma and Myth*, p. 4).
[19] ibid. (ibid., p. 3).   [20] ibid. (ibid., p. 4).

of the New Testament is thus different in principle from that of the people of New Testament times. For the latter, mythology formed an integral part of the current picture of the world and in general they did not see any occasion or possibility, still less any necessity, to opt out of it. They did not have to accept their mythological thought under compulsion, much less 'believe' it; it simply came to them as part of their historical situation. It was their rational, indeed (though it may seem primitive from our point of view) their 'scientific' way of thinking, by means of which they sought to interpret the riddle of their world and their life. For modern man, on the other hand, this way of thinking is obsolete, and he can only accept the conceptions associated with it if he abandons his historical situation.

As that is impossible, we find, according to Bultmann, a sort of schizophrenia in man. In questions of faith he detaches himself from his historical reality and regards this not inconsiderable effort of consciousness as the 'faith' which saves him. In that case, 'faith' is a matter of holding to be true a certain number of statements which contradict contemporary scientific thought, and the believer no longer realizes that this cannot be the faith to which the New Testament refers, because there would be no difficulty at all in 'believing' such statements in the New Testament period.

Alternatively, there is an unbelief which stems from the fact that the 'saving facts', put in mythological terms, and therefore Christian faith, are held to be unacceptable and thus out of date. A man comes up against the mythological expressions of scripture and thinks that he has found in them the scandal of the word of God which is contained in the Christian proclamation. But at this point he has still to be addressed in his own existence. Still less has he come up against the real offence, which is that: 'God's word calls man from all his anxiety and all his self-made security to God, and thus to his *authentic* existence.'[21]

[21] *Kerygma und Mythos*, II, p. 188.

Some of the examples used by Bultmann may clarify what has already been said.

To the mythological view of the world belongs the idea of a heaven to be situated spatially above the earth, which is the abode of God. The statements 'ascended into heaven' and 'descended into hell' present virtually no difficulties for such mythological thought. We no longer accept *this* heaven, and 'the same applies to hell in the sense of a mythical underworld beneath our feet'.[22] In view of this, it would be absurd to demand that Christian faith should frame its confession of the 'ascension' of Christ in such a way as to acknowledge the mythological view of the world bound up with this confession. Christian faith, as we saw, is not and cannot be faith in a past picture of the world; according to Bultmann it is liberation for radical openness to the future, in which God stands before us.

Mythological thought explained the puzzling elements in the world by means of its belief in spirits and demons whose supernatural powers, like the power of God, intervene directly in natural events and, with an effect like that of a natural cause, break through the comprehensible ordering of events. For example, evil is attributed to the Evil One. A 'miracle' in this sense was nothing unusual. Miracles are attested not only by the accounts of the Old and the New Testaments, but also by other accounts throughout antiquity. Both divine and demonic forces alike can perform such miracles. The point at issue was not *whether* there were miracles, but rather who did the greatest miracles, or whose miracles were done in the power of God and whose in the power of the demons. For modern thought, on the other hand, the world represents a closed context of cause and effect. Scientific thought does not allow for miracles. A machine which goes wrong is not exorcized, but repaired. 'Sickness and the cure of disease are likewise attributable to natural causation; they are

[22] *Kerygma und Mythos*, I, p. 17 (*Kerygma and Myth*, p. 4).

not the result of demonic activity or of evil spells.'[23] Anyone who, for example, sets out to explain the New Testament miracles in 'natural' terms, as has happened continuously since the time of rationalism, by referring to suggestion, to hypnotic influence, to deliberate deception, and so on, is merely confirming just how far thought has changed. We attempt to *explain* as yet unexplained processes in cosmic, physical or spiritual events; we do not derive them from uncontrollable supernatural forces. For modern thought, therefore, miracles are a thing of the past. They may not have been a problem for antiquity, but for the modern world they are inconceivable. Anyone who demands belief in the miraculous world of the New Testament and its time because he regards such belief to be the true attitude of Christian piety, should realize that believers in New Testament times could not achieve such a belief because the world of miracles was at the same time their 'scientific' world. He should also realize, thinks Bultmann, that in so doing 'he is making the Christian proclamation unintelligible and impossible for the modern world'.[24]

A third example: for Bultmann, the doctrine of vicarious satisfaction by the death of Christ is also steeped in mythological thought. This doctrine conceived of God's action in terms of the most primitive human ideas of guilt and righteousness. It imagines that God's attitude can be influenced by cultic acts. If one understands the doctrine in the light of ideas of sacrifice, according to which the performance of a sacrifice has some expiatory power, 'what a primitive mythology it is, that an incarnate divine Being should atone for the sins of men through his own blood!'[25] If one were to understand it in legal terms, and to explain 'the death of Christ as a transaction between God and man through which God's claims on man were satisfied, that would make sin a juridical matter; it would be no more than an external transgression of a commandment,

[23] ibid., p. 18 (ibid.).   [24] ibid. (ibid., p. 5).
[25] ibid., p. 20 (ibid., p. 7).

and it would make nonsense of all our ethical standards'.[26] In other words: the doctrine presupposes a historical situation which, with its cultic and juristic patterns of thought, no longer exists—not least because of the influence of the Christian faith itself. What the men of that time took over without reflection from their 'world', simply because it was there, has for our time become not only problematical but even incomprehensible; it can only be restored by an absurd decision which as such has no point of contact with real faith.

One last example: by 'spirit', the Greek understood a divine substance, which could be infused into man to heighten his natural capabilities. Scientific thought does not allow for such a spiritual substance; it is unable to detect it by experiment and the idea that the perceptions and decisions of personal existence could be influenced by such a substance is one which is quite alien to modern man's sense of life. So he no longer understands how sacramental food could communicate spiritual power simply by being eaten, how eating it unworthily could result in physical illness, how baptism with water could bring about a transformation of life, how baptism for the dead could be meaningful and how a virgin's conception by means of the spirit could be possible at all. The average man of the ancient world, on the other hand, took over all these ideas with his view of the world, so that they were essentially unproblematical for him.

It is therefore necessary to demythologize the New Testament message, because modern thought has done away with the mythological picture of the world which governs the New Testament. That is our fate, whether we like it or not, and so demythologizing is our task; for 'in the conflict between the objectifying thought of myth and the objectifying thought of science, the latter is unmistakably the victor'. In one sense, 'the modern picture of the world is the critical standard for the exegesis of Scripture'.[27] The question is, however, how we

[26] ibid. (ibid., p. 8).   [27] *Kerygma und Mythos*, II, p. 184.

are to apply this statement. Is it simply a matter of giving
the modern picture of the world its due? Bultmann disputes
this. His view is rather that it is the Christian faith which is
claiming *its* rightful due. Whether this is right can only be seen
from an investigation of the way in which Bultmann carries
out his programme of demythologizing.

What is the right way to demythologize? Not, according to
Bultmann, simply to *exclude myth*. Mythological thought forms
a unity. If we accept *one* mythological idea, say that of the
sacramental communication of spiritual or physical powers, we
have accepted mythological thought as such. In principle, it
does not much matter then which other mythological ideas we
take over or which we reject. Criticism of New Testament
mythology is made necessary, not by an excess of mythological
ideas, but by obsolete mythical *thinking* as such.

Should all mythological ideas therefore be *eliminated* completely? In this sense, demythologizing would be nothing new.
The problem of myth in the New Testament has long been
recognized, and a solution of the problem has frequently been
attempted. Bultmann himself wrote in 1941: 'All we have said
so far might have been said in much the same way thirty or
forty years ago, and it is really a sign of the bankruptcy of
contemporary theology that it has been necessary to go all over
the same ground again.'[28] The reason why he feels it necessary
to take up the problem all over again, starting from funda-
mentals, is that hitherto demythologizing has not been
attempted in critical theology in an appropriate form, because
the myth has been eliminated instead of being interpreted.

Thus the attempt at *allegorization*, made throughout church history, is seen to be itself a 'mythological', unscientific way of thinking,
but one through which the objective statements of ancient myth were
largely eliminated.
At the end of the eighteenth century, when the concept of myth

[28] *Kerygma und Mythos*, I, pp. 23 f. (*Kerygma and Myth*, p. 12).

was introduced into biblical scholarship, myth used to be regarded as a deliberate 'accommodation' on the part of Jesus and his disciples to the as yet unenlightened attitudes of their contemporaries. To eliminate myth completely in view of the enlightened thought of the present was therefore thought to be in accordance with the intentions of the New Testament writers.

Soon, however, it was recognized that the biblical writers were themselves indebted to this 'unenlightened' way of thinking, i.e. to the mythological world-view of their time, and did not adopt it deliberately or (with personal reservations) on tactical grounds. This made no difference to the verdict on myth: it had to be eliminated, and David Friedrich Strauss did this in a startling way in his *Life of Jesus*. His demythologizing was intended as a positive hermeneutical programme; the elimination of myth cleared the way for seeking and finding the truth of faith in the absolute Idea, understood in the sense of Hegel's philosophy.

The elimination of myth by liberal theology in reaction to Strauss was experienced by Bultmann himself in his student days. According to Bultmann, 'it was characteristic of the older liberal theologians that they regarded mythology as relative and temporary. Hence they thought they could safely eliminate it altogether and retain only the great basic principles of religions and ethics. They distinguished between shell and kernel.'[29] The kernel could be separated from the shell. It consisted in the great moral verities which could be seen in dominant religious personalities. By concern with them, and above all with the moral preaching of Jesus, this kernel could be implanted in one's own soul. In this way the kingdom of God could be realized in the individual.

Even the history-of-religions school which flourished before the first World War and, according to Bultmann, 'was the first to discover the extent to which the New Testament is permeated by mythology',[30] regarded mythological ideas as incidental, unimportant. Its members saw the essentials of Christian faith in its 'religious life, the climax of which is the experience of mystical union with Christ, in whom God took symbolic form'.[31] Such religious feeling which is depicted in the cultic action of the community, is kindled and strengthened by the religious life within the New Testament, not by its objectifying mythological ideas.

[29] ibid., p. 24 (ibid., p. 13).
[30] ibid., p. 25 (ibid., p. 14).
[31] ibid.

Bultmann disputes the legitimacy of all these attempts to eliminate myth; for by excluding myth they also exclude the *kerygma* which, according to Bultmann, does not occur *alongside*, but *in*, the myth. The *kerygma* is not, of course, mystical religious experience, as with the history-of-religions school, or timeless truth, as with the liberal theologians, or the absolute Idea, as with David Friedrich Strauss, or the realization of eternal truths of reason, as with the men of the Enlightenment. The *kerygma* is rather the message of the decisive action of God in Christ. The New Testament 'speaks of an *event* by which God has brought about man's salvation'.[32]

Because this event is spoken of in mythological terms, the question arises whether this event and the person of Jesus, both of which are described in the New Testament in mythological terms, are nothing more than mythology. Can the *kerygma* be interpreted apart from mythology? 'Can we recover the truth of the *kerygma* for men who do not think in mythological terms without forfeiting its character as *kerygma*?'[33]

Hence Bultmann's decisive word in carrying out his programme of demythologizing; *interpretation*. Myth is not to be eliminated, but interpreted, expounded and understood.

This demythologizing interpretation is not to be confused with the radical rejection of mythological language. This rejection is not demanded unconditionally, for many mythological expressions in the Bible have long become metaphors and have lost their original mythical significance, sometimes even in biblical language itself. Bultmann points in particular to the language of the psalms, but he also asks: 'Who ... still understands the statement that God is creator in mythical terms? Who understands statements about the throne of God in heaven and Christ's sitting at his right hand in this way?'[34] 'Especially in the conception of God as Father the mythological sense vanished long ago.'[35] No-one still thinks in terms of a

[32] ibid.   [33] ibid., p. 26 (ibid., p. 15).
[34] *Kerygma und Mythos*, II, p. 186.
[35] *Jesus Christ and Mythology*, p. 69.

physical father. To speak of God as Father means rather to speak of his love, his concern for men, of his claim on us, his action on our behalf. Such language is no longer mythological; it bears witness to our concrete experience of the God who acts towards us. For that reason it is also not merely 'symbolic' language; it describe's God's real 'objective' action. Of course it is not direct language, either, for such language about the God who is never directly accessible to me is impossible. Bultmann terms this way of talking about God 'analogy', for here one 'assumes an analogy between the fellowship of God and man and that of man with man'.[36] According to Bultmann, thinking in analogy in this way is correct; for we can only speak of God's action *authentically* if this action has taken place in our life, if we have experienced God's love towards us, particular people. Such existential experience allows us to speak of the reality of the divine action towards man and at the same time makes such language 'analogy'. This language of 'analogy' is used and understood, quite spontaneously, in an unmythological sense. It *can* be used in this way because myth describes something which is not mythological, and it *may*, according to Bultmann, be used in this way because we cannot speak of God directly.

Now what does myth really mean? How is it to be interpreted? For it is clear that it may only be investigated with a view to understanding what it is meant to mean. Bultmann writes: 'Myth is an expression of man's conviction that the source and limit of the world in which he lives, i.e. the world which he knows and is at his disposal, are to be sought not in it but beyond it, and that this area which he knows and has at his disposal is perpetually dominated and threatened by the uncanny powers which are its source and limit. Myth is therefore also an expression of man's awareness that he is not lord of his own being. He is dependent not only within the known world, but more especially on those powers which hold sway beyond the confines of the known, and in this state of dependence he can be freed from the powers which he knows.'[37] That means that: 'The real purpose of myth is not to present an

[36] *Kerygma und Mythos*, II, p. 196 (*Kerygma and Myth*, p. 197).
[37] *Kerygma und Mythos*, I, pp. 22 f. (ibid., pp. 10 f.).

objective picture of the world as it is, but to express man's understanding of himself in the world in which he lives. Myth should be interpreted not cosmologically but anthropologically, or better still, existentialistically.'[38] In speaking of the other-worldly powers to which man is delivered as though they were worldly, objectifiable entities, in portraying, for example, the transcendent as something that is spatially distant, myth conceals its real intention from our thought and therefore contains within itself grounds for its own criticism. This criticism is practised by Bultmann as the *existentialist interpretation* of myth, i.e. an interpretation which discloses the significance of myth to be 'anthropological', that is, bearing on human existence.

It is therefore clear that the *concept* of 'demythologizing' is only a very inadequate expression of the hermeneutical purpose which is bound up with this concept. Bultmann himself calls it 'an unsatisfactory word, to be sure';[39] for it gives the impression that it is concerned with the elimination of myth. The formula 'existentialist interpretation', which occurs in Bultmann's article of 1941 (though not in the title) as well as in both earlier and later writings, is a more usual designation for the matter, and makes it clear that Bultmann's intention is to interpret myth, to understand it and make it comprehensible, because he is convinced that all myth has an existentialist purpose.

Let Bultmann himself speak again: 'Myth speaks of transcendent forces of demons and gods, as though they were powers on which man knows himself to be dependent, which are not at his control, whose favour he needs, whose wrath he fears. Myth expresses the knowledge that the world in which man has to live is full of riddles and mysteries, that human life itself is therefore also full of riddles and mysteries, and that man is not master of the world and of his life. Myth thus

[38] ibid., p. 22 (ibid., p. 10).
[39] *Jesus Christ and Mythology*, p. 18.

expresses *a particular understanding of human existence*. It knows—as is already indicated by the original connection of myth with the cult—another reality than that of the world, as it is investigated by science. It knows that the world and human life have their source and their limit in a power which lies beyond all that is within the realm of human calculation and control—in a transcendent power.'[40] Thus, for example, the statement that God dwells in heaven expresses 'in a crude manner'[41] the fact that God transcends the world. Or, the idea of Satan as ruler of the world is an expression of the 'deep insight' 'that evil is not only to be found here and there in the world, but that all particular evils make up one single power which in the last analysis grows from the very actions of men, which form an atmosphere, a spiritual tradition, which overwhelms every man. The consequences and effects of our sins become a power dominating us, and we cannot free ourselves from them.'[42]

All myth has such an existentialist significance, and so, too, does myth in the New Testament. Hence 'the importance of the New Testament mythology lies not in the objectifications which make up the content of its ideas but in the understanding of existence expressed in these ideas'.[43]

It is, indeed, the New Testament that makes it clear to Bultmann that such an understanding is demanded by myth itself. For the New Testament is full of mythological ideas which simply contradict each other, if one compares the objectifications in their imagery, though remarkably the contradiction does not destroy the New Testament. Thus, for example, the idea of the Virgin Birth, which occurs only in Matthew and Luke, cannot be reconciled with the idea of preexistence, and the belief in creation contradicts the designation of the devil as the 'prince of this world', etc.

---

[40] *Kerygma und Mythos*, II, p. 183.
[41] *Jesus Christ and Mythology*, p. 20.   [42] ibid., p. 19 (ibid., p. 21).
[43] *Kerygma und Mythos*, I, p. 23 (*Kerygma and Myth*, p. 11).

Moreover, a 'strange contradiction' runs through the New Testament as a whole: 'Sometimes we are told that human life is determined by cosmic forces, at others we are challenged to a decision; sometimes sin is regarded as a doom, at others it is regarded as a fault. . . . In short, man is sometimes regarded as a cosmic being, sometimes as an independent "I" for whom decision is a matter of life and death.'[44] In other words, the objectifying ideas of mythology are constantly accompanied by existentialist expressions in such a way that the latter form the standard for the interpretation of the former.

Hence, finally, it is understandable that 'attempts at demythologization are sometimes made even within the New Testament itself'.[45] This assertion of Bultmann's, which corresponds to his claim that modern scientific thought has its roots in the questions about 'origins' to be found in ancient philosophy, is evidently most appropriate for vindicating the need to undertake an existentialist interpretation of the New Testament myth. It is chiefly defended by Bultmann on the basis of the eschatology of the Fourth Gospel. As our last chapter will be devoted to the problem of eschatology in Bultmann's theology, we shall limit ourselves here to noting Bultmann's claim as it stands.

It cannot be our task here to deal in detail with the way in which the 'existentialist interpretation' of myth is worked out. Were we to do that, we would have to repeat all our previous remarks about Bultmann's theology as exegesis of the New Testament. 'Existentialist interpretation' is not just one part of Bultmann's theological work; his theology as a whole is worked out as existentialist interpretation. Methodological reflection on the right hermeneutical principles, i.e. raising and answering the question how the New Testament is to be interpreted, is *part* of his theological work. If it transpires—as it does for Bultmann—that the appropriate method for the

44 ibid. (ibid., pp. 11 f.).   45 ibid. (ibid., p. 12).

exposition of the New Testament is that of 'existentialist interpretation', then the interpretation as a whole will take the form of this existentialist interpretation.

It is hardly necessary to point out at this stage that *no* hermeneutical method, not even existentialist interpretation, is in a position to bring about faith. 'It goes without saying that an existentialist interpretation does not *produce* an existential relationship between the reader and the text; it merely discloses it. Nor does it *provide* a ground for the truth of scripture; it merely points to it and shows how to understand it. The existentialist interpretation of scripture does not even *provide* a ground for the proclamation of scripture; it provides it with the right concepts. Finally, it does not *provide a ground for* faith, but *shows* what the ground of faith is. In this way it can prevent faith from understanding itself wrongly.'[46] Faith is grounded only in an existential experience which, in traditional concepts, is the work of the Holy Spirit.

In any case, Bultmann by no means thinks that he has said the last word in his existentialist interpretation of the mythological conceptuality of the New Testament. He wants to avoid the impression 'that this is a light and easy task, as if all we have to do is to discover the right formula and finish the job on the spot. It is much more formidable than that. It cannot be done single-handed. It will tax the time and strength of a whole generation.'[47] Of course, as we know, Bultmann is convinced that in the conceptuality used by Martin Heidegger in his analysis of human existence in *Being and Time* he has found the language in which contemporary theology and contemporary proclamation can put their case as unmistakably as possible.

Accordingly, Bultmann describes Christian existence as authentic human existence. Authentic life is life in the moment, in radical openness for the future, and such openness is the

[46] *Kerygma und Mythos*, II, p. 189.
[47] *Kerygma und Mythos*, I, p. 26 (*Kerygma and Myth*, p. 15).

authentic possibility of human existence. Man, however, has always already surrendered this openness, has lost himself as his possibility, by falling victim to the 'they', by living from what is at his disposal. The ultimate depth of this fallenness becomes clear when man claims to be able to free himself from the sin of his fallenness with his own power. According to the New Testament, however, such deliverance of man for his authenticity takes place through an act of the love and grace of God. This unique saving act takes place wherever it is heard, in the Word of Jesus Christ, and the acknowledgement of this saving act in faith brings all human boasting to nothing.

We saw in the chapters on 'The Saving Event' how in the New Testament this saving event is largely described in the language and ideas of mythological thought, but at the same time we have inferred from Bultmann's interpretation of this saving event that New Testament myth is meant to be understood in a non-objective, existentialist way. Bultmann makes this particularly clear in his exposition of the Fourth Gospel, whose author deliberately demythologized the saving event: the saving event is the event of proclamation, which confronts me with the claim of the transcendent God, the source of my life which is not at my disposal. To search behind the word would be to bring the saving event to nothing, because God's saving action necessarily removes itself from objectifying investigation, and for that very reason confronts man radically in decision. God's saving act does not take place *between* worldly actions; it is a particular worldly action, indicated only by the word of proclamation, visible only to the eye of faith, grasped only by resolute obedience.

How far this account of Bultmann's makes sense, how far he has been able to make the saving event clear to us as *event* and as an event of *salvation for us*, how far, then, he has already met his own demand for demythologizing, which in his own words, claims the time and strength of a whole generation, must be left to the verdict of the individual.

To conclude this chapter of Bultmann's theology, however, it would be useful to consider in the short space available an actual example of existentialist interpretation. The one chosen is one which Bultmann himself occasionally uses as an illustration. In 1951, he was asked by some enlightened Swiss theologians to investigate whether the christological confession of the World Council of Churches, 'The World Council of Churches is composed of Churches which acknowledge Jesus Christ as God and Saviour', was in accord with the New Testament.

Can Jesus Christ be designated God? That was the question. The only certain passage in the New Testament in which such a designation occurs directly is John 20.28, where Thomas confesses, 'My Lord and my God'. Otherwise, in all his titles Jesus appears as being of divine nature and divine power, a reflection of the divine nature, say as Son of God, Kyrios or pre-existent Son of Man, but always subordinate to God. Throughout all this, there is never any doubt about his complete 'natural' humanity.

The question which is now raised is whether talk about the divinity of Jesus is meant to say anything about his 'nature', about Jesus 'as he is in himself'. Do the metaphysical titles of Jesus speak of his divine substance or of God's action in Jesus for me? In other words: does he help me because he is the 'natural' Son of God, or is he Son of God for me because he helps me?

The dogmatic theology of the ancient church, under the influence of Greek thought, gave the first 'mythological' answer in its doctrine of the two natures, which is still alien to the New Testament and 'impossible for our thought'.[48] We still stand in that tradition today. In Bultmann's view, however, for the New Testament—at least in its essential character

[48] *Glauben und Verstehen*, 2, p. 257 (*Essays*, p. 286).

—the statements about Jesus' divinity or deity 'are not meant to express his nature but his significance. These statements confess that what he says and what he is do not have their origin within the world: here are not human ideas or events within the world, but God speaks to us in them and acts towards us and for us. Christ is the power and wisdom of God; he became the wisdom of God, righteousness and sanctification and redemption for us (I Cor. 1.30).'[49] Bultmann substantiates this assertion by a number of examples, among others by the fact that in Paul, Christ also appears as judge alongside God, who is obviously the supreme judge of the world. 'It should be clear that Paul did not mean that we have to be responsible before two tribunals or even two persons; he is indicating that our responsibility before Christ is identical with our responsibility before God. God as judge becomes concrete for us in Christ: in him the judge of the world appears as our judge.'[50] Here Paul has in fact given an existentialist interpretation of the mythological idea of the Last Judgment: for 'according to Paul, Christ's judgment of the world has already taken place in the believers—they have received sentence as those who are already justified. (In John the process is taken even further, for the believer has already passed through the judgment.) Judgment takes place in the proclamation of the word—for this word, preaching, spreads death and life abroad (II Cor. 2.15 f.).'[51]

According to Bultmann, all this means 'that the divinity or deity of Christ is revealed in the event in which we are given a place by the message of the gospel, which proclaims him as the grace of God made manifest to us. Conversely, the fact that this message comes to us as the Word which demands faith of us, calls us to responsibility and thus decides about us, finds its expression in the attributes ascribed to Christ; they thus

---

[49] ibid., pp. 252 f. (ibid., pp. 280 f.).
[50] ibid., p. 255 (ibid., p. 283).
[51] ibid.

affirm in truth that God is to be encountered in him and only in him.'[52]

In so far as Jesus is the Word of God, God appears in him, and in so far as God appears in Jesus, Jesus is God. Bultmann therefore thinks it better to avoid the formulas which we mentioned at the start, as it is hardly possible to prevent their being wrongly understood in a substantial, 'natural', objective, even mythological way. Instead of saying 'Jesus is God', we should say what is really meant: Jesus is the Word of God.

This mythological misunderstanding leads to a false offence, the overcoming of which is still not faith: man's offence at the mythological world-picture which represents God in natural and substantial terms. This false offence is to be avoided so that the true scandal may be clearly seen: the demand that man must be brought to nothing if he is to live, the insight of T. S. Eliot, 'In my end is my beginning', which Bultmann is so fond of quoting, Eichendorff's confession:

> Thou art the one who gently shatters
> Around us what we build,
> That we may look above to heaven
> And so I do not grieve,

and the radical recognition of Paul's remark 'When I am weak, then I am strong' (II Cor. 12.10). This true scandal amounts to the fact that man has not to overcome just any offence, but the offence that he presents to himself; he is not to surrender his view of the world but himself; not his ideas and concepts, but he himself is challenged by the *kerygma*.

This true scandal is sharply and unavoidably expressed where a 'particular man, born in Nazareth, whose father and mother are known, asserts that he is the Son of God',[53] i.e. where a natural divine quality of Jesus does not even come into the picture. The divine quality of Jesus expressed in proclamation can only be that of his claim to man, which is unavoidable

[52] ibid., p. 256 (ibid., p. 284).
[53] ibid., p. 260 (ibid., pp. 289 f.).

and to be recognized only in existential decision, where I surrender myself to the call of the *kerygma*, to live God and so to find that God is in Christ.

Because demythologizing, as existentialist interpretation, rules out any possibility of objectifying myth (that is, of making the action of God visible as such to the eye of the beholder and thus controllable and demonstrable), the real scandal is revealed and the false scandal prevented. 'Only against appearances, only in decision is true faith possible—just as the justification of the sinner can only be believed in defiance of the accusations of the conscience.'[54]

As a result, in 1954, in a closing comment on the resounding echo which his demythologizing article of 1941 awakened, Bultmann can say: *'Radical demythologizing is a parallel to St Paul's and Luther's doctrine of justification by faith alone apart from the works of the Law. Or rather, it carries this doctrine to its logical conclusion in the field of epistemology.* Like the doctrine of justification it destroys every false security and every false demand for it on the part of man, whether he seeks it in his good works or in his ascertainable knowledge. The man who wishes to believe in God as his God must realize that he has nothing in his hand on which to base his faith. He is suspended in mid-air and cannot demand a proof of the truth of the word which addresses him. For the ground and object of faith are identical. Security can be found only by abandoning all security, by being ready, as Luther put it, to plunge into the inner darkness.'[55]

[54] *Kerygma und Mythos*, II, p. 207 (*Kerygma and Myth*, p. 210).
[55] ibid. (ibid., pp. 210 f.).

12

Ethics

IN THE PRESENT chapter we are to look for an answer to the
question of how Bultmann provides a theological basis for the
moral conduct of the Christian and what standards his theology sets for this conduct. Our question about ethics is thus
the extremely concrete one of *what* the Christian should do
and why he should do it. It is the question of the imperative,
the 'thou shalt'.

Here too, of course, we must tread extremely carefully and
not take our usual understanding of ethics for granted in
investigating Bultmann's understanding of Christian conduct.
For the average person, the question of ethics is simply the
question of the ethical norms, the concrete guideliness of
moral conduct, i.e. the question of the law. But anyone who
looks for ethical instructions of this kind in Bultmann's writings will very quickly be disappointed. They are nowhere to
be found. That is surprising, because the subject of his writings, the New Testament, is full of such regulations. The real
task of this chapter will therefore be, paradoxically, to explain
the lack of traditional ethical statements in Bultmann's
theology.

Now of course the concept of the 'imperative' occurs quite
frequently in Bultmann's writing. But both the way in which
Bultmann introduces and discusses it and the context in which
he does so are extremely significant. It occurs frequently in the
juxtaposition of 'indicative' and 'imperative', as we saw in

Chapter 5, which dealt with Christian faith as Bultmann understands it. What did the mention of the imperative mean there?

The concept of the 'indicative' includes the reality of the salvation grasped in faith: in faith, freedom from sin has become event. Man is brought back by God's gracious saving act to a right relationship with his Creator and thus to a right relationship with the world; he lives always in the moment, in which alone he can live authentically, from the future of the God who is not at his disposal.

But this salvation is never an assured possession. It is meant to be grasped at each several moment. 'Sinlessness' is not a magical guarantee against the possibility of sin but is itself possibility, namely the possibility disclosed to man by the Word of God, which must constantly be realized afresh in faith. This state of affairs demands and justifies the imperative, which calls man from the world under his control, which can give no true life, to God, from unbelief to faith. For as far as the believer is concerned the world has in no way surrendered its tempting power to promise life.

Thus the imperative does not contradict the indicative, nor does it temporarily deprive the indicative of its force. It results from it, as Bultmann points out in a reference to I Cor. 5.7 f.: 'Cleanse out the old leaven that you may be fresh dough, as you really are unleavened.'[1] The relationship between indicative and imperative is dialectical in the true sense; each of the two terms is only understood rightly in connection with the other. Together they describe the nature of faith.

The imperative understood in this way is therefore not, at any rate directly, the imperative of the law, the 'Thou shalt do this and that', the concrete ethical instruction. It is the summons to faith, the call to turn away from the world of death, the pointer towards life from God. The extent to which it thus *also* summons man to a new form of moral conduct is

[1] *Theologie*, p. 334 (*Theology*, I, p. 332).

something which we must investigate next. But we should be warned against regarding Bultmann's presentation of the relationship between indicative and imperative merely as that between faith and life, or dogmatics and ethics. Rather, faith itself comes about in the dialectic of indicative and imperative. Quite apart from any particular ethical problems, its mere structure is to be grasped only within this tension, which bridges the gap between the 'now already' and the 'not yet' of faith.

This argument of Bultmann's can also be developed in the light of his concept of sin which we noted in Chapter 4. For Bultmann, 'sin', as we said, is 'not identical with moral transgressions'.[2] It is understood more fundamentally as man's attempt to live from what is at his disposal. 'Sinlessness' is therefore not a state of moral perfection, but the deliverance of man by the saving act of God from the *compulsion* of sin, to which he is subject if he looks for his life in what is at his disposal and consequently can only do the works of death; thus 'Paul's remarks about the sinlessness of the man who is justified have nothing to do with an ethic'.[3] The imperative is not the summing up of individual ethical imperatives but the demand derived from the indicative to continue in salvation, to hold oneself open for God's future; in other words, it is an indication that salvation is never under man's control.

Nevertheless, the way from this analysis of the concepts of faith and sin to the problem of ethics is not a very long one. Faith is possible only as existence in the moment, as each man's *concrete* realization of himself. For faith is not a quality of man, nor a particular religious condition of the soul, nor an affirmation of revealed doctrines, nor an exalted moral virtue. Faith is rather an act, an act of obedience, and as such it is as much determined by the fact that it occurs at each particular moment as it is by the fact that it is the act of the *whole* man, who surrenders himself in faith as his own possibility to receive himself back again from God. As we know, Bultmann can say of faith that it 'demands of man the surrender of his previous

[2] 'Das Problem der Ethik', p. 136.   [3] ibid., p. 126.

275

understanding of himself, the reversal of the direction his will has previously had'.[4] He can thus describe faith as an act of the will which continually takes place within the tension of indicative and imperative.

But there is no will which does not realize itself in concrete human existence; therefore there is also no faith which does not actualize itself in the expressions of everyday human life; for faith is the act of the *whole* man and the obedience of faith is *all-embracing* obedience. 'The *whole* man knows that he stands before God, and in so far as he acts, he puts himself at God's disposal.'[5] If it is true of sin, which, according to Bultmann, is not identical with moral transgressions, that 'it can *represent* itself in these transgressions',[6] it is true of faith, though it is not rightly described as a moral condition, that it renews the believer's way of life.

Faith is the forgiveness of sins, and 'the forgiveness of sins is the total; but to understand it as the total, one must see that it is freedom from sin: not only freedom from guilt in the past, but also from sinning in the future'.[7] As we are still not angels, that makes it necessary for the ethical imperative to belong to the total of the forgiveness of sins: 'Its "thou shalt" has been changed to an "I will" in the gift of freedom':[8] ' "So you also must consider yourselves dead to sin and alive to God in Christ Jesus" (Rom. 6.11).' That means: ' "Therefore let not sin reign in your mortal bodies, to make you obey their passions. Do not yield your members to sin as instruments of wickedness, but yield yourselves to God as men who have been brought from death to life; and your members to God as instruments of righteousness" (Rom. 6.12 f.).'[9]

That is the legitimate meaning of the saying about faith which, if it does not have works, is dead in itself (James 2.17);

[4] *Theologie*, p. 136 (*Theology*, I, p. 315).
[5] 'Das Problem der Ethik', p. 138).   [6] ibid., p. 136.
[7] *Kerygma und Mythos*, I, p. 126.   [8] ibid.
[9] *Glauben und Verstehen*, 3, p. 43 (*Existence and Faith*, p. 256).

that is what Paul means when he writes: 'For in Christ Jesus neither circumcision nor uncircumcision is of any avail, but faith working though love' (Gal. 5.6); that, the realization of faith in concrete existence, is what we have to speak about when we discuss ethics.

But how does Bultmann intend us to talk about them? Must we now enumerate the concrete moral norms to which faith has to correspond in its actual realization? Must the imperative now be developed in individual imperatives, as constantly happens in the New Testament? For example, Paul's statement in Gal. 5.25, 'If we live by the Spirit, let us also walk by the Spirit', which Bultmann always quotes as the paradigm for the relationship between indicative and imperative that we have just described, stands in the middle of some quite concrete ethical admonitions. But we have already said that in none of his theological works on the New Testament is Bultmann concerned to establish guidelines of this kind. He speaks of 'the imperative' but not of 'imperatives'—though the imperative clearly includes the imperatives, because the relationship of the believer to God does not exist 'apart from or alongside his concrete action'.[10]

Now of course the quotation from Gal. 5.6 which we have just introduced mentions the *love* through which faith becomes effective, and in referring to this saying of Paul's, Bultmann can write: 'God's demand is for love; it becomes real as the manifestation of faith in living.'[11] Has not Bultmann mentioned at least *one* concrete imperative here, that is, one imperative alongside others, perhaps the highest of all, but still an imperative which, summed up with others, leads to the fullness of Christian ethical norms? This is not the way in which Bultmann sees it.

He discusses the concept of love under the heading of

---

[10] 'Das Problem der Ethik', p. 137.
[11] *Theologie*, p. 345 (*Theology*, I, p. 344).

'freedom', that is, in connection with the discussion of the concept of *faith*, to the elements of whose structure 'freedom' belongs. We have discussed Bultmann's understanding of this freedom of faith in Chapter 5. It is freedom from the 'old man', because the believer no longer belongs to himself, but to God. As freedom of man from himself, it is freedom from sin and from death. It is freedom from everything that promised man life and brought him death: from the world and the law. In all its forms it is the one freedom which God's saving act brought to man. It is therefore wholly and utterly an expression of the *love* of God; it is a gift.

But if it is a gift, this freedom presupposes a bond, a bond to the giver of freedom. And because freedom (this is what the imperative means) is not a possession, but must be constantly achieved anew, this connection is a constant, unceasing one. The freedom of faith is only realized in each new turning towards—and that means obedience to—God as the giver of freedom. The one who is freed by the Lord Christ is at the same time the servant of Christ, as Paul says in I Cor. 7.22. In other words: the freedom achieved by the love of God is only realized in obedience to this love. In calling to faith, the imperative calls to love, to the love of God, to the acceptance of the freedom that has been given.

In so doing, it issues a summons to life *in* love as being for others: 'for surrender to the cross means *positively* that the man who no longer wills to be for himself exists for others. Since what has been opened up to him in the cross is the liberating love of God, the love of Christ also compels him to serve his fellow men (II Cor. 5.14), and his faith is active in love (Gal. 5.6).'[12]

The call to the love of God (the call to the indicative) and the demand to love one's neighbour are not two acts which could be separated from one another. It is rather the case that: 'God is love, and whoever abides in love abides in God and

[12] 'Jesus und Paulus', p. 88 (*Existence and Faith*, p. 199).

God abides in him' (I John 4.16). Bultmann describes this
unity with the words: 'In freeing man from himself, God's
forgiving grace has freed him from anxiety and so for existing
for others, for love!'[13] Anxiety is an expression of the supposed
need to bring life under one's own control; it is thus an expression of self-love which, though senseless, is necessary for the
'natural' man. In deliverance from anxiety through the love of
God, love finds its proper object, the neighbour. For the sake
of the unity of faith and love it is true on the one hand that
'love, as sheer existence for one's neighbour, is *possible* only to
the one who is free from himself—i.e. the one who has died
with Christ, to live no longer for himself but for him who for
his sake died and was raised (II Cor. 5.15)',[14] and on the other
hand that the freedom of the believer from himself is only *real*
in love for the neighbour. Therefore it can be said: 'We know
that we have passed out of death into life, because we love the
brethren. He who does not love remains in death' (I John
3.14). The unity of faith and love is thus complete. Because it
is a summons to faith, the imperative is a summons to love in
its totality. 'In faith it is decided in advance, as it were, that
all one's conduct is to be conduct in love. That is why it is in
love that faith makes good its freedom';[15] what is more, in the
act of love the freedom of faith *is effected*. Though the statement may be exaggerated, it is therefore true of the believer
that 'if he believes, he already loves. . . . In faith the believer
as it were anticipates love's concrete, individual decisions of
love for the future', in such a way that it only becomes clear in
the individual concrete decisions 'whether the decision of faith
in time past was genuine. . . . But this decision (from time to
time) of love is not a second decision alongside that of faith—
the two are one and the same.'[16]

---

[13] *Glauben und Verstehen*, 2, p. 99 (*Essays*, p. 112).
[14] *Theologie*, p. 346 (*Theology*, I, p. 344).
[15] ibid., p. 434 (*Theology*, II, pp. 81 f.).
[16] *Glauben und Verstehen*, 1, p. 150.

Thus the inner unity of indicative and imperative is reflected in the demand to love, if it is rightly understood. 'If the meaning of the *past* was that the encounter with Jesus was experienced as his service, which made the believer free, the meaning of the *future* can only be that in it this freedom is carried forward; and that happens in the fulfilment of the commandment of love. As this commandment and its fulfilment are based on the experience of the love of the revealer, the believer constantly remains bound to the service of the revealer and is never left to himself. Conversely, the believer who has accepted that service can carry it further only in the attitude of the servant, in love. Only as those who love do his own continue to experience his love, as they love and can love only on the basis of this experience.'[17]

All this also shows us how and why Bultmann does not understand the demand of love as a *concrete* ethical demand, still less as *one* such demand among others. For him it is rather the call to faith itself, that is, to a faith which realizes itself as *true* faith in concrete existence in the form of love for one's neighbour. Individual ethical demands are merely a development of this call in respect of each particular concrete situation. That this is so is particularly clear, according to Bultmann, in I Cor. 13, love's 'Song of Songs'. Here love is characterized as the way of all ways, without which the other gifts of the spirit are nothing. 'Though all the Spirit's other gifts will disappear when "that which is perfect" comes, yet love, like faith and hope, will remain—and not only remain, but be the greatest of the three. It can be called nothing less, because in it the possibility opened up by faith and hope becomes reality in concrete existence.'[18] As a result, we can understand how Paul can sum up all particular ethical demands in the commandment of love, as he does in Gal. 5.14 and Rom. 13.8–10: 'Love is the fulfilling of the law'.

[17] *Johannesevangelium*, p. 404.
[18] *Theologie*, p. 346 (*Theology*, I, p. 344).

Because the command to love is identical with the *kerygma*, which issues a call to *faith*, love does not demand *something*, this or that, from man, but man himself, wholly and utterly. It would thus be a terrible mistake to think that the command to love requires *less* of men than the concrete demands of the law. As if the demand of love represented a reduction of ethical demands! 'It really removes man from his own disposal and places him under God's sovereign will. . . . The natural man's real response to the reduction of the law's demands to the commandment of love cannot be to breathe a sigh of relief; it must be to be terrified. And anyone who does not know this terror neither senses the seriousness of the demand nor understands the meaning of liberation.'[19] For in the end he does not know the measure of freedom which God gives man when he frees him from himself.

It would also be an error to think that the reduction of God's will to the commandment of love is a deliverance 'because it seems to direct man's attention to the world and not to require of him that he know of anything beyond the world; i.e. it seems to leave man in his own sphere by simply pointing him to his fellow men'.[20] On the contrary, according to Bultmann, as we saw: 'The commandment to love the neighbour is indissolubly connected with the commandment to love God',[21] though this connection must be understood properly. It is not understood properly if I behave as though the neighbour were only indirectly the goal of my love, which in reality is directed totally to God. On the contrary, as God so wills it, or as I cannot directly love him, the neighbour is used so to speak as an instrument of the love of God. It must be asserted that I can only love God 'while I will what he wills, while I *really love my neighbour*'.[22] But at the same time it is true that 'I *can* love my neighbour only when I surrender my will completely to God's will'.[23] Thus, according to Bultmann, the connection between the two commandments rests on the conviction that 'one cannot see the neighbour as one should if one does not have God in view'.[24] 'As obedient to God, setting aside my selfish will, renouncing my own claims, I stand before my neighbour, prepared for sacrifice for my neighbour as for God.'[25] In turn, that means that without being given freedom from himself, man is not free for the neighbour; the ethical imperative is rooted in the indicative; the call to the neighbour is not to be separated from the call to

[19] 'Jesus und Paulus', pp. 75 f. (*Existence and Faith*, pp. 188 f.).
[20] ibid., p. 77 (ibid., p. 191).   [21] ibid.
[22] *Jesus*, p. 81 (*Jesus and the Word*, p. 86).   [23] ibid.
[24] 'Jesus und Paulus', p. 77 (*Existence and Faith*, p. 191).
[25] *Jesus*, p. 80 (*Jesus and the Word*, p. 85).

God. Anyone who asserts that he loves God while hating his brother is a liar (I John 4.20); and anyone who thinks he can love his brother without loving God is caught up in his own selfishness.

The implication of what has been said in the previous section is that the demand of love, while demanding the realization of faith in concrete existence, is not itself a concrete ethical demand, an ethical norm. Bultmann feels that it is clear that 'the command of love explains nothing about the content of love. *What* must a man do to love his neighbour or his enemy? It is said simply *that* he is to do it.'[26] 'Man is trusted and expected to see *for himself* what God commands.'[27] According to Bultmann, this position is quite appropriate. It is reflected in the complete absence of anything like a material ethic in Bultmann's theological writings, to which we have already drawn attention. But what is the justification for this position?

Faith's demand for obedience is for Bultmann the demand for *radical* obedience. Bultmann sees radical obedience surrendered, if a man allows himself to be told by an outside authority how the gift of love is to be realized on any particular occasion. 'For so long as obedience is only subjection to an authority which man does not understand, it is no true obedience; something in man still remains outside and does not submit, is not bound by the command of God. Criticism can still arise: in itself this does not concern me, in itself these things are indifferent; but I choose to obey. In *this kind of* decision a man stands outside his action, he is not completely obedient. Radical obedience exists only when a man inwardly assents to what is required of him, when the thing commanded is seen as intrinsically God's command; when the whole man stands behind what he does; or better, when the whole man is in what he does, i.e. when he is not *doing* something obediently, but *is* essentially obedient.'[28] So it is entrusted to man himself

26 ibid., p. 67 (ibid., p. 72). 27 ibid., p. 55 (ibid., p. 61).
28 ibid., p. 56 (ibid.).

to decide what must be done as an act of love at any particular moment; for in this way the demand of God becomes clear and the idea of obedience is understood in a radical way. Now man is whole in what he does.

This in itself means that radical obedience is possible only in unconditional openness for the future, i.e. for what encounters a man in each particular moment. For Bultmann, the idea of radical obedience is already surrendered if man thinks that he can have control over part of the future. If *today* he were to determine the principles of his action for *tomorrow* and were to keep to these principles he would be claiming to have control over the possibilities in which God could encounter him tomorrow. And this would make *radical* obedience impossible, for that presupposes God's unconditional freedom in the encounters which present his demands.

It does not matter at this point whether the principles of my action, thus wrongly accepted, consist of a given collection of legal proscriptions, supposedly from God, or of the good which is latent in man himself, as the law of his moral being. In either case man is regarded as a being who from the start has control over any possibilities of his action which he may encounter and over the norms according to which he behaves in this encounter. But that does not correspond to the Christian understanding of existence, according to which man stands absolutely without security over against whatever encounters him. 'A man cannot control beforehand the possibilities upon which he must act; he cannot in the moment of decision fall back upon principles, upon a general ethical theory which can relieve him of responsibility for the decision; rather, every moment of decision is essentially new.'[29] Only in this way does Bultmann find a guarantee that the ethical demand is really *God's* demand, the demand from beyond myself, the demand which comes quite simply from the future and which is as such the unconditional demand of the moment:

[29] ibid., p. 61 (ibid., p. 66).

'For man does not meet the crisis of decision armed with a definite standard; he stands on no firm base, but rather as it were alone in an empty room. This it is which shows the requirement of the good to be actually the demand of God— not the demand of something divine in man, but the demand of God who is beyond man.'[30]

The *divine quality* of the demand and the *radical quality* of the obedience demanded thus both require equally that only insight into the demand of the moment itself should show *what* is to be done, or rather, *how* faith has to take definite form in love, though not that of a law understood or grounded in some way. The concrete demand arises out of the situation of decision. Only if I encounter my *neighbour*—not the concept of the neighbour or the command to love my neighbour—do I experience *what* I should do.

'Also from Phil. 4.11 f., it is evident that the Christian life is not regulated by fixed prescriptions. Paul says: "I know how to be abased and I know how to abound; in any and all circumstances I have learned the secret of facing plenty and hunger, abundance and want." Or he says to the Corinthians: "To the Jews I became as a Jew . . . to those under the law I became as one under the law . . . to those outside the law I became as one outside the law . . . to the weak I became weak . . . I have become all things to all men . . ." (I Cor. 9.20–22). The same freedom in responsible decision is expressed in the statement: "All things are lawful for me, but not all things are helpful. All things are lawful for me, but I will not be enslaved by anything" (I Cor. 6.12), and again in the discussion of whether it is allowable to eat meat offered to idols (I Cor. 8.1–13; 10.23–31). And it can only be a matter of decision how to obey the demand: "Do all to the glory of God" (I Cor. 10.31).'[31]

Insight into this situation frees man 'from the endless and useless task of searching for commands and prohibitions which he must know in order to act rightly; from the fear of having failed here and there because he did not know the scriptural precept or its right interpretation'.[32] In this respect the

[30] ibid.   [31] *History and Eschatology*, p. 46.
[32] *Jesus*, p. 59 (*Jesus and the Word*, p. 64).

demand for radical obedience relieves man of a considerable burden. Such obedience is also easy, 'because it frees a man from dependence on a formal authority and therefore frees him also from the judgment of the men whose profession it is to explain this authority'.[33]

Of course, this situation is at the same time terrifying. 'For to the weak man it is a relief to have the judgment of good and evil and all responsibility taken away from him.'[34] Bultmann, on the other hand, sees that this is the responsibility which is shifted on to man in the New Testament.

'The crisis of decision is the situation in which all observation is excluded, for which *Now* alone has meaning. *Now* man must know what to do and what not to do, and no standard whatever from the past or from the universal is available. *That* is the meaning of decision. It does not, of course, mean that man lacks insight into the empirical possibilities of his conduct or its consequences as empirical processes. Decision is not dice-throwing; its character becomes plainer, the more clearly the empirical possibilities are understood. Decision means that the choice between the possibilities is not determined by insight into them but is free and responsible. Anyone who sees man in the crisis of decision and recognizes this as the essential of human existence, assumes that man knows what is good and evil *now*; as has already been said, he knows, not on the basis of any past experience or rational deductions, but directly from the immediate situation.'[35] In other words: the demand of love, the 'fact' of it, is made concrete and given definite content only in the moment in which *this* content is to be put into effect by me. I never know what is to be done on each several occasion as an onlooker. I know it as one who has to do it. In this way Bultmann sees a radical departure from the subject-object pattern in the realm of the particular moral action.

In that case, what is the significance of the countless concrete moral demands which occur in the New Testament? To answer this question, Bultmann draws attention to the antitheses at the beginning of the Sermon on the Mount as an

---

[33] ibid., p. 60 (ibid., p. 65).   [34] ibid.
[35] ibid., p. 63 (ibid., p. 68).

example of the fact that it is wrong, 'to look to Jesus for concrete ethical requirements or for his attitude towards concrete ethical problems'.[36] The significance of these radical demands is to be sought somewhere other than in the institution of specifically Christian precepts. 'In all these passages the decisive requirement is the same; the good which is to be done is to be done *completely*. Anyone who does it partially, with reservations, just enough to fulfil the letter of the law, has not done it at all. The man who indeed refrains from murder but does not master anger has not understood that his decision must be complete. The man who indeed avoids adultery, but keeps lust in his heart, has not understood the prohibition of adultery, which requires of him complete purity. The man who simply refrains from perjury has not seen that absolute truthfulness is demanded. The man who divorces his wife has not understood that marriage requires of him a complete decision, but thinks of it as a relative action which can be annulled. The man who takes revenge for injustice does not realize that by so doing he himself upholds injustice; to reject injustice completely also means not to retaliate. The man who is kind only to friends does not know what love means; for complete love also includes love of enemies.'[37]

According to Bultmann, then, the ethical demands of the New Testament are not meant to lead to the fulfilling of a sum of particular norms of conduct; they are the *concrete* expression of the demand for *radical* obedience, as the antithetically formulated demands of the Sermon on the Mount make quite clear. Otherwise the demand of God would not be identical with his gift, the gift to man of his own self, in radical freedom for the future at each particular moment. If this were not so, man's obedience would be a work, alongside which he stood, which he could weigh up, which he could confirm. Rather, God demands man totally, and that also means that in each new situation he demands anew the decision for *what* is to be

[36] ibid.   [37] ibid., p. 65 (ibid., p. 70).

done *now*. In other words, he calls for a responsible examination of the question of what the reality of faith in fact means in the situation now presented to me, how I have to live now from the love which has been given to me. This, however, I do not know outside and before my action, but only in it. Only here, as we saw, does Bultmann see a guarantee that God demands man himself and not a particular action of his which has been determined beforehand; only in this way does man really live in the freedom that has been given to him.

Consequently it would be a misunderstanding to regard the concrete ethical demands of the Bible as formal legal regulations with which a man complies if he fulfils them to the letter in every situation. 'Unless the decision which is demanded in these sayings arises out of a present situation, it is not truly the decision of obedience.'[38] In concrete terms: 'Anyone who refuses to dissolve an unendurable marriage by appealing to a word of Jesus; anyone who offers the other cheek to one who strikes him, because Jesus said so, would not understand Jesus.'[39] The paraenetic instructions of the New Testament are no generally valid ethical principles by which a man can guide himself once for all. Anyone who understands them in this way deprives himself of the possibility of that radical obedience with which he boldly decides afresh in his obedience *in* each new situation about what is demanded and thus, by putting himself completely at risk, opens himself completely to the future.

If the Christian always has to decide *what* is to be done in the concrete situation, then in view of what has been said he does not necessarily have to decide in each particular situation which of the rules that he knows and affirms (as he thinks, by an act of faith) he is now to follow. The sole question is how he is to put into effect the demand that is identical with God's gift, the demand of love. Here, of course, he can learn from

[38] ibid., p. 66 (ibid., p. 71).   [39] ibid.

the norms of conduct that are known to him, for he does not live outside history. But every norm that holds in a given situation is itself created in encounter and to that extent is constantly new. In that case, however, is there still such a thing as a specific Christian morality? Like his teacher Wilhelm Herrmann, Bultmann replies to this question with an emphatic 'no'. We must now investigate this 'no'.

Bultmann argues, above all, that the command to love one's neighbour is not a specifically Christian command. The commandment of love—however it is grounded—occurs frequently in Jewish and pagan paraenesis. According to Bultmann, the reason for this becomes clear if we note that the neighbour is anyone who 'is always already there. I always have him and I do not need to look for him first.'[40] Man's being-with others is thus an existentialist determination of humanity, Heidegger's well-known 'being-in-the-world'. I am myself only *with* others. 'It is not, then, the case that people stand in the world as isolated subjects, as in an empty room, and that one subject looks round for another, makes contact with him, comes to him later. It is not the case that people first have to ask how to get to others, and what to do with them. My being is from the start a being-with-others; human being is being-with-one-another, and thus it is historical being, as opposed to the being of nature.'[41]

So it is not in fact surprising if the concept of the neighbour and the demand for a loving relationship to him are generally recognized; for 'if the neighbour is the one who is always already there, then everyone always has a neighbour. And to the extent that human community has never completely misunderstood itself, it has always in some degree seen the demand of love. So the demand of love does not emerge in Christianity as something entirely new in the history of the spirit; the demand of love in Christianity takes it for granted that everyone really ought to know what love is and that every-

[40] *Glauben und Verstehen*, 1, p. 231.   [41] ibid.

one knows who his neighbour is when he is told: Love your neighbour as yourself.'[42] Because being-with-man is an *essential* part of human existence, a knowledge of love is part of a man's being. And because man cannot totally free himself from his bond with the 'thou', he knows of faithfulness, truthfulness, righteousness and other elements of the loving I-Thou relationship even if he denies them in his conduct.

Now if the commandment to love is not a specifically Christian commandment, and if the New Testament is aware of this, then it is all the more understandable that the New Testament should also presuppose that everyone knows or can know *what* is demanded of him if he is to act lovingly: 'For what it means to love *himself* he knows very well, without any theory or system about the self. For self-love is not a principle of morality, but the attitude of the natural man. If a man, then, is to love his neighbour as himself, he knows very well how to direct his conduct in the concrete situation,'[43] and, 'The example of the merciful Samaritan shows that a man can know and must know what he has to do when he sees his neighbour in need of his help.'[44]

When the commandment of love is actualized in certain situations in the New Testament, when there is a *concrete* summons to life in love, the New Testament thus resorts without further reflection to the well-known ethical norms. 'Not only the moral commandments of the Old Testament, but also the catalogues of virtues and vices from the paraenetic tradition of Hellenistic Judaism are valid.'[45] 'If we look at the content of the moral imperatives, we shall find that there is no specifically Christian ethics; and if we want to call, say, the commandment of love a specifically Christian commandment, we should remember that St Paul describes the commandment of love a summary of all the commandments, indeed a

---

[42] ibid., p. 236.   [43] *Jesus*, p. 81 (*Jesus and the Word*, p. 86).
[44] *Theologie*, p. 18 (*Theology*, I, p. 18).
[45] 'Das Problem der Ethik', p. 138.

summary of the Law. These commandments can be known to every man before he has heard the Christian message. Every man has a conscience, and can know what is good and what is evil. True Christian preaching does not have special demands to make with respect to ethics.'[46] Christian faith brings no new moral ideal into the world. Nothing is demanded of the Christian that is not also demanded of the non-Christian who affirms the demand of love. The actual accomplishment of this demand is therefore grounded in perspectives which arise from and in each particular situation. In so far as they make definite the content of what is demanded on each occasion, moral decisions are rational decisions; that is, they are made on the basis of an insight into a particular situation which is accessible to all. 'The rightwised man is only asked to do what is good, acceptable and perfect, whatever is excellent and worthy of praise' (Rom. 12.2; Phil. 4.8),[47] i.e. what even a pagan judgment would recognize to be good. Only for this reason, Bultmann feels, can Christians also be asked to commend their faith to 'outsiders' by their moral behaviour (I Thess. 4.12; I Cor. 10.32).

In that case, is there no perceptible difference between the conduct of the believer and that of the unbeliever? Certainly not, if it is thought that the believer puts into practice moral standards quite alien to the unbeliever. It is true, rather, of the believer that, 'for him, moral demands have no new content, and his moral behaviour is different from that of others only by virtue of the fact that it has the character of obedience'.[48] This is the difference between moral action in faith and in unfaith: the believer realizes the demand of love as an *act of obedience* in the radical sense described above, and not as a work, an accomplishment, a compulsion or an expression of general humanity. In other words: for the believer, the imperative of love is at the same time grounded and made possible in the

[46] *Glauben und Verstehen*, 3, p. 125 (*Religion and Culture*, p. 238).
[47] 'Das Problem der Ethik', p. 138.   [48] ibid.

indicative of revelation; obedience in love is identical with the obedience of faith, which is grounded in the saving act of God and is possible only on this basis; in faith man finds freedom from himself, and such freedom makes him free to love his neighbour. Love *as obedience* 'becomes our possibility of existence only if we grasp our existence as being grounded, or newly grounded, by Christ in God'.[49] Love as an act of obedience presupposes the saving event. For, according to Bultmann, man's freedom from himself which makes possible the radical obedience expressed in his love for his neighbour, is 'not a natural attribute of man; it is always event, and it becomes event only when man is freed from himself by the word of forgiveness and so becomes open for the demanding question which he encounters in his neighbour'.[50]

In so far as the indicative of the divine saving action *demands* the act of moral obedience, it is obviously true 'that if a person really acts in obedience under God, the seriousness of the moral demand as the commandment of God takes on new life, and his way of life *is in fact a new one*'.[51] True, the mark of existence in faith is not that the Christian follows unheard-of norms of conduct but that in so far as he does not deny his faith he realizes in practice the demand of love. In the light of this we can understand Paul's conviction 'that the life of the believer is clearly different from his earlier way of life and from that of his pagan surroundings',[52] an observation which acknowledges that under some circumstances pagans, too, can do what is demanded on occasion by love and is *also* done by Christians out of obedience. Moral behaviour is in no way a proof of faith.

In so far as the indicative *makes possible* the achievement of moral obedience, because it brings about the 'reversal of the

---

[49] *Glauben und Verstehen*, 1, p. 243.
[50] *Glauben und Verstehen*, 3, p. 126 (*Religion and Culture*, p. 239).
[51] 'Das Problem der Ethik', p. 139.
[52] ibid., pp. 138 f.

course of life of the natural man' who holds fast to himself,[53] it is true that 'the attitude of obedience which matches the demand is at the same time the gift of God, achieved through the spirit, though without robbing the demand of its character as imperative'.[54] As an act of obedience, the concrete, tangible moral act can never become a work, a human contribution; or, put in another way, it is an act of obedience in that the agent does not regard it as a work.

The mere fact that for the Christian the imperative, 'Love your neighbour', is rooted in the love of God, explains why the command of love can be called a 'new commandment' (I John 2.8), although it has long applied, or at least has been recognized as a demand. 'For this newness is not its relative historical novelty, for that, of course, would quickly cease to be new. And anyhow from the world's point of view, to which the epistle shifts for a moment, it is not new, but old (I John 2.7).'[55] The commandment is *new*, because love 'has become reality in the love of God brought about through Christ'[56] and therefore the new existence of faith is realized in the fulfilment of the commandment to love, and the obedience of faith demonstrates itself again and again in love. The commandment to love is *new* in that 'we come into our "now" as those who are loved and thus are free to love in return'.[57]

Consequently, the answer to the question of a specifically Christian morality, which introduced the last section, is an emphatic 'no'. 'There are no special works of faith and love, but all our acts in the fulfilment of our daily duty can become such',[58] i.e. when we act from the obedience of faith. The specifically Christian element is that the good is done in obedience, that is, in realization of the indicative. But in that case, with Bultmann 'we must speak of the *concealment* of Christian love in the sense that a loving action can never confront the

---

[53] *Glauben und Verstehen*, 1, p. 238.
[54] 'Das Problem der Ethik', p. 140.
[55] *Theologie*, p. 434 (*Theology*, II, p. 82).
[56] *Glauben und Verstehen*, 1, p. 243.
[57] *Glauben und Verstehen*, 3, pp. 28 f. (*Existence and Faith*, p. 85).
[58] *Glauben und Verstehen*, 1, p. 111.

outsider as such, can never be pointed out as an action from and in love';[59] for how will anyone demonstrate that his acts of love are done in obedience? He can never *himself* claim that character for his action, unless he wants to put himself alongside his works of love, and as one who is obedient that is just what he cannot do. Christian love, love as an expression of obedience, can never be demonstrated; it can only be performed: 'There is no such thing as a Christian science or a Christian ethic; there is no political or social programme of Christian faith. There is no Christian art, or culture, or educational system—no "Christian humanism". Of course, all these things do exist so far as Christians pursue them, or so far as they select their materials from the thought-world and history of Christianity—this is true, for example, of art and science. But it is an abuse of language to go on to speak of "Christian" science of art; for there is no "Christian" method in any of these spheres of intellectual life. There are certainly Christian cobblers: but there is no Christian shoemaking.'[60]

We can now understand why for Bultmann there is no such thing as theological ethics, in the sense of instructions for concrete moral action. He describes such an ethic explicitly as a 'misunderstanding of the original I-Thou relationship',[61] which is real only in the liveliness of accomplishment and would throttle man's own liveliness were it to replace the demand of the neighbour by some sort of demand from the law. The ethical injunctions of the Bible are to be interpreted in the light of the *radical* demand presented in them. As *concrete* demands, they are determined by their situation, i.e. they are bound up in the situation which produced them and thus belong to the past. Whether they were appropriate in their original situation is a question for theological criticism,

[59] ibid., p. 239.
[60] *Glauben und Verstehen*, 2, pp. 137 f. (*Essays*, p. 156).
[61] *Glauben und Verstehen*, 1, p. 234.

but the answers it gives do not say whether they are also possible in our situation. This question can only be decided in each new moment of decision, over which the theologian has no control in his scholarly work. 'Ethics' in the traditional sense is therefore distinct as a discipline from historical and systematic theology.

That does not mean that it should be excluded from proclamation, i.e. from pastoral activity in the widest sense. It is of the very nature of proclamation that it is related to the situation. Thus in 1926, in a comment about plans for the reform of theological study, Bultmann thought it appropriate to separate 'ethics' completely from historical and systematic theology and to give it an appropriate place in practical theology. But there, even in Bultmann's view, 'ethics' *does have* a place, as limited as it is necessary.

The limits set to ethical reflection, even in 'practical theology', become clear when one remembers that an insight into what is commanded on each particular occasion *in* the church can only be achieved *outside* it, i.e. through a rational insight into the situation. This insight cannot be derived from the Word of God; the preacher can only give a personal verdict, arrived at in a responsible way, which does not relieve any of his hearers of the responsibility of making his own decision, but rather entrusts him explicitly with it. The task of preaching is to guide the hearer to the responsibility of making his own decision.

Bultmann clarifies this problem at one point by an example from political ethics. The church must reject any pressure for it to make detailed political pronouncements; for 'a political judgment in a concrete political situation is not the word of God. Theology must watch very carefully that Christian faith is not confused with a political programme.'[62] This is not because the Christian does not have to act in a politically responsible way. On the contrary, he *is* to act responsibly, but

[62] *Glauben und Verstehen*, 3, p. 195.

the Church cannot relieve him of this responsibility. God's word is there to urge him on. 'He has reason in order to be able to come to an independent judgment and to make his own decisions',[63] i.e. by informing himself as completely as possible about the different political programmes and by looking in a critical and inquisitive way for opportunities of discussion with others. It is the duty of theology and of the Church to make this responsibility clear to him and to emphasize it in their proclamation.

The extent to which and the way in which a person is to speak in *concrete* terms can only be decided by him in a particular situation. For example, the pressure of propaganda might rule out relevant discussion and the possibility of an independent judgment, cloud the mind and make manipulation inevitable. It goes without saying that in any concrete remarks the preacher is constantly at risk: is his judgment, however responsible, the right one at the time? Will the hearer understand it rightly, as a summons to his own responsibility, and not wrongly, as a norm of Christian ethics? It also goes without saying that to refrain in principle from making concrete remarks is often an evasion of pastoral responsibility. At any rate, Bultmann himself has not been afraid of being quite concrete on occasion, not only in incidental remarks during his lectures especially when dealing with the paraenetic sections of the New Testament, but also in taking a public stand on fundamental questions, as for instance in the *Merkur*, in 1952, on the question of 'The German People and Israel', or in his comments on the Jewish question during the Third Reich. In this context, the section on 'Jesus before Pilate' from Bultmann's commentary on the Gospel of John is particularly worth reading. It appeared in 1941, and amounts to a thoroughgoing controversy with the perverted authority of the National Socialist state approach.

It is worth paying closer attention to *one* instructive example.

[63] ibid., p. 196.

On May 2, 1933, Bultmann began his first lecture in the summer semester with the words: 'On principle, I have never spoken in my lectures about the politics of the day, and I do not expect to do so in the future. But today it seems quite wrong to ignore the political background against which we begin this new semester.'[64] Bultmann is concerned to indicate to popular talk the limits set to it by faith: 'No state and no people is so distinct a group, is so free from sin, as to be able to derive God's will clearly from the mere fact of its existence. No people is so pure and clean that any movement of the popular will may be proclaimed directly to be the will of God. Like nature, our whole human society, including the people, has become uncanny to us through sin. From it come beautiful and noble actions; but from it, too, break forth the devilries of sin.'[65] Such a critical view, Bultmann immediately continues, can never lead to a fight over abstracts, 'for we cannot disguise the fact that state and people consist of particular men and women, who are our neighbours'.[66]

Bultmann illustrates what he means by three examples. First, he attacks the premature haste of the 'New Marburg Assembly for State Order', 'which in its first session recognized no more urgent duty for the new time than to give new names to certain streets and places.' Such laurels for the new time and its leader, Bultmann feels, 'nourish a peculiar feeling of security which is not to be confused with *faith* in the future' —he even goes so far as to call it 'frivolous'. His second example warns against the rampant denunciation, e.g., the baskets of letters sent daily to the Minister of Culture, which 'suppresses the free and honest words of men' and teaches them to lie. In his third example, Bultmann attacks the defamation of the Jews: 'As a Christian I must deplore the injustice done to *German* Jews by such defamation'; here Bultmann sees 'demonic distortion', and not the spirit of love at work.

[64] 'Die Aufgabe der Theologie', col. 161.
[65] ibid., col. 164.   [66] ibid., col. 165.

He ends his bold lecture with a warning that everyone, including his students, should at all times be ready to face the 'either-or' of faith; his words, particular as they are, should remind them of this decision, 'so that it can be made clearly and conscientiously'.[67]

Bultmann soon had an opportunity to defend the position on the Jewish question adopted in this lecture in a more important form. The General Synod of the Church of the Old Prussian Union had passed a law regulating the appointment of pastors and church officials, according to which the bearers of these offices had (1) 'to give unconditional support to the national state', and (2) to be, along with their wives, 'of Arian descent in accordance with the provisions of the State laws'. On September 11, 1933, the Kirchentag of the three church districts of Upper Hesse, meeting in Marburg, asked the theological faculties at Marburg and Erlangen for an opinion on this church law. Whereas the faculty at Erlangen, in the opinion subscribed to by Paul Althaus and Werner Elert, agreed in essentials to the regulations in question, the Marburg faculty unanimously opposed them in its opinion of September 19, 1933. This opinion derives essentially from the pen of Rudolf Bultmann, who composed it in agreement with Heinrich Schlier and Hans von Soden; later, he not only defended it in writing but also published at about the same time a memorandum on 'The New Testament and the Race Question'.

The opinion states, *inter alia*, that the pastor is in duty bound 'to give appropriate expression in some cases even to critical opinions of events in the life of church and state', regardless of the fact that he has to be a loyal citizen.[68] For example, it comments on the introduction of the Arian paragraph into the church: 'Anyone who refuses to follow the Apostles and the Reformers in recognizing the complete unity between Jewish and non-Jewish Christians in the church, as

[67] ibid., cols. 165 f.   [68] ibid., col. 291.

it is developed most clearly in the Epistle to the Ephesians, and refuses to allow this unity to be expressed in the composition of the church, deceives himself if he confesses that the Holy Scripture is God's Word for him and that Jesus is the Son of God and Lord of all men. Beyond all question, God has proclaimed his Word in the world not only in the Old Testament but also in the New, and has chosen his Son from among the Jews.'[69] Bultmann counters the argument that such statements are a scandal to the 'popular consciousness' by pointing out: 'The church can only be a blessing to Church and State in the New Reich if it fulfils its peculiar task boldly and without swerving; it must not forget that its task of criticism keeps it in constant tension with the popular consciousness. If its task entails the constant possibility of scandal, if this task can be fulfilled in some circumstances only at the cost of mistrust and enmity, the church can at least be quite certain that people and state will see where firmness of character and faithfulness prevail. A church which does not look to right or left performs the one true and genuine service for people and state, which it alone can offer.'[70]

I shall conclude with two examples from Bultmann's Marburg sermons. In 1937, he attacked the 'blood and soil' myth with the remark that man easily falls victim to the conceit 'that he too is also a divine being. He feels that a divine energy and a sacred will are expressed in his blood, and in the impulses to which it gives rise. God lives within him, he thinks, inasmuch as he belongs to the community of his people with its natural roots in blood and soil, and its solidarity flowing from oneness of blood and one sacred energy throbbing within it. God in the race, God in man! For Christians it is a matter of course that a belief such as this violates the majesty of God, and the Christian recoils in horror from the consequences to which such a blasphemous doctrine leads.'[71]

[69] ibid., col. 293.   [70] ibid., col. 369.
[71] *Marburger Predigten*, p. 34 (*This World and the Beyond*, pp. 43 f.).

In a sermon from Advent 1938, a few weeks before the Night of Crystal, which ushered in the 'Final Solution' of the Jewish question, we find the words: 'Christians realize that whenever any system is established in this world, however noble and lofty its aims and however much it may be inspired by the will to good, it is only possible through sheer power, and that in the process of setting up any secular order, whether nationally or internationally, human beings are sacrificed and crushed. The prosperity of some is purchased only at the expense and indeed often the destruction of others. That is the way things inevitably go in this world. But Christians refuse to be satisfied with this inevitability; they feel as a painful burden the sorrows and the tears of those to whom violence is done. And *if* this is the unalterable way of things in this world, *if* the way of secular government is a way which always leads through blood and tears, then we conclude that this very fact is a sign that the dominion of men is never the dominion of God, nor can it ever lead to the dominion of God.'[72]

Such words sound easy enough today. In their time they were brave words. If there are any theologians in our country who can look back without shame to what they said and wrote in 1933 and afterwards, Rudolf Bultmann is among them.

We introduced this situation at the end of the present chapter to present the subject of the chapter in a *comprehensive* way. We have been concerned with the problem of ethics in Bultmann's theology. We said at the beginning that Bultmann develops no 'ethics' in his theological work. In the course of the chapter we have shown how and why Bultmann will not hear of a specifically Christian ethic. Finally, we attempted to avoid the false impression that as a result, ethical behaviour was a voluntary matter or that the preacher was prevented from taking a particular stand in ethical questions.

We may all have our own views about Bultmann's discussion

[72] ibid., pp. 91 f. (ibid., p. 105).

of ethical questions; be this as it may, we are concerned here with the *foundation* of ethical decisions in Bultmann's theology and not with their elimination. If this has not become clear in the 'abstract' part of the present chapter, the 'concrete' part hardly leaves room for doubt.

13

Eschatology

IN TRADITIONAL dogmatics, 'eschatology' is the 'doctrine of the last things', the last things in time, i.e. of the end of the world, the resurrection of the dead, the immortality of the soul, life after death, etc. For obvious reasons, these questions are usually discussed at the end of any outline of Christian doctrine. Therefore our last chapter, too, has this title, which represents one of the most central and most-used concepts in Bultmann's theology.

We must, however, immediately guard against a misunderstanding. In Bultmann's writing, 'eschatology' does not describe the last things which are still to come in time, or the doctrine of the last things. The concept of the eschatological, as Bultmann uses it, has undergone a change which is characteristic of his whole theological thought. *For Bultmann, 'eschatological' does not describe the final goal of the saving action of God which has still to take place in time; it describes any occasion which is itself bound up in this final action.*

After what we have said so far about Bultmann's theology, this statement can be understood in principle, but we shall have to clarify its details. This much, however, is already plain: the reason for discussing eschatology at the end of this book is not that we have now to talk about the future and about hope in a way which in principle goes beyond what we have so far said about man and the saving act of God—which gives future and hope. For it is characteristic of Bultmann's view of the nature of eschatology that eschatology is not a special area of dogmatics, the doctrine of the last things; for Bultmann, the Christ event in its completion, the Word of God which proclaims it as such in the present, and Christian existence as a whole are all eschatological phenomena. The concept of eschatology thus holds together the whole structure of Bultmann's theology as though at a focal point. In this final chapter, therefore, we shall once again keep to the centre of Bultmann's theology, so as to clarify his concept of the eschatological (which we have so far avoided as far as possible) and its relationship with what usually falls under this heading in traditional eschatology.

How are the 'last things' understood in the New Testament? The believer expects the dawn of the kingdom of God. This dawn is identical with the future 'Day of our Lord Jesus Christ'. The trumpet of God will sound, and at his command Christ will descend from heaven. The dead will be raised and will appear together with the living before the judgment seat of the Lord. The righteous will enter into eternal joy, the wicked will be given over to everlasting torment. This event is set in the context of a cosmic catastrophe which brings an end to the 'old world' and calls forth a new world from the hand of God. The details of the description of these events of the end-time vary considerably in the New Testament—a sign that people were not really interested in the particulars of these events—but by and large the picture of the end-event is clear. Bultmann first of all points out that this picture of the future is not specifically Christian. It derives from late Judaism, and from the apocalyptic stream within it. In numerous late-Jewish apocalypses which still survive, the course of the end-events is depicted in the same way as in the New Testament. The only difference is that either God himself or his still unknown 'Son of Man' takes Christ's place as the coming judge of the world.

This apocalyptic picture of hope is drawn from many sources. One of these sources is the Old Testament. In the Old Testament, too, history is already understood as a course of events leading to a goal. The difference is that in the Old Testament the salvation history is not world history, but the history of the people of Israel; moreover, the goal of this history is imagined to be within the world: God will lead his people, if they remain obedient, through all national catastrophes into a glorious future in which they will live in peace on earth under the rule of the Messiah from the house of David. With the help of non-Israelite influences, which we cannot go into here, the Old Testament picture of history was then transformed into the apocalyptic one.

Bultmann describes the characteristic differences between Old Testament and apocalyptic eschatology as follows: 'In the Israelite view of history the goal of history is promised, but the realization of the promise is conditional on the obedience of the people. In the apocalyptic view the end of history comes with necessity at the time determined by God. According to the first view, the course of history becomes clear by the knowledge of divine justice which guides history to its goal. In the second view, the course of history is revealed by the knowledge of the secret counsel of God. In the first view the responsibility of the individual coincides with the responsibility of the whole people, a responsibility in face of the possibility of future welfare *or* judgment. In the second view the individual is responsible for himself only, because the end will bring welfare *and* judgment at the same time, and the individual's future will be decided according to his works.'[1]

There is no doubt that the New Testament picture of hope is in essentials that of apocalyptic. The apocalyptic description of the end-event is, however, in Bultmann's view, *mythological*. This characteristic must now be investigated.

[1] *Glauben und Verstehen*, 3, p. 94 (*New Testament Studies*, I, 1954, p. 7).

It will be remembered that Bultmann uses 'mythological' to describe a way of speaking in which the other-worldly appears and is presented as this-worldly, the beyond in terms of this side. Now in his view this is exactly what happens in the apocalyptic outline of the future rule of God. In the expectation that the salvation of God will descend from the cosmic realm of the heaven situated above the earth, we find 'the other and divine world of salvation and light' conceived of as 'a sphere within cosmic *space* above our earth'.[2] But Bultmann also argues that the apocalyptic understanding of *time* is mythological, in seeing the end of the world ushered in by the sudden invasion of supernatural powers. Here the divine action is imagined as analogous to human action, superior to it only in force and incalculability.

Bultmann writes: 'This mythological method of representation is foreign to modern man, whose thinking is determined by science to whatever extent, if any, he himself actively participates in scientific research and understands its methods. We have learned the meaninglessness of speaking about "above" and "below" in the universe. We can no longer honestly accept the thought of Christ coming on the clouds of heaven. We are accustomed to understanding cosmic processes as natural ones; and when we consider an end to the world, then it is an end brought about by natural processes, natural catastrophes. And when nowadays the fearful thought crops up that through man's misuse of atomic power our habitable earth could be turned into a chaos, then that is something altogether different from an end brought about by divine intervention—quite apart from the fact that it would only be a question of the end of the earth, and not of the universe.'[3]

Hence Bultmann sees the need to demythologize the New Testament conceptions of the future, i.e. the need for their 'existentialist interpretation'. 'For that is now the problem of

[2] ibid., p. 83 (*Expository Times*, 65, 1954, p. 229).
[3] ibid., p. 84 (ibid.).

"demythologizing", whether with the elimination of mythological concepts the final word has been spoken, or in them some enduring truth has found expression; whether there lies at their roots a viewpoint, indeed a knowledge, of the nature of human existence which may not be the only possible understanding of human existence—for there are many such, and to choose one is always a matter for decision—but which is a possibility which ought never to lose its claim to be considered. Does such an understanding lie at the basis of these mythological concepts? And how would it be expressed in the concept and speech of modern man?'[4] It is therefore not enough to surrender the mythical *elaboration* of the apocalyptic picture of hope and to retain the hope itself, without further interpretation, as an event beyond our everyday existence; for myth in general, as a whole, is the way in which ancient man thought, and, according to Bultmann, is obsolete as far as the modern world is concerned. It must be possible to express what is said in mythological form in a modern way without eliminating its content, and if apocalyptic eschatology can be understood in this way as a 'happening in existence,'[5] we shall have a real theological understanding, for theology has to do with man.

Bultmann is fond of attempting to work out the 'existentialist content' or the 'existential significance' of the New Testament apocalyptic picture of hope by comparing it with other ideas about the course of history. The contemporary Greek historical writers offer a particularly good point of comparison. In Greece, Bultmann says, the realm of history was understood by analogy with the realm of nature, 'and is not seen as an independent world alongside the world of nature, which is the *cosmos* in the Greek sense. There is no realization that the history of man and of the human community represents a special sphere of life—a sphere of life in which the present is the time of decision, burdened with its inheritance and its

[4] ibid., p. 85 (ibid., pp. 329 f.).
[5] *Kerygma und Mythos*, I, p. 125.

responsibility towards the past and the future.'[6] Greek history-writing is therefore interested in the pragmatic association of cause and effect in particular historical events; in this way a moral may also be drawn from history, for what once happened will—as in nature—happen again in the same way, so that history-writing can be of general value in education and be particularly instructive for politicians. The Greek historian, however, 'does not reflect on possible future eventualities, nor does he regard the present as a time of decision in which man must assume responsibility towards the future. The Greek historian does not raise the question of meaning in history.'[7] In other words, the process of history is not understood 'as a process in which individuals as well as peoples or nations *receive* their character by their actions and experiences.'[8] This character is rather already brought by them into each historical situation. Man is a spiritual, rational person and incorporated in a cosmos which is shaped by the ordering law of the same spirit. He must strive to put himself in harmony with the time-less nature of this cosmic order. 'Man cannot really be touched by encounters, but encounters can only be for him occasion and material for unfolding and shaping his timeless nature. In principle the future cannot bring anything new in so far as man is independent of time in realizing his real nature.'[9] True, the individual acts as a person, he makes history. But he himself is not a historical being. He does not *become*, he always *is*. He stands, timeless and unalterable as a person, over against history. In Greece, the nature of history is there-fore not thought of as an independent theme of philosophers, but only as the subject of scientific history writing.

It is clear that the understanding of history in apocalyptic presupposes an essentially different picture of history and of man. Its basis is the quesion of the *meaning* of history. This meaning is revealed for the apocalyptist only in the light of the

[6] *Glauben und Verstehen*, 2, p. 241 (*Essays*, p. 267).
[7] *History and Eschatology*, pp. 15 f.   [8] ibid., p. 17.   [9] ibid., p. 94.

end of history, and that means that his end is appointed, in the apocalyptic understanding, by God, from beyond history. God, who guides history to its goal, is the demanding and forgiving God, and accordingly man must hope within history for this grace and agree to this demand, if he wishes to achieve a good destiny. In all his actions he is related to what is beyond himself, to God, in so far as he understands himself rightly. 'There is at the same time the understanding that his real nature transcends the world in which he now lives—the knowledge that "this world is not the only world" (Franz Werfel).'[10] In other words: the apocalyptic understanding of history expresses knowledge of the historicity of man himself, and the mythological question of the meaning of history in its total course is—existentialistically interpreted—the question of the significance of each particular moment in which man exists historically.

In this way we have come up against the concept of 'historicity', which is one of the most characteristic concepts in Bultmann's theology. It is the central anthropological concept: the nature of man is his historicity. True, we have so far avoided this concept, as it is best understood *as a concept* in the context of a discussion of the problems of history. But we have dealt at length with its *content* in Chapter 3, when talking about man. We must repeat some of what was said there, and it may now be more easily understandable.

Man exists historically, because his authentic nature is not always already determined in a timeless way, and he does not therefore realize himself at the farthest possible remove from concrete historical encounters. Because he is his own possibility, he finds his way to himself as his own realized possibility only in actual historical encounters which demand his decision on particular occasions. His historicity does not consist in the fact that he 'makes history', or even in the fact that

[10] *Glauben und Verstehen*, 3, p. 88 (*Expository Times*, 65, 1954, p. 277).

he is involved in a series of historical events, far less in the fact that he 'enters history'. It consists in the fact that he is *himself* only *in* history, that is, in historical encounters; that he always seeks and has his own history in which he realizes himself. His existence is historical, 'and by the historicity of human existence we understand that his being is a being-able-to-be. That is, man's being is removed from his control and stands at risk from time to time in the concrete situations of life. It is involved in decisions in which man does not choose *something for himself*, but chooses *himself as his own possibility*.'[11] Authentic human existence is not given beforehand, naturally, but surrendered historically, handed over to human decisions. 'In these decisions man becomes himself, whereas the life of animals does not evolve through decisions but remains in the pattern given by nature. The single animal is only a specimen of its genus, whereas the single man is an individual, a person. Therefore the life of a man is always one which stands before him and acquires its character as forfeited or as real by his decisions. What a man chooses in his decisions is basically not this or that, but is himself as the man he is to be and intends to be, or as one who has forfeited his real life.'[12] At another place Bultmann says the same thing in other words:

'Man is not involved in the causal connection of natural events in the same way as a natural being; he has to take over himself, he is responsible for himself. That means that human life is history; it leads through decisions at particular times to a future in which man chooses himself. . . . "History" is the field of human decisions.'[13] Man would lose himself were he to detach himself from history; for he would surrender himself as his possibility if he were to objectivize the historical event which is the determination of his potentiality instead of keeping radically open to his encounter. Only in the *encounter* with history will he experience its meaning and its truth. 'If the enquiry into truth, by which human existence is basically motivated, is for the

---

[11] *Glauben und Verstehen*, 1, p. 118.
[12] *History and Eschatology*, pp. 43 f.
[13] *Glauben und Verstehen*, 4, p. 129.

Greeks the enquiry into the undisguised disclosure of what is in being as an organized whole, the enquiry into truth is for the biblical man one into the significance of the moment that confronts him—what it demands and what it offers.'[14]

The 'temporality' of man is part of 'historicity' understood in this way. 'Temporality' does not mean that man has a particular span of life or that the elements of his decision, his authentic being at any given time, add up to a course of time—though this, of course, is also the case. Time as an elapsing sequence of time is only a secondary aspect of original time. The primary nature of time, 'temporality', consists in the fact that man has his authentic time in each particular 'now' of his historical existence, a time which is determined and filled by past and future. Existence in the moment as authentic human existence is therefore not timeless, but determined by the past which man brings with him and the future which now encounters him decisively, i.e. in calling him to decision. For man, to be a temporal being thus means that at any given moment he only has time as filled time.

Bultmann writes: 'Man is indeed a temporal creature; his present is always confronted by a future.'[15] 'Historicity' and 'temporality' therefore belong with futurity as elements of the structure of human existence. 'Futurity', properly understood, does not mean that man still has something to expect—though that is, of course, also true; at least death is still to come, and man is constantly occupied by the question of what the future will bring—but that in his present existence he is determined by the future, i.e. by what is coming to him, what encounters him. Man's authentic being is 'futurity' in this sense.

In this context it is important to recognize that according to Bultmann the concepts 'historicity', 'temporality' and 'futurity' paraphrase what the mythological concepts of the rule of God *really* (i.e. in an existentialist interpretation) mean in

[14] *Glauben und Verstehen*, 2, pp. 110 f. (*Essays*, p. 125).
[15] *Marburger Predigten*, p. 15 (*This World and the Beyond*, p. 23).

apocalyptic terms. In this connection I would like to introduce a lengthy quotation from *Jesus and the Word*:

'The future kingdom of God, then, is not really something which is to come in the course of time, so that to advance its coming one can do something in particular, perhaps through penitential prayers and good works, which become superfluous in the moment of its coming. Rather, the kingdom of God is a power which, although it is entirely future, wholly determines the present. It determines the present because it now compels man to decision; he is determined thereby either in this direction or in that, as chosen or as rejected, in his entire present existence. . . . The kingdom of God is genuinely future, because it is not a metaphysical entity or condition, but the future action of God, which can be in no sense something *given* in the present. None the less this future determines man in his present, and exactly for that reason is true future—not merely something to come "somewhere, sometime", but destined for man and constraining him to decision. The coming of the kingdom of God is therefore not really an event in the course of time, which is due to occur sometime and towards which man can either take a definite attitude or hold himself neutral. Before he takes any attitude he is already constrained to make his choice, and therefore he must understand that just this necessity of decision constitutes the essential part of his human nature. Because Jesus sees man thus in a crisis of decision before God, it is understandable that in his thought the Jewish Messianic hope becomes the absolute certainty that in this hour the kingdom of God is coming. If men are standing in the crisis of decision, and if precisely this crisis is the essential characteristic of their humanity, then every hour is the last hour, and we can understand that for Jesus the whole contemporary mythology is pressed into the service of this conception of human existence. Thus he understood and proclaimed his hour as the last hour.'[16] 'Then it becomes obvious that the attention is not to be turned to the contemporary mythology in terms of which the real meaning in Jesus' teaching finds its outward expression. This mythology ends by abandoning the fundamental insight which it conceals, Jesus' conception of man as forced to decision through God's future act. To this mythology belongs the expectation of the end of the world as occurring in time, the expectation which in the contemporary situation of Jesus is the natural expression of his

[16] *Jesus*, pp. 38 f. (*Jesus and the Word*, p. 44).

conviction that even in the present, man stands in this crisis of decision, and that the present is for him the last hour.'[17]

According to Bultmann, it is particularly clear from Paul that the intent of the apocalyptic picture of history for primitive Christianity lay in *anthropology*; for Paul deliberately interpreted the apocalyptic picture of history, which in late Judaism depicted the history of salvation (or doom) essentially as the history of the nation and mankind, in the light of anthropology: according to Rom. 5.20, the law given by Moses has the task of making sin powerful, so that grace can also be powerful. The law, like the sin provoked by it, thus has a positive significance, which has as its goal the salvation of the believing *individual*. In this unique interpretation of history is expressed, according to Bultmann, the fact 'that man can receive his life only by the grace of God, but he can receive the divine grace only when he knows himself annihilated before God; therefore the sin into which man is plunged is paradoxically the presupposition for the reception of grace',[18] in short: eschatological salvation meets man in his *historical* situation.

Bultmann believes that in this way he has found the reason why Jesus and the primitive Christian tradition in general do not usually portray the coming rule of God in descriptive pictures. 'That would be to take away the essential character of the beyond. The kingdom would be a creation of human desire and imagination; it would not be the kingdom of *God*',[19] which is strictly related to the historical existence of man.

Bultmann thus infers the structures of authentic human existence from the apocalyptic expectations of the future in the New Testament. One could also say that he finds these structures again in apocalyptic eschatology, for Bultmann is indeed convinced that it is in the end the task of *philosophy* to demonstrate the structures of existence by means of an existential analysis. The concepts of historicity, temporality and futurity are therefore not expressions developed *ad hoc* by Bultmann; he takes them over directly from Heidegger and indirectly from a long philosophical and theological tradition. This tradition is not Christian by chance, but at the same time it need

[17] ibid., pp. 41 f. (ibid., p. 47).
[18] *History and Eschatology*, p. 41.
[19] *Jesus*, p. 42 (*Jesus and the Word*, p. 47).

not necessarily be Christian. The fact that the existentialist contribution to this interpretation of the biblical picture of the future does not produce anything specifically Christian (at this point we are still short of dealing with the saving event), corresponds to the fact that this picture of the future is itself older than the Christian faith and has simply been taken over by it.

Does that mean that the demythologizing of the apocalyptic expectation in the New Testament has been satisfactorily achieved? Bultmann answers, Yes and No. Yes, in so far as that expectation is no different from that of Late Judaism. No, in so far as the apocalyptic picture of the future in primitive Christianity was a *modified* form of that of Judaism. It is Bultmann's conviction that the New Testament decisively altered the late Jewish picture of hope under the influence of the saving event. In examining this modification and its significance, we move from Bultmann's understanding of the historical to that of eschatology. This step matches the one we took between the fifth and sixth chapters, when we left the analysis of human existence and turned to the exposition of the saving event in Bultmann's theology. It is the step from an ultimately *philosophical elucidation* of existence to a description of the *achievement* of existence in *faith*.

Bultmann calls this modification 'a kind of demythologizing'.[20] In other words, it is the beginning of the process of demythologizing in the New Testament itself. As is well known, there have been numerous attempts at demythologizing New Testament apocalyptic. The best known is the secularization of the teleological picture of history in apocalyptic by Hegel and his followers, in particular by Karl Marx: the classless society is the kingdom of God without God. Here, as in apocalyptic, the future is seen as what is still to come. But the decisive idea of the old hope is surrendered, knowledge of

[20] *Glauben und Verstehen*, 3, p. 89 (*Expository Times*, 65, 1954, p. 277).

the fact 'that the fulfilment of human life cannot be the result of human effort but is rather a gift from beyond, the gift of God's grace'.[21] This is a course which exactly meets up with that taken by the New Testament itself when it demythologizes the apocalyptic ideas which it finds to hand. For in this transformation of the apocalyptic picture of the future, its one-sidedly future character is given up under the impact of the saving act known in faith, and the *extra noes* of God's saving act on each occasion is stressed all the more strongly.

We must first look at the eschatology of *Paul*, as Bultmann interprets it. For Paul, the Kingdom of God is 'righteousness and salvation and joy in the Holy Spirit' (Rom. 14.17): that means, 'the conception of bliss is thought of with regard to the individual'.[22] To this degree Paul simply follows the intent of the apocalyptic expectation of the end. But the 'Holy Spirit' has now already been poured out over the community; righteousness, salvation and joy in the Holy Spirit are therefore presently experienced realities. The kingdom of God is, at least in a certain way, already present. 'The believer who has received baptism is "in Christ". Therefore it is true that "if anyone is in Christ he is a new creature" (II Cor. 5.17) and that "the old has passed away; behold, the new has come" (ibid). The New Aeon is already reality, for "when the fullness of the time was come, God sent forth his Son" (Gal. 4.4). The time of bliss, promised by Isaiah, is present: "Behold, now is the acceptable time: behold, now is the day of salvation" (II Cor. 6.2). The gift of the Spirit, which the Jews expected to come at the time of the end, is now bestowed upon believers; therefore they are now already "sons of God" and free men instead of servants (Gal. 4.6 f.).'[23]

'For the believer who is "in Christ" the decisive event has already happened. Neither death nor life nor any hostile power shall be able to separate us from the love of God which

[21] ibid., p. 88 (ibid.). [22] *History and Eschatology*, p. 42.
[23] ibid.

is in Christ Jesus our Lord (Rom. 8.35–39). Whether we live or die, we are the Lord's (Rom. 14.7–9). The believer is even now free and master over all destiny:

> For all things are yours . . .
> whether the world or life or death,
> or the present or the future,
> all are yours;
> and you are Christ's, and Christ is God's (I Cor. 3.21–23).'[24]

In other words, the saving act of God in Christ is the real eschatological event; the resurrection of Jesus is the beginning of the general resurrection (I Cor. 15.20); the existence of the believer is eschatological existence; history is swallowed up in eschatology; the time is fulfilled, because Christ is the end of history; real history now takes place in the realization of human historicity; the world history which is now taking place is not salvation history, but profane history, whose end does not interest the believer.

We have still to ask why in addition Paul still holds on to the apocalyptic expectation of the future. But first we must note the modification of the expectation of the future in *John*, who radically surrenders the hope presented in mythological terms. According to Bultmann this later caused offence, so in some places an 'ecclesiastical redaction' reintroduced the ideas of traditional eschatology. John himself, on the other hand, describes eschatological salvation as already present:

'For John the resurrection of the dead and the last judgment are present in the coming of Jesus. It is evident that he formulates this statement in opposition to the traditional apocalyptic eschatology when he explicitly says:

> And this is the judgment,
> that the light has come into the world,
> and men loved darkness rather than light (John 3.19).

John understands the "judgment" as the separation which happens in the hearing of the word of Jesus:

[24] ibid., p. 43.

> For judgment I came into the world,
> that those who do not see may see,
> and that those who see may become blind (9.39).
> He who believes in the Son has eternal life,
> and he who does not obey the Son shall not see life,
> but the wrath of God rests upon him (John 3. 36).

The believer has already passed the judgment, and he who does not believe is already condemned (3.18). The believer is already resurrected from death:

> Truly, truly, I say to you,
> he who hears my word and believes him who sent me,
> has eternal life;
> he does not come into judgment,
> but has passed from death to life.
> Truly, truly I say to you,
> the hour is coming and now is,
> when the dead will hear the voice of the Son of God,
> and those who hear will live (John 5.24 f.).

Especially clear is the thought of the author in the dialogue between Jesus and Martha where the traditional idea of the resurrection is explicitly corrected. Jesus assures Martha who is mourning for the death of her brother: "Your brother will rise again." Martha understands this in the traditional sense: "I know that he will rise again in the resurrection at the last day." But Jesus corrects her:

> I am the resurrection and the life;
> he who believes in me, though he die, yet shall he live,
> and whoever lives and believes in me, shall never die
> (11.23–26).'[25]

'It is not that John denies the Parousia, which others expect as an event occurring in time . . . John rather opens the eyes of the reader to see that the Parousia is already present. . . . If its real coming were still delayed, then Jesus' actual coming would be misunderstood. It is understood only where men see

[25] ibid., pp. 47 f.

315

that *this* coming is the turn of the ages. Whatever cosmic catastrophes may come, things can never be different from what they are on every day of the world. Even though men may rise up from their graves, it will be no different from men rising up every morning from their sleep. The decisive event has already happened.'[26]

The quotations are sufficient. They make us understand Bultmann's conviction that the apocalyptic expectation in the New Testament was essentially modified, in that the expected saving event in the coming of Jesus has already taken place, and salvation is present.

We cannot repeat here the details of what we said about the saving event in detail in earlier chapters. In this context, however, it is essential to note that the divine saving act described in detail earlier has an *eschatological* character: it does not promise salvation, but brings salvation. The time *post Christum natum* is a time of salvation, the life of the believer is life in salvation. Jesus' coming 'is an event which signifies the end of world history. Those who believe in him are lifted out of the flux of time into eternity.'[27] 'To be a Christian, to believe, means to have anticipated the time span of this world, to stand already at the end of this world.'[28]

Nor can we repeat in detail what we said about the authenticity of human existence as existence in salvation. We may recall that according to Bultmann, man is transported to the authenticity of his existence only by the gracious saving act of God. As this saving act has an eschatological character, the authentic existence of man is naturally *eschatological* existence. Believers 'have truth, purity, life; as pain and death have no further power to reduce them to despair, so the evil around them and within them can no longer make them afraid. It is engulfed in the divine grace.'[29] 'Thus eschatological existence

[26] *Glauben und Verstehen*, i, pp. 144 f.
[27] *Marburger Predigten*, p. 96 (*This World and the Beyond*, p. 110).
[28] ibid., p. 171 (ibid., p. 190).   [29] ibid., p. 96 (ibid., p. 110).

has become possible. God has acted, and the world—"this world"—has come to an end. Man himself has been made new.'[30] The believer exists *eschatologically*, because he is freed from his sin, his past, i.e. from himself as the old man who desired to live from what was at his disposal; the man who wants to live was redeemed from what brought him only death. In opening himself in such freedom to the future radically and without any assurance, he finds true, eternal life in constant encounter with God; for God, who freed him from the slavery of sin, gives him in this freedom the eternal future, the everlasting 'coming-to-him' of God. To be on the way in such openness for God means at the same time to be constantly at the goal.

'The existentialist meaning of the mythological statements about the turn of the age' which has taken place in Christ is consequently that the past, with which it is at an end, 'is not only a cosmic situation—although it is also this for mythological thinking—but rather my particular past in which I was a sinner. And the future for which I am freed is likewise my future.'[31]

In view of this demythologizing interpretation, we can understand the characteristic and particularly frequent use of the concept 'eschatological' in Bultmann. 'Eschatological' is the traditional designation for the last, the decisive, the once-for-all saving act of God which is taking place. Following Paul and John, Bultmann explains that this eschatological saving act has taken place in the Christ event, or rather continually takes place in the proclamation of the Christ event. 'According to the New Testament the decisive significance of Jesus Christ is that he—in his person, his coming, his passion, and his glorification—is the eschatological event.'[32] The Word of God in which this event becomes present is the eschatological Word

[30] *Kerygma und Mythos*, I, p. 39 (*Kerygma and Myth*, p. 32).
[31] *Glauben und Verstehen*, 3, p. 42 (*Existence and Faith*, p. 255).
[32] *Jesus Christ and Mythology*, p. 80.

and the once-for-allness of the Christ event is the once-for-allness of this eschatological event which takes place in the Word here and now. 'Where this Word resounds, the end of the world becomes present to the hearer in that it confronts him with the decision whether he will belong to the old or to the new world.'[33] The *kerygma* qualifies every present as eschatological time. Faith is always an eschatological phenomenon. Christian existence is eschatological existence, for the way of the believer is 'already his end'.[34] The believer not only receives the certainty of an invisible world but is himself transported into unworldly, eschatological existence. 'To live in faith is to live an eschatological existence, to live beyond the world, to have passed from death to life.'[35] Eschatology, as a doctrine of the last things, thus speaks not about what is still to come but about what is taking place.

We must follow Bultmann for one last step in his exposition of the New Testament picture of hope. Despite his conviction that the decisive saving event has already taken place and that the turn of the ages has already taken place in the appearance of Jesus, Paul holds fast to his expectation of the cosmic end-event. John surrenders this form of the mythological expectation of the end, but he too 'looks forward to a future perfection of the present life of the believer';[36] not of course to a cosmic catastrophe, but to the consummation of the individual believer after his death. Here he speaks in the language of gnostic eschatology: 'The traditional idea of the parousia is transformed: Jesus promises to his disciples that he will come again and receive them to himself into one of the many heavenly mansions (John 14.2 f.).'[37] Thus for both Paul and John the present life, or rather the time of this world *post*

[33] *Glauben und Verstehen*, 3, p. 129 (*Religion and Culture*, p. 242).
[34] *Johannesevangelium*, p. 467.
[35] *Jesus Christ and Mythology*, p. 81.
[36] *History and Eschatology*, p. 49.   [37] ibid.

Christum natum, is an intermediate period, even though it is eschatologically qualified.

What does that mean? Bultmann thinks that we must see that this time is to be taken as an intermediate time in more than a *chronological* way, as more than a time between the 'once' and the 'one day'. This 'between' in fact characterizes the *manner* of being of the believer as dialectical being between the 'no longer' and the 'not yet', of which we have spoken before. This dialectic of 'no longer' and 'not yet' does not contradict the eschatological situation of the believer, but corresponds to it in a special way; for the fact that the present existence of the believer is eschatologically qualified does not mean that the believer has nothing more to expect. On the contrary, it means that he has true future. It is the 'old man' who has nothing more to expect. His nature is to live from what he already has, from what he has at his disposal; he lives from the past, and *his* grasp for the future is guided by the intention of securing himself against the future; what he hopes for, he hopes to be able to hold. So he loses his future by already qualifying it as past.

The 'new man', on the other hand, lives from God. Freed from his past as sinful striving to secure his life from what is at hand or what is hoped for as a possession, he wins a true future in constant readiness for encounter with God; for true future can only be future from each new encounter with God. The very knowledge of such a future and the constant expectation if its coming-to-us is expressed in the 'not yet' of eschatological existence, which cannot and may not be overcome if the future of the believer is to remain *true* future. The eschatological consummation of human existence is its *constant* openness for the future of God; the 'not yet' is therefore an inalienable characteristic of the being which is 'now already' consummated. Put paradoxically: 'what we never are here and now— precisely that is our true being'.[38]

[38] *Glauben und Verstehen*, 3, p. 79 (*Existence and Faith*, p. 281).

319

Bultmann can also express the same state of affairs in the following way: in holding fast to the 'not yet', man keeps the gracious gift of his authentic life from 'again becoming a phenomenon of the world. He does not have his authenticity in what could be realized at any time within the world, in experiences, in achievements, or in his personality, nor does he have it in his believing; he has his authenticity in what he is *not* in the sense of being within the world—he has it in what he is only with God; his existence is eschatological and transcendent.'[39] Bultmann is thus convinced that for Paul even the 'vision' still to come does not do away with the 'not yet' of eschatological existence. The radical openness of human existence also remains in the consummation beyond temporal and earthly existence, as I Cor. 13.13 makes clear: But now *remain* —i.e. when we see 'face to face'—faith, hope, love, these three characteristics of authentic, eschatological existence in the 'now already' *and* the 'not yet': for 'faith and hope are the dispositions of those who are always looking for the grace of God as a future possibility'.[40] Paul 'can conceive of no state of perfection in which the unworldly is a mere possession. The openness of Christian existence is never-ending.'[41]

But true future from God is at the same time a future which is not at man's disposal; for God is not at man's disposal. It is thus always true of each new future that '. . . It is *not yet* manifest what we shall be' (I John 3.2). This 'not yet' is indeed done away with in concrete encounter with God on each particular occasion, because I now know how God encounters me *now*—which I could not have known before. But because for the believer each new 'now' is eschatologically qualified both in life and in death, the 'not yet' of the 'it is not yet manifest' is a matter of principle and remains permanently.

As a result, Bultmann consistently refuses to say anything

---

[39] *Glauben und Verstehen*, 2, pp. 97 f. (*Essays*, p. 111).
[40] *Das Urchristentum*, p. 174 (*Primitive Christianity*, p. 221).
[41] ibid., p. 195 (ibid., p. 246).

about *what* is still to come; for if he did, God's future would have been placed at man's disposal and would have ceased to be *God's* future. *God* is *the one* who is still to come: this is the legitimate way of talking about the 'last things'. True, Bultmann can say that in life and death I cannot come anywhere where God has not already been before me; that means that there is no future for man in which God cannot be present: the future 'can only be understood in the light of God's grace as the permanent futurity of God which is always there before man arrives, wherever it be, even in the darkness of death'.[42] But only God has control over the 'whether' and 'how' of each particular encounter.

Bultmann writes: 'Even in death, man is not released from the hand of God, and he has to encounter death as the encounter with God, whether for his salvation or his damnation. God is the God who comes; that is true even in the face of death. Therefore it does not matter in the end what mythological ideas men have of the "eschatological" event, of the resurrection of the dead and the last judgment.'[43] It is enough for the believer to know that in any event God is his future. He must therefore keep himself open for any encounter with God. For Christian faith does not look for this or that, but for God himself. 'Therefore, this hope or this faith may be called readiness for the unknown future that God will give. In brief, it means to be open to God's future in the face of death and darkness;'[44] for 'faith knows that God encounters us at the very point where the human prospect is nothingness'.[45] But it is a *hopeful* openness for the man who has opened himself in faith to the forgiving grace of God, 'because he has in fact already left death behind him and has passed from death to life (John 5.24; I John 3.14)'.[46] 'The only certain thing in

[42] ibid. [43] *Glauben und Verstehen*, 3, p. 164.
[44] *Jesus Christ and Mythology*, p. 31.
[45] *Kerygma und Mythos*, II, p. 203 (*Kerygma and Myth*, p. 205).
[46] *Glauben und Verstehen*, 3, p. 164.

man's future is that every man is faced with death. For the man who is open to all future as the future of the coming God, death has lost its fear.'[47] This is not because the earthly life of the believer 'would be well-rounded and meaningful in itself; rather, it is because his life is not confined within the limits of temporal-historical existence'.[48] Really to live from the future means 'to overcome the anguished fear of it in the certainty that whatever it brings can only serve our ultimate good. And the final proof of the Christian attitude would not be to shudder and recoil at the thought of the death which the future will assuredly bring to every one of us, but rather to go forward to meet it undismayed in the assured conviction that "neither death nor life, nor angels nor principalities, nor things present nor things to come . . . will be able to separate us from the love of God".'[49]

But the believer 'will refrain from painting in the future which God bestows in death, for all pictures of a glory after death can only be the wishful images of imagination, and to forgo all wishful images is part of the radical openness of faith to God's future'.[50] 'Do we know any higher life? Do we know anything of the future, of the transcendent? If we are honest we must admit that we have no direct *experience* of it, and we *know* nothing about it. What we do know, and what we have immediate experience of, is ever and only our life up to the present; our life here below, the life of our earthly destiny, the life of our plans and projects. But to reckon with eternity means just this: to view our familiar life as a provisional, unfulfilled and unfulfillable life, and to live it in preparation for a future, fulfilled and true life which God wills to bestow on us. If we were to try to picture the future to ourselves, we should only fill it out with the images suggested by our wishes and

---

[47] ibid., p. 90.   [48] *Johannesevangelium*, p. 399.
[49] *Marburger Predigten*, p. 67 (*This World and the Beyond*, p. 79).
[50] *Glauben und Verstehen*, 3, p. 90 (*Expository Times*, 65, 1954, p. 278).

dreams. Now it is just these fantasies which we are to surrender. To be ready for God's future means to walk trustfully into the darkness, ready for the purpose which God in his wisdom designs us to fulfil.'[51]

Regardless of this, the mythological conception of the resurrection of the body or 'the flesh' is better than that of the immortality of the soul; for the Christian hope may not be understood 'as a clinging to what one has and is, to the provisional, but rather as the surrender of all this. The man of faith stands under the sentence of death (II Cor. 1.9), and he must take this death upon himself. Thus he enters into utter darkness. But the Christian hopes precisely where there is no hope (Rom. 4.18), namely, in God who raises the dead and calls into existence the things that are not (Rom. 4.17; cf. II Cor. 1.9).'[52]

In this context, Bultmann is fond of pointing to Martin Luther, who in his *Lectures on the Epistle to the Romans* writes, on Rom. 8.25, that the man who hopes 'does not know what he hopes for and yet knows what he does not hope for'—i.e. not death, because he hopes on God—and paraphrases this sentence as follows: 'Christian hope knows *that* it hopes, but it does not know what it hopes for.'[53] Luther further says, on Rom. 8.28, that on the uppermost level of God's election stand those who behave in accordance with the will of God even in the doom of hell, 'as perhaps happens with many in the hour of death. They are most completely cleansed by their own will and by the wisdom of the flesh.' That, says Bultmann, is what he means, taken to the utmost extreme: 'The believer must be determined to accept damnation to hell at the hand of God, provided that it is God who damns him to hell.'[54]

In a radio discussion with Bultmann, Friedrich Karl Schumann put it like this: 'The Christian hope is kept in God,

---

[51] *Marburger Predigten*, p. 135 (*This World and the Beyond*, p. 153).
[52] *Glauben und Verstehen*, 3, p. 28 (*Existence and Faith*, p. 85).
[53] Bultmann and others, *Die christliche Hoffnung*, p. 58.
[54] ibid.

and so it can be quite silent. It does not need to talk over-much and to spend its days in gossip. Let it praise this God, as it is already doing on earth.'[55] Bultmann agreed with this. 'Quite correct,' he says. So it seems to me quite to the point to end the chapter with this remark; these concepts may be inadequate, but what they express will serve to describe all Bultmann's theological work: to praise at the right time and to be silent when necessary.

[55] ibid., p. 59.

BIBLIOGRAPHY

This bibliography lists, in chronological order, details of the English translations and original versions of works referred to in the present book. It thus covers Bultmann's main publications. A full bibliography of Bultmann's writings to 1965 may be found in Charles W. Kegley (ed.), *The Theology of Rudolf Bultmann* (London: SCM Press and New York: Harper & Row, 1966), pp. 289–310.

Works by Rudolf Bultmann

'Die Bedeutung der Eschatologie fur die Religion des Neuen Testaments', *Zeitschrift für Theologie und Kirche*, 27, 1917, pp. 76–87.

'Ethische und mystische Religion im Urchristentum', *Christliche Welt*, 34, 1920, cols. 725 ff.; 738 ff.

Die Geschichte der synoptischen Tradition (Göttingen: Vandenhoeck und Ruprecht, 1921 [1961⁵]); ET by John Marsh, *The History of the Synoptic Tradition* (Oxford: Basil Blackwell, 1963).

'Karl Barths *Römerbrief* in zweiter Auflage', *Christliche Welt*, 36, 1922, cols. 320 ff.; 330 ff.; 358 ff.; 369 ff.

'Das Problem der Ethik bei Paulus', *Zeitschrift für die neutestamentliche Wissenschaft*, 23, 1924, pp. 123–40.

'Das Problem einer theologischen Exegese des Neuen Testaments', *Zwischen den Zeiten*, 3, 1925, pp. 334–57.

Jesus (Berlin: Deutsche Bibliothek, 1926; Siebenstern-Taschenbuch, 17, 1964); ET by Louise Pettibone Smith and Erminie Huntress Lantero, *Jesus and the Word* (New York: Charles Scribner's Sons, 1934; London: Fontana Books, 1958).

'Die Frage der "dialektischen" Theologie', *Zwischen den Zeiten*, 4, 1926, pp. 40–59.

'Besprechung von Hans Windisch: *Der Sinn der Bergpredigt*', *Deutsche Literaturzeitung*, NF 6, 1929, cols. 985–93.

Introduction to the Theology of Bultmann

'Die Geschichtlichkeit des Daseins und der Glaube', *Zeitschrift für Theologie und Kirche*, 11, 1930, pp. 339–64. (For ET see *Existence and Faith* below.)

'Die Aufgabe der Theologie in der gegenwärtigen Situation', *Theologische Blätter*, 12, 1933, cols. 161–66; 'Gutachten der Theologischen Fakultät der Universität Marburg', ibid., cols. 289–94; 'Der Arier-Paragraph im Raume der Kirche', ibid., cols. 359–70.

Glauben und Verstehen. Gesammelte Aufsätze (Tübingen: J. C. B. Mohr [Paul Siebeck]), 1 (1933), 1961[4]; 2 (1952), 1961[3]; 3 (1960), 1962[2]; 4, 1965. ET as follows: I (major articles) by Louise Pettibone Smith, *Faith and Understanding* (London: SCM Press and New York: Harper and Row, 1969); II by J. C. G. Greig, *Essays Philosophical and Theological* (London: SCM Press and New York: The Macmillan Company, 1955); translations of some essays from volume 3 may be found in: Schubert M. Ogden, ed., *Existence and Faith* (Cleveland: The World Publishing Company, 1960; London: Fontana Books, 1962); further translations are available as follows: 'Die christliche Hoffnung und das Problem der Entmythologisierung' in: *Expository Times*, 65, 1954, pp. 228–30, 276–8; 'Geschichte und Eschatologie im Neuen Testament' in: *New Testament Studies*, I, 1954, pp. 5–16 (first published in English); 'Allgemeine Wahrheiten und christliche Verkündigung' in: *Journal for Theology and the Church*, ed. Robert W. Funk, 4, 1967, pp. 153–62.

'Der Sinn des christlichen Schöpfungsglaubens im Rahmen der Schöpfungsmythen und der Wissenschaft', *Zeitschrift für Missionskunde und Religionswissenschaft*, 51, 1936, pp. 1–20; ET in *Existence and Faith* (see above), pp. 206–25.

'Jesus und Paulus', in: *Jesus Christus im Zeugnis der Heiligen Schrift und der Kirche* (Beiheft zur Evangelischen Theologie 2) (Munich: Christian Kaiser Verlag, 1936), pp. 68–90; ET in *Existence and Faith* (see above), pp. 183–201.

Das Evangelium des Johannes, Kritisch-exegetischer Kommentar über das Neue Testament (Meyers Kommentar) II Abteilung (Göttingen: Vandenhoeck und Ruprecht [1941], 1962[17]); ET by G. Beasley-Murray et al. (Oxford: Basil Blackwell, in preparation).

Kerygma und Mythos, I (Hamburg: Reich Verlag [1948], 1960), ed. H.-W. Bartsch (including *Offenbarung und Heilsgeschehen*, originally published as Beiträge zur Evangelischen Theologie 7 [Munich: Christian Kaiser Verlag, 1941]).

Bibliography

Kerygma und Mythos, II (Hamburg: Reich Verlag, 1952); ET of extracts from these two volumes by Reginald H. Fuller in: *Kerygma and Myth* (London: S.P.C.K., 1953).

Kerygma und Mythos, III (Hamburg: Reich, 1954).

Kerygma und Mythos, VI. 1 (Hamburg: Reich, 1963).

Das Urchristentum im Rahmen der antiken Religionen (Erasmus-Bibliothek) (Zurich: Artemis-Verlag, 1949 = Rororo -rde, 157–8, 1962); ET by Reginald H. Fuller, *Primitive Christianity in its Contemporary Setting* (London: Thames & Hudson, 1956 = Fontana Library, 1960; New York: Meridian Books, 1956).

Introduction to Adolf von Harnack, *Das Wesen des Christentums* (Stuttgart: Ehrenfried Klotz Verlag, 1950 = Siebenstern-Taschenbuch, 27, 1964); ET by Salvator Attanasio and Ephraim Fischoff in: Adolf von Harnack, *What is Christianity?* (New York: Harper & Brothers, 1957).

Theologie des Neuen Testaments (Tübingen: J. C. B. Mohr [Paul Siebeck], [1948–1953] 1961⁴); ET by Kendrick Grobel (New York: Charles Scribner's Sons, I [1951]; II [1955] and London: SCM Press, I [1952]; II [1955]).

(with Karl Jaspers) *Die Frage der Entmythologisierung* (Munich: Piper-Verlag, 1954).

(and others) *Die christliche Hoffnung und das Problem der Entmythologisierung* (Stuttgart: Evangelische Verlagswerk, 1954).

Marburger Predigten (Tübingen: J. C. B. Mohr [Paul Siebeck], 1956); ET by Harold Knight, *This World and the Beyond* (London: Lutterworth, 1960).

History and Eschatology (The Gifford Lectures 1955) (Edinburgh: The University Press, 1957—first published in English).

Jesus Christ and Mythology (New York: Charles Scribner's Sons, 1958 and London: SCM Press, 1960—first published in English).

Das Verhältnis der urchristlichen Christusbotschaft zum historischen Jesus (Sitzungsberichte v.d. Heidelberg. Acad. Wiss., Phil.-hist. Klasse, 3. Abhandlung, 1960); ET by Carl E. Braaten and Roy A. Harrisville, ed., in *The Historical Jesus and the Kerygmatic Christ* (Nashville: Abingdon Press, 1964), pp. 15–42.

'Der Gottesgedanke und der moderne Mensch', *Zeitschrift für Theologie und Kirche*, 60, 1963, pp. 335–48 (= *Glauben und Verstehen*, 4 [see above], pp. 113–27; ET 'The Idea of God and

Modern Man', by Robert W. Funk in: *Journal for Theology and the Church*, 2 (1965), pp. 89–95 (reprinted in R. Gregor Smith (ed.), *World Come of Age* (London: Collins and New York: Harper and Row, 1967), pp. 256–73.

Works by other authors

Martin Heidegger, *Sein und Zeit* (Tübingen: Neomarius Verlag, 1963¹⁰); ET by John Macquarrie and Edward Robinson (London: SCM Press, 1962 = ²Oxford: Basil Blackwell, 1967 and New York: Harper and Row, 1962).

Karl Barth, *Rudolf Bultmann, ein Versuch, ihn zu Verstehen* (Theologische Studien, 34, 1952); ET by Reginald H. Fuller in: *Kerygma and Myth*, II (London: S.P.C.K., 1962), pp. 83–132.

Friedrich Gogarten, *Entmythologisierung und Kirche* (Stuttgart: Friedrich Vorwerk Verlag, 1953); ET by Neville Horton Smith, *Demythologizing and History* (London: SCM Press and New York: Charles Scribner's Sons, 1955).

INDEX OF SUBJECTS

Numbers in **bold type** refer to the chapter in which a concept is discussed at length; numbers in *italics* refer to passages in which the relevant concept is discussed thematically.

329

INDEX OF BIBLICAL REFERENCES

Index